# VALUES & VISIONS

A Merck Century

# FOREWORD
P. ROY VAGELOS, M.D.


## PART I VALUES
BY LOUIS GALAMBOS

CHAPTER I  ROOTS OF THE MERCK TRADITIONS
*In which the company's central traditions — global enterprise, innovation, service to the health needs of society — are highlighted against the background of a brief historical sketch of the firm's origins and evolution.*

CHAPTER II  MERCK PEOPLE
*In which the company's values are described by way of sketches of thirteen of the people who work for Merck, in the United States and abroad.*

CHAPTER III  RESEARCH: THE MERCK STYLE OF INNOVATION
*In which the history of Merck research and the people who made it successful are described and the firm's major contributions to the therapeutic revolution are discussed.*

CHAPTER IV  ON THE TECHNOLOGICAL EDGE: QUALITY AND EFFICIENCY IN MANUFACTURING
*In which the development of the company's manufacturing capabilities, from the earliest days at Rahway and St. Louis, are examined and its goals — quality, productivity, safety, environmental protection — are set in historical context.*

CHAPTER V  GLOBAL MARKETING
*In which the transformation of Merck & Co.'s sales and marketing operations during the past century is treated, the leading innovators are discussed, and their policies are briefly described — ending with a flourish and a glance at the global outlook.*

## PART II VISIONS
MICHAEL S. BROWN, M.D., AND JOSEPH L. GOLDSTEIN, M.D.,
"THE NEW BIOLOGY: NEW TARGETS FOR THE NEW MEDICINE"

CONCLUSION
P. ROY VAGELOS, M.D.,
"MERCK'S SECOND CENTURY"

APPENDIX
ACKNOWLEDGMENTS
INDEX

For a hundred years, Merck men and women around the world have shown exceptional creative energy in discovering and developing products of genuine value, manufacturing them to meet ever-higher standards of quality, and marketing them effectively to reach those who need them. To all those Merck people, this Centennial History is dedicated with admiration and gratitude.

They deserve our admiration for their individual contributions to establishing the Company's global leadership in a highly competitive industry.

They also deserve gratitude from the millions of people who have benefited from Merck innovations — for example, products that reduce the risk of a stroke or heart attack or fatal infection . . . protect pregnant women against the rubella that could impair their unborn children . . . preserve elderly persons' eyesight from glaucoma . . . help ranchers and farmers improve their herds and crops . . . and increase industrial efficiency through hundreds of specialty chemical applications.

I believe readers in every country and every occupation — not only Merck people — will find much to interest them here. The book shows how people now working for the Company and those who came earlier — all the way back to 1891 — built the extraordinary organization that is Merck today. In these pages every reader will meet a number of memorable individuals and get the flavor of their personalities and accomplishments through their own words and the words of people who worked with them.

I am sure that Merck employees and retirees will understand that because the book had to cover so many years in so few pages, only a small number of people could be identified by name. Those mentioned, however, represent thousands of others at all levels. So, as you Merck people read this volume, nearly all of you will recognize somewhere the kind of activities that you have engaged in personally. Learning more about how those activities evolved over time will, I hope, add to your understanding of your own role at Merck. I know the history has helped me more fully appreciate the people and the flow of events that have established the Merck tradition of service to health and society, and thus it has strengthened my determination to nourish and expand that tradition.

Turning from the Company's past to its future, I believe the Merck philosophy and work environment will attract and develop people just as able and dedicated as those who have created our splendid record. Biomedical science will advance more in the next twenty years alone than in all of the last hundred. This will present enormous opportunities for the Company to achieve rewarding growth for employees and stockholders. I am confident that Merck will continue to innovate and prosper at the leading edge of our industry's progress in the Twenty-First Century.

*Roy Vagelos*

P. Roy Vagelos, M.D.

# CHAPTER ONE

# ROOTS OF THE MERCK TRADITIONS

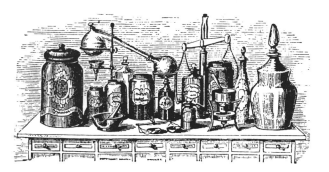

As Merck honors its centennial in 1991, a few of the company's scientists will probably be doing some extra celebrating. Not all of them. But Edward Scolnick, who presides over the Merck Sharp & Dohme Research Laboratories (MSDRL), hopes that a couple of his research teams will be celebrating as they shepherd new medicines through their final tests. Scolnick thinks that veteran chemist Gary Rasmusson might be one of those who will have a special toast to drink in 1991.

Rasmusson has been with the firm since the 1960s. "When I began working for Merck," he recalls, "I was brash, intense and tightly focused on a narrow area of science." You can understand why he was brash. He had already made it out of tiny Clark, South Dakota. Made it through St. Olaf College's chemistry program and then into the big time at Massachusetts Institute of Technology. At MIT his research on steroids and carbocyclic synthesis had been promising enough to get him a postdoc at Stanford University, where he worked on terpenes. Then he

*Good people, good ideas, and good research have given Merck the products that have placed the company at the forefront of the world's pharmaceutical industry.*

made the decision that would define the rest of his scientific career. Already familiar with pharmaceutical research as a result of summer jobs, he decided to accept Merck's offer to join the company's laboratories at Rahway, New Jersey. Thirty years later, he is certain he made the right decision.

Today Gary Rasmusson is still intense. Still well organized. But a good deal broader in his approach to science and more tolerant of those with whom he works. He has learned to take advantage of the opportunities for intellectual cross-fertilization in a lab that blends the efforts of microbiologists, organic chemists, virologists, biophysicists, and other scientists and technicians in an intense search for new therapeutic agents. One of these agents is *Proscar*, which promises to become the world's first effective drug for treating enlargement of the prostate gland. Gary Rasmusson has devoted the better part of sixteen years to *Proscar*, and that experience tells you much about his career and about the trials of modern drug research.

When he started at Merck, Rasmusson could not use his knowledge of steroids. The firm's scientists knew steroids were potent. But these drugs had produced the kinds of side effects that had persuaded Merck to shift its attention elsewhere. Only one scientist, Glen Arth, had kept the light flickering in steroid research, and Arth's tiny group was unable in the mid-1970s to convince management to press forward with a compound they thought might be useful in treating acne, the scourge of teenagers. Instead, MSDRL's president, Dr. Roy Vagelos, steered their research toward solving the problems of prostate enlargement.

Shortly, Rasmusson took over the project following Arth's untimely death. Within a year, the lab was off and running with a promising compound, but eight years would pass before Merck had a patent covering the chemical. Elaborate safety tests were conducted. Tinkering with the molecules improved the drug's potency and metabolism. By 1990, sixteen years and many millions of dollars later, *Proscar* was still only in Phase III of its clinical trials. Only one out of every ten thousand compounds studied even make it this far. *Proscar* showed great promise. But as Rasmusson and Scolnick knew, it could still fail to clear its final hurdles. If that happened, sixteen years of research would go down the drain. But if *Proscar* succeeded, Merck would have a unique product that will relieve an irritating condition afflicting most of the world's older men.

Risky indeed. Incredibly painstaking and expensive. In Merck's centennial year the company is spending close to a billion dollars to stay

*Molecular model of finasteride, the active ingredient of* Proscar.

*Dr. Lewis H. Sarett and Dr. Glen E. Arth on the cover of* Merck Review, *1958.*

*Dr. Gary H. Rasmusson (left), Senior Investigator, Synthetic Chemical Research, MSDRL, and Dr. Edward M. Scolnick, President of MSDRL, 1990.*

## GEORGE MERCK

His family had been in business in the central German city of Darmstadt for almost two centuries when this second son of Wilhelm Ludwig Merck was born in 1867. His father and mother (née Lina Moller, daughter of an architect) had a secure status and comfortable life. Wilhelm, who ran E. Merck's fine chemicals factory, sent the fun-loving, sometimes mischievous George to the local Gymnasium, a secondary school. When he was sixteen, George began his business training. He was apprenticed to the wholesale druggist firm F. A. Budingen in Frankfurt am Main. Two years later he joined E. Merck and continued his practical education with the company's representatives in Paris and London.

A more polished and mature young businessman emerged, ready for a difficult assignment in the United States. There had been a problem which threatened E. Merck's reputation for high-quality products: the company's labels had illegally been placed on chemicals made by other businesses. Theodore Weicker, who ran the New York sales office, had seen the agency through that crisis, but the parent firm wanted a trusted family member to promote its interests in the United States. Hence George's trip to New York and the organization in that city in 1891 of Merck & Co.

Although posted in the new world, George Merck did not turn his back on Darmstadt. He returned for a visit in 1892 and continued to hold a commission as a lieutenant in the German army. In 1893, he married Fredericke Schenck, whose family had long resided in Darmstadt but were currently living in Antwerp.

Abandoning his bachelor quarters, George and Fredericke bought a home at Llewellyn Park, West Orange, New Jersey, where they became neighbors and friends of the inventor Thomas Edison. While George would continue to visit Germany, he now put down deep roots in the United States. In 1902 he became an American citizen, and he sent his only son, George Wilhelm, to local schools and then to America's premier academic institution, Harvard University.

George Merck's business career in the United States was not an uninterrupted voyage into success and prosperity. Two years after he established Merck & Co., the national economy dipped into a four-year depression, the worst the nation had ever experienced. Having sailed through that storm, George found himself at loggerheads with his own best customers, the German druggists of New York and vicinity. This fight began in 1897, when Merck & Co. opened its own stylish pharmacy in downtown Manhattan. It ended two years later when George Merck bowed to the demands of his customers and closed his elegant apothecary. Later, the war with Germany in 1917 created a far more serious crisis, one which threatened to wrest control of Merck & Co. from its founder's hands.

George Merck guided his company successfully through these rough seas and following WWI permanently severed his formal ties with the German parent firm. While steadily building the company's sales, he enhanced Merck & Co.'s reputation for high-quality products and became a manufacturer as well as distributor of fine chemicals (as opposed to bulk industrial chemicals). He purchased one of his plants, the St. Louis factory, from Herf & Frerichs and built the other, much larger operation on the north side of Rahway, New Jersey, from the ground up. By the time he passed the helm to his son, Merck & Co. was one of the "Big Three" fine chemical producers in the United States. A year later, on October 21, 1926, the company's founder died at his home in New Jersey.

GEORGE W. MERCK

He was the embodiment of "Merck restraint." Tall, blue-eyed, blondish, and impeccably dressed, George W. Merck looked the part he was born and bred to play. After completing his secondary education in local New Jersey schools, he attended Harvard University, where he became an editor of the Lampoon and "occasionally made gay but not wild expeditions to Boston theatres and cinemas. . . ." Graduating in 1915 with a BA and a "moderate working knowledge of chemistry," he heeded his father's advice not to venture to wartorn Europe for graduate work. "Come on into the shop," George Sr. said, "You can get your degree later."

Ten years later, George W. Merck would be president of Merck & Co. and launched on a career that would involve some of the most exciting innovations in the firm's history. As president and later as chairman of the board, he guided the company through its two most decisive mergers. The first, in 1927, with Powers-Weightman-Rosengarten, more than doubled the company's sales and freed it from dependence upon Germany for its supply of such alkaloids as morphine and quinine. The second, in 1953, with Sharp & Dohme, was the making of the modern Merck corporation, a fully integrated, multi-national producer and distributor of pharmaceuticals as well as specialty chemicals.

The 1953 merger was decisive to the company's future and tricky to administer. A lesser man than George W. Merck might have drifted into retirement without taking on that challenge. He had after all spent a quarter of a century as president and three vigorous years as chairman of the board. Now he had to oversee the transformation of a chemical company into a full-line producer and distributor of ethical pharmaceuticals. The customers were different. As were the two companies' products and cultures. There was as well the new emphasis on global operations, a transformation that called for a new corporate structure, a new breed of managers, and heavy investments in countries whose political economies were subject to sudden, unpredictable changes. The successful consummation of the merger with Sharp & Dohme was one of the two major accomplishments of George W. Merck's long business career.

The other was the creation within the firm of a new and unusually effective research organization. While averring that he "was not a scientist," he carefully built within Merck the team of scientists and the strategy of scientific innovation that would characterize the company from the 1930s to the present day. He made certain that Merck was "alive to its larger obligations" so the company could "play the part of a true partner with medicine. . . ." He blended outstanding scientists and technicians into an effective team that produced significant accomplishments in the synthesis of vitamins, in antibacterials and antibiotics—including the sulfa drugs, penicillin, and streptomycin—and in hormone research.

Living the cooperative ideals he proclaimed, George W. Merck served his country as well as his company and community. During World War II, he was director of the War Research Service and a special consultant to the Secretary of War. In the postwar years he served under two presidents as a member of the board of the National Science Foundation. At Merck during these years, he had shifted day-to-day operational responsibilities to his carefully chosen successors. But he remained chairman of the board and was deeply involved in the firm's evolution until his death on November 9, 1957. Merck restraint. Merck innovation. Merck teamwork. All were embodied in the firm's second executive leader and last of his family to head the business.

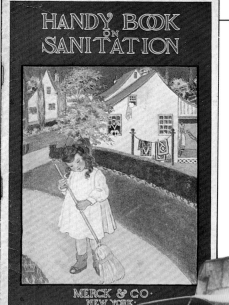

*A 1917 pamphlet designed to give consumers "useful information on the sanitary care of the household and of domestic animals" and guidelines for using Merck's* Creolin-Pearson, *a coal-tar, creosote-based disinfectant.*

*The masthead of* Merck's Market Report, *1892.*

*One of Merck's growing fleet of delivery vehicles outside company headquarters in New York City, circa 1908.*

*George W. Merck (seated), President of Merck & Co., Inc., confers with his brother-in-law George W. Perkins, Merck Executive Vice-President and Treasurer, 1947. Photograph for* Fortune *by Barrett Gallagher, © 1947 Time Inc. All rights reserved.*

"on the tip"—as Rasmusson puts it—in this kind of research on human and animal health products. Without that effort, revolutionary drugs like *Proscar* could never be developed. You stay "on the tip" in microbiology and organic chemistry by nurturing scientists like Gary Rasmusson. You provide them with first-class facilities and equipment. You develop a spirit of cooperation, of teamwork in research and development. Good people, good ideas, and good research have given Merck the products that have placed the company at the forefront of the world's pharmaceutical industry. Merck's deepset traditions have sustained that effort.

## THE TRADITION OF GLOBAL ENTERPRISE

Merck, an enterprise in the top 100 of the *Fortune 500* today, began a century ago as a small branch of a European fine chemical firm, E. Merck. In this, as in many other ways, America has always been an amalgam of people, ideas, and resources from around the world. Europe provided this commercial outpost of E. Merck with its initial vision, its leadership, its capital, and its base of scientific knowledge. All of these came from Germany where E. Merck, an established Darmstadt company, traced its origins back to the seventeenth century. By the late nineteenth century, the Darmstadt business was exporting many of its four thousand products to the United States, where the pharmaceutical industry being served by E. Merck was relatively backward.

Germany at this time led the world in generating new chemical knowledge and synthetic organic products. American scholars who wanted to understand the most advanced scientific techniques routinely

MERCK'S
ARCHIVES
OF
MATERIA MEDICA
AND DRUG THER.
A MONTHLY JOURNAL

TOLUENE M.
(TOLUOL)

— 17 —

and inorg. salts and besides h
suffered by fermentation an
slow and insufficient dry

Analytical Methods

I Tartaric acid determina

**Merck's Report**

Reflects the onward steps made anywhere in pharmacy as a science, an art, a business.

It records the achievements of leading scientists, and disseminates the views of prominent educators.

It gives the current history of all valuable experience in pharmacy.

It keeps constant track of all the newer materia medica, and of technical improvements.

It increases profits from prescription trade, counter sales, and specialty manufacture.

It helps establish congenial relations with physicians, and tells how druggists win the influence
doctors.

... is published monthly, the
... being $2.00 a year, payable

... copy, address

... MERCK'S REPORT

New

**Merck's Report Ready-Reference**

DESIGNED FOR USE AT THE PRESCRI
COUNTER AND PHARMACEUTICAL
LABORATORY

CONTAINING

MPORTANT INCOMPATIBLES, ARRANGED
THE COMMONER POISONS, AND THEIR
LE, COMPRISING OVER 2400 PREPARATI
OLDER, AS WELL AS THE NEWE
SYSTEM, WITH TABLES
Y OF TERMS OCCURRI
RAN PRESCRIPTION
LUTION CHART
UTION. OTHER

MERCK
MERCK

Specify MERCK'S
on your orders

ATE OF SOD

ANILINE IODEOSINE

GUARANT

1 OZ.
IODINE

1 OZ.
THYROIDIN MERCK

part—about 5 parts fresh

Distributors
and Guarantors

ANTIPYRINA

1 OZ.
IUM LACTATE

U. S. P. VII

MERCK

RY MER

TECHNICA

went to Germany to study. Many of them returned to the United States with knowledge that seeded entrepreneurial ventures in the domestic chemical industry. It was in this context that E. Merck reorganized its tiny sales office in the United States as a separate firm.

The task fell to Wilhelm Merck's second son, George Merck, who journeyed to New York City in 1891. Only twenty-three years old when he set up shop on William Street, George Merck quickly established his reputation as an astute businessman. Deliberate and attentive to details, he worked hard to enhance the company's reputation as a reliable supplier of high-quality chemicals. His major customers were the apothecaries of New York and vicinity. Within a few years George had doubled the branch office's sales and moved into his own six-story building at University Place and 8th Street. By 1897, he had boosted sales to over one million dollars.

Turn-of-the-century America was prosperous and confident. George was convinced that these favorable conditions would continue and that he would be able to turn his fledgling firm into a replica of its parent enterprise, E. Merck. He looked south to New Jersey, where he was able to buy 120 acres of wooded countryside near Rahway. Shortly after he became a U.S. citizen in 1902, he started manufacturing his own fine chemicals at Rahway and in St. Louis, where he bought a factory that was already making iodides and other staple pharmaceuticals. No longer merely a branch office, George's business, Merck & Co., gradually expanded its product line of American-made narcotics—including morphine and cocaine—bismuths and iodides. By 1905 sales pushed past $2 million. By 1910 past $3 million. Merck & Co., an offspring of Germany, was soon manufacturing more than it imported, and in 1912 it set up its own foreign subsidiary in Canada.

Merck & Co. was coming of age in America, but its ties to Europe were still strong. George Merck used to his advantage the manufacturing processes of E. Merck, which held a controlling interest in the

*Twenty-nine-year old George Merck in 1896.*

*Merck's Rahway manufacturing site, circa 1903.*

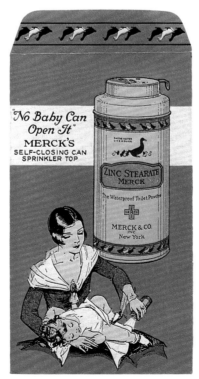

*Package for zinc stearate baby powder, an early Merck consumer product. Courtesy William H. Helfand.*

*(Opposite) Products, publications, and manuscripts representative of Merck & Co. activities in the United States before 1920.*

## JAMES J. KERRIGAN

Kerrigan well deserved the Horatio Alger Award that he received in 1952. Given to honor those who rose from humble beginnings, achieved great success, and were of great service, the awards that year were bestowed upon a Nobel Peace Prize winner and a distinguished university administrator, as well as Merck's president.

Kerrigan fitted the pattern. Born in Brooklyn in 1894, he had spent his early childhood in Ireland. Returning to the United States alone at the age of 13, he landed a job with Merck as an "order-bench boy," delivering small orders by hand through the streets of New York. In the next few years, he worked his way up through nine different positions. Ambitious and energetic, this red-haired Irishman attracted the attention of the company's president. George Merck soon had the 17-year-old Kerrigan on a fast track. First, Merck sent him to Canada in 1911 to help organize the new sales office in Montreal. A year later he was assistant manager of the Montreal branch. Two years of success in Canada brought him a promotion to chemical buyer in New York.

George W. Merck agreed with his father's evaluation of Kerrigan, who became vice president in charge of sales and purchasing and a member of the board of directors in 1927. While he held those positions, Merck & Co. experienced an increase in sales large enough to persuade George W. Merck to name Kerrigan commercial vice president in 1945. Five years later, George

W. Merck bestowed the presidency on this former messenger boy and product of the "old boy" network in sales.

Kerrigan held the presidency during five of the most decisive years in Merck's history. There was the merger with Sharp & Dohme in 1953 and the subsequent turn to global operations under the auspices of Merck Sharp & Dohme International. New drugs were beginning to spur the company's growth. By 1955, when he retired, the firm which had employed only 300 when he joined it had a work force of over 10,000. When Kerrigan died in 1956, he had been honored by his country for wartime service and by the National University of Ireland, which had given him an honorary Doctor of Laws degree in 1951. He had served as a member of the executive and development committee of the Columbia University College of Pharmacy and Fordham University's advisory board of research. He had earned his Horatio Alger Award.

*(Opposite) A view of the new Merck & Co. works in St. Louis, Missouri. This picture is from the August 1903 announcement in the* Oil, Paint and Drug Reporter *that Merck had acquired the chemical business of Herf & Frerichs. Among the products made in St. Louis were iodides, bromides, salicylic acid, and bismuth salts.*

*Henry W. Johnstone, Vice President for Operations (right), and James J. Kerrigan, Vice President for Sales (center), chat with Charles B. Llewellyn at the first Merck Family Day in Rahway, May 1939.*

## MERCK & CO.'S WORKS AT ST. LOUIS, MO.

*Chemical operator using a respirator and protective gear at the Rahway plant in the 1920s.*

American company. Frequently, George looked to Darmstadt for counsel and to German immigrants for employees. His Rahway, New York, and St. Louis operations all had a strong Teutonic flavor. Reminiscing about the St. Louis branch, factory worker Anson Veazey recalled that he and his brother were the only ones on the staff who did not speak German. The summers were hot, he said, and in the early years they had a "beer break" twice a day in the warehouse and factory. Every worker had his own pail, which was hung on a pole studded with nails to keep the buckets from sliding off. Merck—mindful of the firm's reputation for high quality products—abandoned this St. Louis ritual around 1910, and in subsequent years the ethnic ties to Europe were gradually loosened.

In 1917 when the United States entered the First World War, the German phase of the Merck company's history abruptly ended. To the distress of many immigrants, the German Empire was now the enemy. George Merck had no choice but to break formal ties with his family and E. Merck after the U.S. government seized the Merck & Co. stock owned by the Darmstadt firm. Fortunately, George had positioned his business so that it could weather this crisis. With help from New York investors, he was able to purchase from the U.S. government the stock formerly owned by E. Merck. Belts had to be tightened for several years. But by 1924, George Merck had total sales edging up toward $6 million. He pushed past that mark in 1925, when he turned over the presidency to his son, George W. Merck.

The "roaring twenties" were good to most U.S. companies, despite the trade protectionism that frequently crimped the overseas business. Merck & Co. extended its line of U.S.-made chemicals and concentrated for some years on building its coverage of markets at home. Meanwhile, the company cautiously moved forward in those foreign nations hospitable to American products. One of the areas was the Caribbean. There, the firm began to establish new distributorships and to compete on an equal basis with the older, established European and English companies. By the end of the decade, Merck was making good sales in the Caribbean and was successful in promoting its subsidiary in Canada as well. These markets were not nearly as important as domestic demand, but they enabled Merck & Co. to keep a presence in international trade during the twenties and the depression-ridden 1930s.

For Merck the nineteen-forties brought a vigorous return to globalism. At the end of the Second World War American producers of chemicals and other goods were in a powerful position. Many of their overseas competitors had been savaged, their plants bombed or diverted entirely to military products. With their credit impaired and their distribution networks thrown awry, foreign companies were preoccupied for several years with the tasks of reconstruction. That left U.S. businesses dominant in many of the world's markets.

Merck firmly grasped this opportunity. The company launched its global expansion by establishing two organizations, Merck North America and Pan America. These were marketing agencies which strengthened the system of distributorships that the company had begun to create before WWII. Under the leadership of a new president, James J. Kerrigan, these two organizations boosted exports to about twenty percent of the firm's sales by the early 1950s.

Then began one of the most exciting eras of Merck's drive to globalism. The foundation was laid when the company merged in 1953 with Sharp & Dohme. This eminent pharmaceutical company had long been a customer for Merck's fine chemicals. Sharp & Dohme brought to the merger a well-established network for distributing pharmaceutical products overseas. As management consolidated the two firms, they used this network as the base for creating an entirely new entity, Merck

*Postcard honoring Merck's contributions to the war effort sent by George W. Merck to all company employees then in the Armed Forces, 1943.*

*Packaging penicillin in Rahway, 1943. These ampules were shipped to Allied service men and women around the world.*

*A Merck poster honoring the contributions of pharmacists to national welfare (prepared for National Pharmacy Week, October 1941).*

"I was the first member of the family ever to go to college...," Connor said. But his parents expected him "to go to college and then, hopefully, to graduate school." He did not disappoint them. Graduating magna cum laude from Syracuse University in 1936, he went to the Harvard Law School, where he compiled a good record, was a member of the Legal Aid Bureau, and received his degree in 1939. For the next three years, he practiced law in New York, followed by an extended period of government service: first with the Office of Scientific Research and Development (OSRD); then in the Marine Corps; the Office of Naval Research; and finally the office of Secretary of the Navy James Forrestal, to whom Connor was a special assistant.

This circuitous path led to Rahway, N.J., by way of Vannevar Bush (head of OSRD and later chairman of Merck's board of directors) and George W. Merck, who was also serving the government in Washington, D.C. Both men were impressed with Connor. They persuaded him to join Merck in 1947 as general counsel and secretary. Three years later he was appointed vice president, and in 1955 he became president and Chief Executive Officer (CEO).

Connor would lead Merck through a decade of expansion and administrative change. His first and most pressing task was to carry to completion the consolidation of the Merck and Sharp & Dohme organizations. Of particular interest to the new CEO were the international operations, where he himself had been working before 1955. Here he brought new and dynamic leaders to the fore and sought to make the firm a "Free world Enterprise based in the United States."

The first of Merck's professional managers, Connor created a new decentralized structure and vigorously promoted research and development. He introduced management by objectives in 1955, as well as formal profit planning and long-term strategic planning. In 1957, he organized The Merck Company Foundation to manage the corporation's philanthropy. At MSDRL he moved Dr. Max Tishler, "the consummate leader," into the top position. The new products that came out of the labs under Tishler were crucial to the success of Connor's program at home and abroad.

John Connor also led Merck's defense when the Federal Trade Commission charged it, along with four other companies, with price fixing. Although the trial judge dismissed the suit, Senator Kefauver pursued this issue before the U.S. Senate's Subcommittee on Antitrust and Monopoly

for the next three years. Connor, who brilliantly defended the drug companies, considered the resulting Kefauver-Harris Drug Amendment Act (1962) as a victory for the industry. But he recognized that Merck and its competitors would have to improve their public relations if further attacks were to be avoided. Only forty years old when he became CEO, Connor retired in 1965 to go to Washington, D.C., as Secretary of Commerce under President Lyndon B. Johnson. Two years later he resigned that post and became president and a director of Allied Chemical Corporation, a position he held until 1979. Later, he renewed his ties to Merck, serving on the board of directors from 1981 to 1987.

## JOHN T. CONNOR

*Holding a molecular model of cortisone, Nobel laureate Edward C. Kendall of the Mayo Clinic testifies with Merck President John T. Connor (right) at the Kefauver hearings in Washington, D. C., December 1959. John J. Horan, then Merck's Director of Public Relations, is seated in the background.*

# POWERS-WEIGHTMAN-ROSENGARTEN

"Sulphur from Louisiana, Bromines from the salt wells of Michigan, cinchona bark from the mountain slopes of Java, Araroba found in the decaying forests of Brazil, nux vomica from the jungles of India, bismuth from Bolivian mines, iodine from Chile, cloves from Zanzibar, lemon juice from Sicily and the West Indies, Spanish Quicksilver and Chinese nut galls." These were some of the exotic raw materials that Powers-Weightman-Rosengarten used in the 1920s to produce its extensive line of fine chemicals. The firm's lineage, like its raw materials, had a global cast. One branch could be traced back to the English pharmacist, John Farr, who had started a chemical business in Philadelphia in 1818 and subsequently learned how to manufacture cinchona alkaloids, especially quinine. In 1836 he used this knowledge as the basis for creating a new company in Philadelphia with his nephew William Weightman and with Thomas H. Powers. Although Weightman's sons and son-in-law later joined the firm, he survived them all, leaving his daughter, Ann M. Weightman Walker, as sole family member on his death in 1904. Unwilling to run the business on her own, she agreed to merge with Rosengarten & Sons in 1905.

Rosengarten & Sons also had deep roots that could be traced back to early nineteenth-century Europe. The company began as a partnership in Philadelphia between two Swiss chemists, Zeitler and Seitler, in 1822. George D. Rosengarten, an accountant from Alsace-Lorraine, later purchased a share in the business and formed Zeitler & Rosengarten. He wisely sent his sons to the University of Pennsylvania for the best American training in chemistry and then back to Europe to work with the leading chemists of the day. When they joined the firm in 1854, it became Rosengarten & Sons.

By the 1920s, this company was— like Merck—a "long-line chemical house," with a large business in quinines and synthetic drugs, including neosalvarsan. Its assets and sales were greater than Merck's, but the four surviving Rosengarten heirs wished to be relieved of the burden of managing the firm after their father's death (1921). They turned to George W. Merck, who arranged the merger with his business in 1927. Frederick Rosengarten, the youngest of the sons, became chairman of Merck following the merger, and the family was last represented on the Board by Adolph G. Rosengarten, Jr., who died in 1990.

*Powers-Weightman-Rosengarten headquarters in Philadelphia, 1915.*

*(Opposite) East view of Schuylkill Falls plant of Powers & Weightman. The East Falls site was in continuous use for chemical production from 1846 until 1952. Courtesy Philadelphia Museum of Art, William H. Helfand Collection.*

*(left to right) Thomas H. Powers, William Weightman, and Henry D. Rosengarten.*

*The Merck office building at University Place and Clinton Place in New York City, 1896.*

# Part I

# VALUES

By W. H. Rease.

East View of Schuylkill Falls Laboratory.

# POWERS & WEIGHTMAN

## MANUFACTURING CHEMISTS,

## PHILADELPHIA

OFFICE AT CITY LABORATORY
NINTH & PARRISH STS

NEW YORK OFFICE
Nº 56 MAIDEN LANE.

Sharp & Dohme International (MSDI), to promote the company's trade in pharmaceuticals around the world.

A new cadre of leaders emerged in the late 1950s to guide the international division's aggressive expansion. John T. Connor, who became chief executive officer at Merck in 1955, was an ardent advocate of increased involvement overseas. He saw to it that MSDI's first president, James H. Sharp, had the resources and the personnel he needed to put some muscle in his new organization. Supporting Sharp and then becoming president of the division in 1956 was an unusual man who would do much to set the tone of Merck's international operations for the next two decades.

Dr. Antonie T. Knoppers had little experience in business when he joined Merck in 1952. An academician, a physician, an avid chess player, a lover of classical music, he would have been out of place in prewar Merck. But at MSDI he proved to be an ideal choice to head the company's fastest growing division. Dutch-born and educated, Knoppers had been teaching pharmacology at the Free University of Amsterdam when he came to Merck's attention.

At MSDI, Knoppers built a like-minded team of managers. Familiar with the customs and languages of the nations whose markets they served, they were urbane spokesmen for a corporation transforming itself from an exporter to a multinational. Knoppers emphasized the development of strong subsidiaries throughout the world, each with its own national character. By giving the subsidiaries considerable leeway to build their own organizations, MSDI was able to blend the Merck emphasis upon high quality products, the marketing skills of Sharp & Dohme, and the national talents of the division's many indigenous businessmen. During this entrepreneurial phase at MSDI, the keynotes were rapid expansion, local autonomy, and aggressive, innovative salesmanship.

*Dr. Antonie T. Knoppers (left), President of MSDI, discusses European initiatives with Merck President John T. Connor, 1961.*

*Cover of a 1933 Merck information pamphlet.*

*Handling boxes of Merck products in the shipping department of the Rahway plant, 1951.*

"During a period of eight years," Ernst Stauffen said, "I had no vacation except an occasional week-end trip to Mr. Sharp's county seat on the eastern shore of Maryland." Stauffen had been working at Sharp & Dohme's Baltimore offices since 1876. By that time the original "Retail Drug Store" that Alpheus P. Sharp had started in 1845 had grown into two buildings and a lively business manufacturing various "extracts, elixirs, syrups, cordials, [and] solutions. . . ." Sharp and his partners, Louis and Charles E. Dohme, sold their "Ethical Pharmaceutical Products" through wholesale druggists in Maryland, Delaware, Pennsylvania, and Virginia. In addition to the hard-working Stauffen, the company in the 1870s employed four salesmen and one detail man who called upon doctors.

*Ernst Stauffen.*

In the years that followed, Sharp & Dohme steadily extended its markets, product lines, and work force. The firm established agencies in New York, Chicago, Boston, Philadelphia, and other domestic commercial centers. Its chemists developed a new "soluble hypodermic tablet," a gelatin-coated pill, and numerous other innovative products. The firm's managers pushed their network of agencies overseas, making important inroads in Latin American markets.

In 1929 Sharp & Dohme merged with H. K. Mulford Co. of Philadelphia and subsequently moved its central offices to that city. Mulford brought to the merger a well-established biological laboratory which had been the first in this country to develop commercial forms of diphtheria antitoxin, smallpox vaccine, pneumococcic antibody serum, and various bacterial vaccines. Strengthened by this alliance, Sharp & Dohme experienced a tenfold increase in sales in the decade following 1942. The company produced important innovations in sulfa drugs, in techniques for dehydrating biologicals, in plasmas, and in well known over-the-counter products such as throat lozenges Sucrets. The company also made antiseptic powders and solutions (*S.T. 37* and *B.F.I.*), antibiotics (*Penalev* and *Remanden*), and dietary aids (*Altepose* and *Melozet* wafers).

It was this profitable and growing institution, with sixteen domestic branches, operations in over fifty different countries, five hundred products, almost four thousand employees, and total sales of more than fifty million dollars, that opted in 1953 to merge with Merck & Co. The moral of the story? Something about hard work, because Ernst Stauffen finished his career as Sharp & Dohme's chief operating officer.

*H. K. Mulford pioneered with diphtheria antitoxin in 1892. Courtesy William H. Helfand.*

*Mulford automatic tablet compressing machine, 1905.*

*July 1891 price list for Sharp & Dohme products.*

"I saw in them no signs of the horns or tail...," Professor Richards later commented. He had met with George W. Merck, George W. Perkins, and Dr. Randolph T. Major to discuss the future of research at Merck & Co. "I could detect no difference between their attitude toward the development of the sciences contributory to medicine and that to which I had been exposed in universities and on the advice of the heads of my university accepted the proposal." He would act as a consultant to the business, an undertaking that was in 1930 despicable to many of his fellow academics.

Pharmacology was a relatively new field, and research training in this branch of chemistry was itself still controversial at many American universities. R. H. Chittenden, Richards's chemistry professor at Yale, had been trained to meet the rigid requirements of German laboratory research. Richards, who also took a university course at Strasbourg, had gone on to acquire an international reputation for his research courses in clinical pharmacology at Northwestern University and then at the University of Pennsylvania.

Still, it was controversial for a scholar of Richards's renown to work for a business. The American Society for Pharmacology and Experimental Therapeutics (ASPET) had a clause in its constitution barring from membership pharmacologists who worked for industry. Richards, a charter member of the Society, tendered his resignation on accepting Merck's offer.

Richards plunged ahead with his efforts to create a first-class laboratory at Merck. He helped the firm land Dr. Hans Molitor of Austria as the first head of its new pharmacological laboratory, dedicated in 1933 as the Merck Institute of Therapeutic Research. Richards headed a board of advisers who encouraged the company to emphasize basic research and to allow its scientists to publish their results. In this way Merck was able to attract top scientists and move to the cutting edge of several areas of medical research.

Over the years, academic scorn for industry dissolved. Richards was reinstated in ASPET and honored for his wartime service to the nation. From 1947 to 1950, he served as president of the U.S. National Academy of Sciences. In 1948 at age 72, he retired as vice president of medical affairs of the University of Pennsylvania and joined Merck's board of directors. From 1949 to 1956 he chaired the board's scientific committee. Having done as much as any one scientist to shape his discipline and to develop scientific research at Merck & Co., he finally retired from the firm's board of directors at age eighty-four.

ALFRED NEWTON RICHARDS

## THE TRADITION OF INNOVATION

*Sharp & Dohme's Baltimore laboratory at the turn of the century.*

*An ad for a popular Sharp & Dohme consumer product circa World War I.*

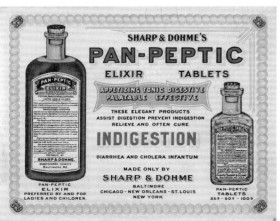

Of course Merck's strategy of innovation long predated MSDI and was by the 1950s embodied in every aspect of the company's operations. Science-based innovation from within is a central component of the Merck way, as is the tradition of capitalizing on opportunities for growth outside the firm. Both approaches have made essential contributions to Merck's expansion during the past century.

In the mid-1920s, after George W. Merck took over the presidency, he guided the company through a 1927 merger with Powers-Weightman-Rosengarten (PWR), a family business whose heirs chose to leave active management. PWR was a successful Philadelphia producer and distributor of pharmaceutical chemicals. It was actually a larger organization than Merck, with a somewhat different product line. The two firms thus complemented one another, and the merger fostered economies of scale both in production and in marketing. This larger organization—with sales in 1929 over $13 million—also created new opportunities to innovate because the firm could now afford to make a heavy investment in research and development.

The crucial move into science-based innovation came in the 1930s. These were dire times for the United States, which was caught in the worst depression in the nation's history. But paradoxically, despite the millions on relief, the medical sciences in America were thriving. This was an era of dramatic accomplishment in science, and several of the breakthroughs were to have an important impact on the Merck enterprise.

George W. Merck was attentive to the events taking place on the frontiers of science. Once he had the merger with PWR under his belt, he set out to create within the firm an institution that would enable Merck to link its future to the therapeutic revolution. Working closely with George W. Perkins, his brother-in-law and chief operating officer, and with the distinguished University of Pennsylvania pharmacologist,

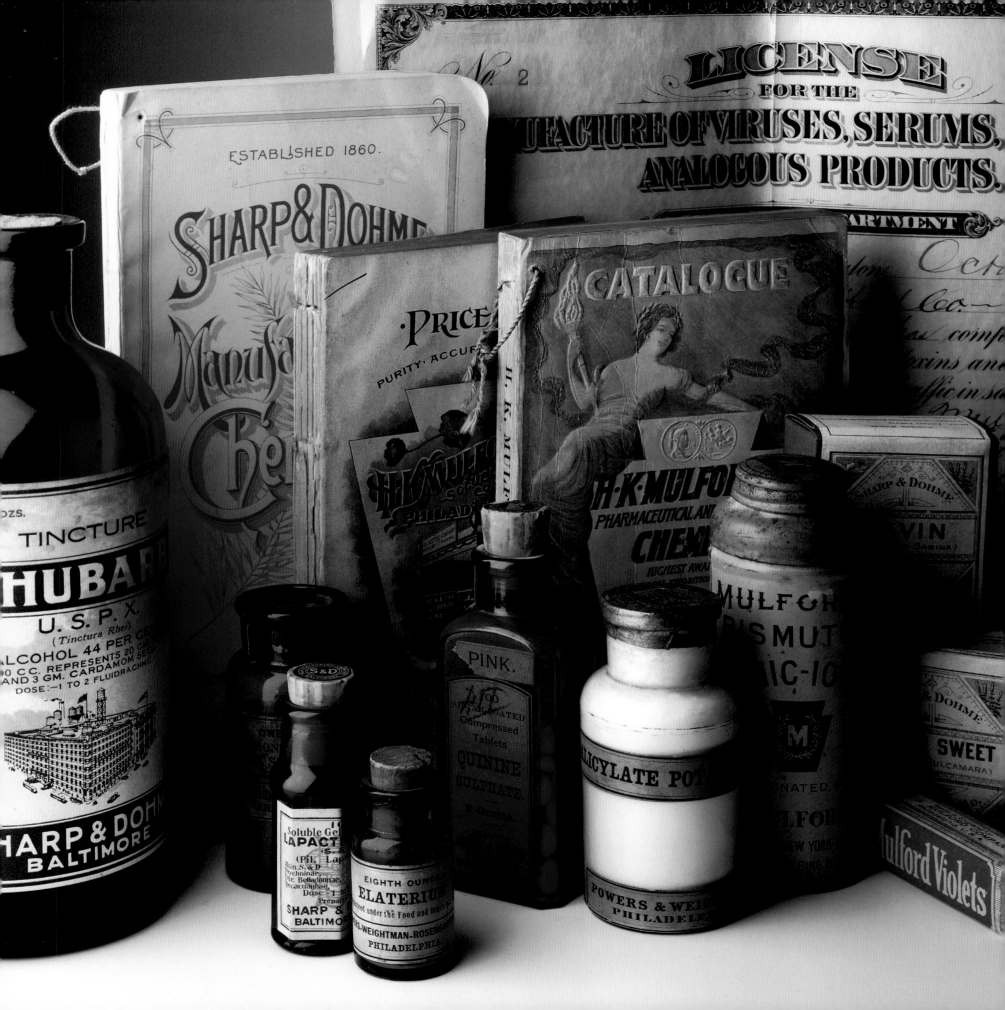

*These artifacts and documents illustrate the range of products sold by Powers & Weightman and its successor Powers-Weightman-Rosengarten, H. K. Mulford, and Sharp & Dohme, all of which became part of Merck & Co., Inc. through mergers and acquisitions.*

*Artist's sketch of the new building of the Merck Institute for Therapeutic Research dedicated in 1953.*

*(Left to right) Randolph T. Major, Alfred Newton Richards, Hans Molitor, George W. Merck, and James J. Kerrigan at the ground-breaking ceremony for the new Merck Institute building, October 1951.*

Dr. Alfred Newton Richards, he began in the early 1930s to build a new type of research team within the company.

First he needed the right scientist, one with the potential to become a science manager and advocate in the company for research. With the help of Richards, he was able to hire Dr. Randolph T. Major, a promising young chemist teaching at Princeton University. Major guided Merck into "fundamental chemical studies," including research on the identification and synthesis of vitamins. George W. Merck and Major encouraged the company's researchers to publish the results of their studies as well as to develop commercial products. As of 1933, they had an up-to-date, central research laboratory in which to work. With new facilities, an excellent staff, and strong financial support, they soon positioned Merck at the front edge of research on anesthetics, antibiotics, and vitamins.

Recognizing that he needed full-time support from a trained pharmacologist, George W. Merck dipped into the international market for scientific talent. The company found in Vienna the young scientist it needed, Dr. Hans Molitor. In Rahway, Molitor became head of the Merck Institute of Therapeutic Research. He would remain in that important post until 1956, building his staff from three to more than 150 researchers while actively pressing forward with his own investigations into subjects ranging from analgesics to synthetic vitamin $B_1$.

As the Molitor-Major-Richards research team got under way, it began to define the growth path of the corporation. Up to this point, Merck was still manufacturing fine chemicals and synthetic products which it sold to medical institutions or to other companies to be processed and packaged. But in the 1940s, the firm's laboratories conducted a series of breakthrough research projects involving penicillin, streptomycin, vitamin $B_{12}$ and cortisone. So successful were these undertakings

27

## HENRY W. GADSDEN

He was the master operating officer. Armed with a photographic memory and an intense distaste for misinformation, CEO Henry Gadsden could produce managerial tremors when reports had to be presented to Merck's top officers. He had been in the industry since 1937—four years after receiving a BS in economics from Yale University—starting at Sharp & Dohme as an analyst in sales research. Twelve years later, he was vice president and a director of the company, positions he held at the 1953 merger with Merck. As the two firms' officers were blended together, Henry Gadsden became first an administrative vice president and then executive vice president in the Rahway headquarters of Merck, second in command to John T. Connor. The two men maintained a fruitful relationship that climaxed for Gadsden with his appointment in 1965 as Merck's president and chief executive officer.

As CEO, Gadsden charted a new growth path for Merck. In his view, Sharp & Dohme's successful expansion before 1953 could be attributed first to its skill in marketing new products of research, second to its ability to maintain its market share in existing products, and only then to its capabilities in production and applications research. Concerned in the mid-sixties that new regulations would impede the growth of the drug industry, he decided to make a series of selective acquisitions. Merck diversified into related fields which involved high technology and promised to create significant synergies. Gadsden planned to achieve this goal without shifting Merck's primary focus away from the animal and human health field. He acquired established research facilities in Canada (Charles E. Frosst & Co., Montreal, which also produced and distributed pharmaceuticals) and in France (Chibret Laboratoires) and for veterinary research, Hubbard Farms in New Hampshire. He expanded into industrial and agricultural chemicals (Metalsalts Corporation) and into the health-related field of environmental control with the acquisition of Calgon Corporation, Baltimore Aircoil Company, and Pacific Pumping Company. In 1972, Merck acquired both Solar Laboratories and Kelco Company.

Sometimes these experiments worked. Sometimes they failed. When diversification was unsuccessful, Gadsden corrected the situation quickly and forcefully. But throughout, he remained dedicated to expansion. Sales under his leadership grew from $158 to $457 million. He continued to support strongly the expansion of the company's overseas division, MSDI, despite significant difficulties in repatriating profits due to exchange fluctuations during the 1960s. Sales outside the United States had increased to 44% of Merck's total sales by 1976.

When he retired as CEO in April of 1976, he said the company's growth record was his greatest satisfaction. Second was the reliance on long-range planning. "The emphasis in all this planning was getting people to think in terms of when Merck was going to be Number One. Now, Merck is one of the companies leading the pharmaceutical field." Four years later, Henry Gadsden died at his home in Short Hills, New Jersey.

*Henry W. Gadsden inspecting sheep during a visit to Hillgrove Station, a Merck research farm near Armidale, Australia, October 1973.*

*John T. Connor (left), President of Merck & Co., Inc., and Henry W. Gadsden, Executive Vice President, 1955.*

that Merck's officers began to consider whether the company should formulate and market finished products. The sales were substantial. And some of Merck's best customers were beginning to produce their own chemicals and synthetics instead of buying them from the Rahway plant. That prompted Merck's leadership to look into the possibilities of a second strategic merger, this time with a pharmaceutical firm. The new strategy would be risky. But George W. Merck and the Board decided to bet the company on a decisive merger.

Merck found the ideal prospect close at hand in Philadelphia, where Sharp & Dohme was headquartered. It would be hard to imagine more complementary partners. The chairman at Sharp & Dohme, John S. Zinsser, as well as the president, William L. Dempsey, both had once worked for Merck. Their organization brought to the merger extensive pharmaceutical knowledge and marketing skills honed by over a century in the business. Its field sales organization was an important asset, as were its new manufacturing, warehousing, and research facilities at West Point, Pennsylvania. Both of the research organizations had experience with sulfa drugs, but Sharp & Dohme had also done extensive research with blood plasma, vaccines, and other biologicals. In part, these latter activities had been acquired when Sharp & Dohme combined with H. K. Mulford Co. in 1929. After that merger, Sharp & Dohme (S&D) had continued to emphasize biological research.

Although some of the managers at S&D and Merck knew each other well, the 1953 merger was not painless. Each of the firms had a deeply rooted culture. Their officers and employees were proud of their accomplishments, certain of their abilities. It was no easy task to bring these two operations together and, indeed, vestiges of their separate identities persist today. Seen from suburban West Point, the Rahway headquarters is the "Emerald City." From the New Jersey perspective,

*The Merck Board of Directors meets at West Point, Pennsylvania, September 22, 1953. Members included (clockwise from left) Walter E. Sachs, Adolph G. Rosengarten, Jr., James H. Sharp, Alfred Newton Richards, Vannevar Bush, Edward H. Green, James J. Kerrigan, George W. Merck (chairman), John S. Zinsser, William L. Dempsey, Frederic Rosengarten, Henry W. Johnstone, Edward Reynolds, Charles S. Garland, Charles D. Dickey, and George S. Currie.*

*A molecular model of chlorothiazide, promotional item for* Diuril, *and samples of the tablet and syrup forms.* Diuril, *introduced in 1958, was the first major product in Merck's new line of cardiovascular drugs.*

*Installation of an axial flow fan in a Baltimore Aircoil Company cooling tower, 1970.*

managers transplanted from Pennsylvania are part of a sales-oriented "West Point Gang."

Still, the merger was a success for both businesses, and Stuart Henshall, controller at Merck, played a central role in managing that delicate process. Turning for advice to Zinsser and Dempsey, who understood both corporations well, Henshall skillfully guided the teams from the two organizations as they ironed out the problems of coordination. Shortly the combined venture began to yield unanticipated synergies.

One came in research. The West Point and Rahway labs were different. Merck's scientists—including in particular Max Tishler and Karl Folkers—had by the 1950s logged a number of outstanding accomplishments in chemical research. Sharp & Dohme had extensive experience in biologicals and in sulfa drugs, but its labs did not have a comparable reputation in the national scientific community. Indeed, some researchers in the "Emerald City" were patronizing to West Point science. But they had badly underestimated their new partners. One of the first breakthroughs after the merger came when Karl Beyer, James Sprague, and others in the West Point labs developed a new diuretic (*Diuril*). Condescension gave way to cooperation. In the years that followed, the labs together generated a long series of therapeutic innovations that have been crucial to the firm's success.

By the 1960s Merck was a fast-growing company with a high level of technical skill, a shelf full of profitable products, and an impressive bundle of managerial ability in manufacturing, research, and marketing. It was also a firm with most of its resources in an industry which increased government regulation threatened to make less profitable. This challenged Henry W. Gadsden, who became CEO in 1965, to experiment with diversification. During these years many American businesses were adopting the strategy of developing related lines of

business in an effort to sustain high growth rates and open new areas in which to apply the corporation's resources. Merck was no exception. In 1968 it acquired Calgon Corporation, one of the nation's leading suppliers of water treatment chemicals and services. Other acquisitions followed in quick march.

Like many of its peers, Merck discovered that other businesses were frequently easier to acquire than they were to run at a profit. Earlier, the company had ventured into consumer products without much success. Some of the diversifications of the 60s and 70s encountered similar problems. One of these was Baltimore Aircoil, a manufacturer of equipment for refrigeration and industrial cooling. This was, unfortunately, an investment that carried the firm far from its core operations in chemicals and pharmaceuticals. Merck eventually sold the business.

There were also successes, one of which was Kelco, still today a highly profitable division. This West Coast operation processed kelp—that is, brown seaweed—to produce alginates and other specialty chemicals. Kelco subsequently extended its line of products to include the xanthan gums used in large amounts by the food industry and manufactured by a fermentation process in its Okmulgee, Oklahoma, plant. Kelco also expanded overseas, acquiring for example Alginate Industries Limited of London in 1979. Like other profitable divisions, Kelco has long had its own research and development facilities. As Kelco and Merck's other successful divisions and subsidiaries matured, each of them acquired a unique set of capabilities. This is certainly the case in Merck's profitable animal health division, Merck Sharp & Dohme AGVET (MSD AGVET). Merck researched its way into the animal health and agricultural chemical business in the years following WWII. By 1979 this enterprise was so successful that it was established as a separate market-

Executives of Merck and Johnson & Johnson celebrate the signing of the joint venture agreement at Branchburg Farm, March 28, 1989. (L to r) Joseph R. Chiesa, J&J ture for Merck; Ralph S. Larsen, J&J Chairman and Chief Executive Officer, and A. E. Cohen, Merck Senior Vice President.

ing division. Today, MSD AGVET is a major source of growth and of new products for Merck.

Joint ventures have provided another doorway to new opportunities. Some of these have been overseas. One of the longest lasting was Nippon Merck-Banyu, which from 1954 to the 1980s gave the American company the opportunity to acquire a secure footing in the rapidly growing Japanese pharmaceutical market. In 1983, Merck purchased a majority share in Banyu—the first such purchase by any U.S. firm operating in Japan. Another current venture, with AB Astra, enables Merck to market in the U.S. the innovative products of this Swedish firm. A third, with Johnson & Johnson, eases Merck into the over-the-counter market and helps it launch a new campaign to transform selected prescription drugs into widely available over-the-counter remedies. A fourth alliance is with the chemical giant, Du Pont. Merck and the Delaware corporation are cooperating in research and marketing

## " We try never to forget that medicine is for the people. It is not for the profits. The profits follow, and if we have remembered that, they have never failed to appear."

Company Group Chairman; Edward F. Chase, Vice President of McNeil Consumer Products Company and General Manager of the joint venture for J&J; Francis H. Spiegel, Jr., Merck Senior Vice President; Dr. P. Roy Vagelos, Merck Chairman and Chief Executive Officer; G. Theodore Mascott, Vice President, Merck Consumer Healthcare, and General Manager of the joint ven-

Yoshie Suzuki inspects ampules on a packaging line at Nippon Merck-Banyu's Okazaki plant, 1968.

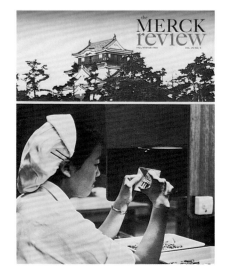

efforts for a series of Merck products and new agents to treat heart disease and high blood pressure. More recently they have signed a second agreement, joining forces to create a new, independent, research-driven pharmaceutical firm.

Each of these complex arrangements blends some of Merck's special skills or products with those of a carefully selected partner company. ''We're trying to be creative,'' senior vice president Francis H. Spiegel says, ''in a merger-mania world.'' As Merck's ''top dealmaker,'' Spiegel has worked with CEO Roy Vagelos to develop these several new ways to combine the company's two major sources of innovation: the quest for science-based discoveries from within and the search for good business partners outside the firm.

## THE TRADITION OF SERVING THE HEALTH NEEDS OF SOCIETY

Innovation at Merck is keyed primarily to the company's third and strongest tradition, that of serving the health needs of society. This tradition—like globalism and innovation—has evolved over the past century, gradually acquiring a broader meaning and more subtle tones. In the early days, when Merck was manufacturing fine chemicals for pharmaceuticals, the primary means of serving society's health needs was by providing high quality products. From George Merck's first days in New York, as we saw, the company stressed the purity of its chemicals. By publishing such standard reference works as *The Merck Index* and *The Merck Manual* (joined in 1990 by the inaugural edition of *The Merck Manual of Geriatrics*), the firm reinforced its commitment to quality and to the provision of full information about its products. At the Rahway plant, quality control was an important function from 1903 on, and George W. Merck reaffirmed his adherence to that tradition in the 1930s by building a modern analytical laboratory to monitor the purity and uniformity of Merck's products.

A modern lab was needed because the founder's son was transforming the company. Science-based innovation and the decisive 1953 merger with Sharp & Dohme accelerated the firm's growth and dramatically increased its potential to serve society's health needs. The Merck concept of service began in the years that followed to acquire new meaning.

In manufacturing there was a new emphasis upon protecting the health and welfare of its own employees and the many communities in which it operates. The dedication to quality in products and services— symbolized by Merck Sharp & Dohme's "Pride in Quality" plan— remained a central feature of the corporate mission, but in the years since WWII, Merck & Co. has taken a far more active role in serving the health needs of those closest to its operations. As manufacturing processes became more intricate and drugs more potent, Merck steadily increased the resources devoted to safety and environmental programs.

WHAT'S WRONG WITH THIS PICTURE?

NATIONAL SAFETY COUNCIL

*This cartoon from the June 1943* Merck Review *accompanied the announcement of a safety competition among Rahway plant departments.*

*George W. Merck (right) with his son, George W. Merck, Jr., and seven-year-old grandson Tony Merck at the Merck Institute groundbreaking, 1951.*

The company introduced new training courses and controls to ensure that neither its employees nor surrounding communities would be endangered.

In marketing as well as manufacturing, the service concept has broadened and deepened since the pivotal 1953 merger. John J. Horan, John Lloyd Huck, and John E. Lyons—all three of whom were in the domestic pharmaceutical division, MSD—led the efforts to devise new and more effective ways to communicate with pharmacists, health organizations, and doctors. Their policies transformed MSD marketing. In dealing with doctors, in particular, Merck became a leader in the pharmaceutical industry. Its extensive training programs stress the goal of ''fair balance,'' that is, providing physicians with full information on side effects and potential problems, as well as the benefits of the company's new drugs.

Those new products flowing out of the Merck Sharp & Dohme Research Laboratories have of course been the primary means of serving the health needs of society and of promoting the company's growth. Profits and progress have been delicately interwoven. The company's second chief executive officer, George W. Merck, found a simple but powerful way to express the company's approach to that relationship. ''We try never to forget,'' Merck said, ''that medicine is for the people. It is not for the profits. The profits follow, and if we have remembered that, they have never failed to appear.''

Illustrations abound. Take *Sinemet*, the unique product Merck researchers developed for treating Parkinson's disease. In this case, Rahway's chemists and West Point's biological experts combined forces in a complex research and testing effort that evolved out of the company's earlier work on hypertensives. In 1975—two years after it had been introduced in Europe and fifteen years after the research had begun—the FDA approved *Sinemet* for use in the United States. The history of *Timoptic*, the first breakthrough in the treatment of glaucoma,

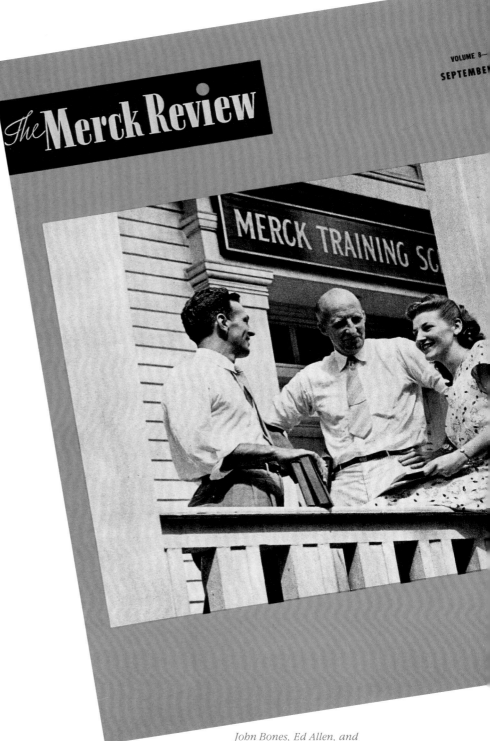

*John Bones, Ed Allen, and Anne Smith on the porch of the Merck Training School, September 1947.*

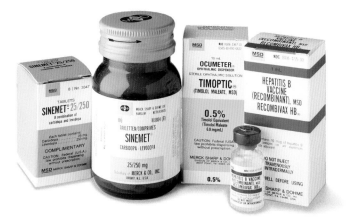

*MSD executives congratulate Dr. Maurice Hilleman (in white lab coat) on the successful introduction of* Pneumovax, *Merck's vaccine against pneomococcal pneumonia, in early 1978. Left to right are Eugene F. McCabe, Vice President for Marketing; John E. Lyons, President; Robert F. Hendrickson, Vice President for Operations; and Franklin W. Costner, Vice President for Sales.*

was similar. In this case, however, the research was multinational as well as multidisciplinary: scientists in Canada, France, and the United States made vital contributions to the development of this important drug.

A third example of the Merck blend of service and profits is provided by the vaccines the firm has developed for inoculating against the debilitating liver disease hepatitis B. This was a particularly dangerous disease because it could cause cancer. Merck's vaccine was *Heptavax-B* (1982), which Dr. Maurice R. Hilleman and his associates derived from human plasma. To free the company from dependence on blood supplies, MSDRL then mounted a new research campaign which resulted in *Recombivax HB*, the first genetically engineered vaccine approved for use in humans. These vaccines, along with *Sinemet* and *Timoptic*, have been profitable to Merck, as has *Mevacor*, the company's leading cholesterol-lowering agent. These drugs have as well benefited millions of people throughout the world.

But what happened when profits did not follow? Merck has frequently developed drugs which promised significant benefits in health care but which for one reason or another could not pay for themselves. The ''orphan drugs'' for treating diseases which affect only a tiny part of the population have, for instance, been introduced under conditions that rule out profits. So too with the amazing drug *Mectizan*, which has already been administered to over eight hundred thousand people in more than a dozen equatorial countries.

The only effective, practical means of preventing a parasitic disease (onchocerciasis) that has blinded millions, *Mectizan* grew out of the company's innovative research in animal health products. Ivermectin—which Merck discovered—is used to control parasites in livestock, horses, and dogs. Finding that a human formulation, *Mectizan*, could be used to prevent river blindness, Merck was left with a quandary. The product simply could not be sold or distributed effectively where it was needed. African and Latin American populations could not afford to buy *Mectizan*. Nor did their governments have the delivery systems or funds necessary to ensure that the more than eighty-five million people at risk would be treated.

CEO Roy Vagelos made the only choice consistent with Merck's traditions: the company would give away the drug. An independent committee of experts was established to review and approve public and private treatment programs, all of which received the drug free. Through these efforts, the countries at risk have begun to make inroads against this pernicious disease.

*Mectizan* and the orphan drugs are of course the exceptions; *Sinemet, Timoptic, Recombivax HB*, and *Mevacor* the rule. Therein lies the story of Merck's astonishing growth in the 1980s. Worldwide sales increased from $2.7 billion to $6.6 billion by the end of the decade, giving Merck the largest single share of the global market for prescription drugs. Already the leading U.S. firm in the animal health and agricultural fields, Merck now seeks to achieve global leadership in this market too. This era of expansion enabled CEO Roy Vagelos and the Board to increase the firm's investments in research to a billion dollars in this centennial year. Echoing George W. Merck, Vagelos has reminded us that the company has been successful because it "provides products of extraordinary <u>value</u>, both human and economic. That," he says, is Merck's "primary corporate mission."

As the company celebrates its centennial, its managers and employees have much to look forward to and a past that they should understand and appreciate. Merck's traditions are important. It is today completely committed to global operations and to innovation. It has reaffirmed and broadened its concept of service to the health needs of society. In the pages that follow, we will see how those traditions have manifested themselves in research, manufacturing, and marketing. But first we must look to the people who breathe life into the traditions and make this company successful.

Mectizan, *Merck's treatment for onchocerciasis, was introduced in 1987. This anti-parasitic promises to save millions of children in tropical regions from the threat of eventually going blind.*

(Opposite) Thanks to Mectizan *these children in Sikoroni, Mali—shown leading their blind elders—can now be spared the ravages of onchocerciasis, "river blindness". Photograph by Eugene Richards, 1989. Reprinted with permission.*

*Dr. Halfdan Mahler (left), then Director-General of the World Health Organization, Merck Chairman Dr. P. Roy Vagelos (center), and Albert D. Angel, Merck Vice President for Public Affairs, meet the press in Washington, D. C., after the announcement of Merck's decision to donate* Mectizan *to combat river blindness, October 1987.*

*The Merck baseball team, Rahway, New Jersey, 1933.*

# CHAPTER TWO

# MERCK PEOPLE

**M**erck's century of accomplishment is a tribute to the talented, dedicated men and women who discover, develop, manufacture, and market its products, who manage and provide staff services to its factories and laboratories, who guide and conduct its complex, global operations. In the previous chapter you met some of those who have helped build the firm and its enduring traditions. Here our interest is the present.

While we can only meet a handful of Merck's employees, even that small sample can help us understand why this company is so productive, innovative, and successful. Let's start in England, where Ricki Flower works.

"I probably talk too much. I'm told I'm a typical Leo in that I'm a bit bossy, but that gets the job done." Ricki Flower is administrative assistant to the managing director of Merck Sharp & Dohme Limited (MSDL) in Hoddesdon, England. She remembers her first "awe-inspiring" day with Merck as a junior cost clerk. She was 15 years old, with her head down on the table, thinking, "I'm never going to get the hang of it." Determined to "make a go of it," she became a skilled clerk and started her move up through the ranks. Encouraged by her superiors, she took outside courses—three years of night classes in typing and two years of shorthand at college.

"I was moving up all the time," she recalls. Between 1962 and 1972, she was promoted four times. In 1971 she became secretary to the financial controller, and the following year she got her first shot at "the Big League." Secretary to the finance director and then personal secretary to the marketing director, Ricki loved the "hyperactive" pace, the work on new products, and the interaction with the sales people in the field.

## "IN THE BIG LEAGUE" WITH RICKI FLOWER

The next break came in 1980 when Albert D. Angel (now Merck's vice president for public affairs), became MSDL's chairman and managing director. "I applied to work for him," she recalled, "and I got the job. I had made it!" Angel remembers Ricki's help when he was still learning how to deal effectively with the people and organization at MSDL. "The thing about Ricki is that from Day One she really wanted me to succeed, and she wanted to do everything in her command to help the company succeed." She was, he says, "enormously efficient without being officious."

Teamwork is important to Ricki. At a sales conference to launch the analgesic *Dolobid*, she found that the sales packets for the professional representatives were incomplete. They had to be in "hunky-dory order" the following morning when the meeting opened. "It was all hands to the pump," she says. They improvised an assembly line which included the vice president of MSD Europe, the managing director of the U.K., the marketing director, the visiting Americans, and of course, Ricki. Top Brass to secretary, they worked until 2:00 a.m. There were "a lot of 'Hay Points' in this line," she recalls, and "it was such fun!" From her clerkship to the Big League, Ricki Flower has been having just that kind of "fun," the kind that "gets the job done."

# THE STAFF AT MERCK

The organization charts so dear to the hearts of business school professors are supposed to show you how a corporation like Merck functions. But as any experienced executive can tell you, the charts miss the personal ties, the cooperative spirit, the team effort that makes a business successful. At Merck the various staffs are a crucial part of the team. They hire and develop personnel, provide financial and planning expertise, offer legal guidance, give counsel on public affairs, and implement the company's communications and information programs. At Merck after the 1953 merger, staff organizations like Human Resources steadily became more important as the company became larger, more complex, and more global in its operations. In a sense, Human Resources is responsible for all of the Merck employees who are profiled here and the thousands who are not—each of whom contributes to the firm's success.

*Mrs. E. R. Dryer, Merck & Co.'s first secretary, began work at the young firm in 1894.*

# HUMAN RESOURCES

In 1988, John E. Lyons, vice chairman of the board, nailed down "the essence of Human Resources." It involved treating people with integrity, encouraging dedication, sharing a vision, and above all showing respect: "Respect people for what they do and respect all people for what they are." It sounds simple, but companies—like the people they hire—have to learn things, and Merck's current-day approach to human resources was many decades in the making.

In the "old days," when Merck was a fine chemical manufacturer, management had a paternal concern for its employees. But like most companies of the pre-World War II era, it left personnel matters largely in the hands of supervisors and of departmental offices. The firm helped employees attend work-related college courses and ran its own training programs. It instituted retirement and savings plans. But personnel services did not begin to acquire its contemporary characteristics until Merck introduced modern techniques of management in the years following 1945.

Then, in a few decades, the company's leaders transformed the personnel function. In 1956, CEO John T. Connor appointed John J. Radigan the first director of corporate personnel relations, directing him to coordinate and improve this aspect of Merck's staff work. Radigan introduced new incentive plans and training programs, while devoting a substantial share of his and his organization's energy to labor relations. In the 1960s, as interest in affirmative action on behalf of women and minorities increased throughout the nation, Merck (under chief executive Henry Gadsden) developed new affirmative action initiatives. The company—with the industry's first office of minority affairs—became a leader in this important area of personnel services.

CEO John J. Horan revamped the organization again in 1977. He gave it new leadership: Walter R. Trosin. And a new name, Human Resources, to reflect its new and broader mission. The focus was now upon selecting and training the best employees in the industry and upon maintaining the best possible supervision at all levels of the firm. In 1990 CEO Roy Vagelos launched the global phase of Merck's human resource policies. With Steven M. Darien at the helm, Human Resources set out to make more effective use of the firm's people, emphasizing flexibility through flex time, flex benefits, and flexible pay. Greater emphasis is now given to careful evaluation of results and to making rewards commensurate with outstanding performance. It is the award-winning programs of Human Resources that have enabled Merck "to attract, develop and keep talented people" (*Fortune*), one of the keys to the firm's performance in recent years.

*On June 21, 1990, President George Bush presided at the opening of The Children's Inn, a guest house for desperately ill children and their families on the campus of the National Institutes of Health in Bethesda, Maryland. Shown at the ribbon-cutting ceremony are (left to right) First Lady Barbara Bush; P. Roy Vagelos, M.D., Merck Chairman and Chief Executive Officer; President Bush; and Louis Sullivan, M.D., Secretary of Health and Human Services.*

## PUBLIC AFFAIRS

Professional standards have also been at the heart of the change that has taken place in public affairs. The task of dealing with Merck's external environment was for many decades handled on an ad hoc basis, usually by the company's top officers. They received back-up from within the corporation and from without, but a higher level of in-house capability was not needed by a fine chemical manufacturer with limited dealings with the public or with government organizations.

As the labs began to turn out innovative products in the 1930s and 1940s, however, Merck's enhanced public profile created a new need for public affairs expertise. Cortisone was front-page news, as was vitamin $B_{12}$. Under Tom Jennings, the public affairs staff became larger and more talented as the company moved into the limelight. Then came a shock. In the 1950s—now a fully-integrated pharmaceutical company—Merck came under fire from public authorities and the media. Charged with price-fixing and later attacked in the hearings before Senator Kefauver's Subcommittee on Antitrust and Monopoly, Merck clearly needed a more sustained and professional public relations program. As director of public relations, John Horan began the task of building up a stronger professional staff to handle Merck's public affairs. Continuing this effort from 1961 to 1979 was John E. Fletcher, who became vice president for public affairs. Fletcher—with strong support from Henry Gadsden and Horan—provided the firm with the staff and organization it needed to cope with the more complex and demanding environments in which this global corporation was operating by the 1970s.

In recent years Public Affairs has again been transformed as Merck became a truly "high profile company," in the United States and abroad. Now the organization—under the leadership of vice president Albert D. Angel—developed a new strategic perspective and a more positive set of goals. Instead of merely reacting to external developments in the public sector, Merck and its employees are attempting to anticipate change, to shape an environment favorable both to the firm and to the societies in which it operates. By becoming "a significant player on the public policy scene," Merck is using its expertise to ensure that public attitudes and policies which encourage innovation and thus better service to the health needs of society prevail at home and abroad.

When the United States entered World War II in 1941, hundreds of thousands of factory workers were called to military service and women took their places, keeping American industry productive. Remember "Rosie the Riveter"? Well, after the war, most of the "Rosies" either lost their positions to men or decided to leave their factory jobs behind them. Not for long, however. The next few decades witnessed one of the most revolutionary changes in American history, as women poured back into the work force, battled

## THE "CAN-DO" ATTITUDE WITH LESLIE KRONE-SPECK

listened carefully to the company's experienced workers, the people on the shop floor. "Men. . .in their sixties [were] reporting to me and knew the factory like the back of their hand. . . .Before I became their boss, I worked very closely with them. And I think they recognized me for the expertise I brought to the whole factory. And I certainly recognized their expertise, too, and. . .relied on their good judgment for a lot of things."

What kind of a boss did she become? Leslie characterizes herself as "a very participative manager." She enjoys

their way into the professions, and finally began to make inroads into the executive ranks. "Rosie" may not be back, but Rahway has her modern-day counterpart in Leslie Krone-Speck, manufacturing area head, Merck Chemical Manufacturing Division (MCMD).

Leslie began her career at Merck in 1979 as a chemical engineer at the Stonewall plant in the Shenandoah Valley where her uncle Herb had worked during the 1950s as an engineer. Her first project was unique and exciting. She helped set up a new process for the separation of the anti-infective *Mefoxin* from fermentation broth. The process was complex. It was MCMD's first such use of a large-scale ultrafiltration operation (the largest in the world), and Leslie doubts that it could have been done without a programmable computer controller. Later, she worked on another difficult problem: maximizing the *Mefoxin* fermentation process. At first, she says, it was a bit like "black magic." Again, they used the computer creatively to achieve the best possible yield and to maintain "perfect" control.

At Stonewall and throughout her career, Leslie has always

finding ways to get her employees "excited about their jobs and working towards improving things." She senses "a major change in the attitude in the. . .factories that I've been working in as far as just having the 'can-do' attitude when confronted with bleak situations. Being creative and coming up with a way to do what we're supposed to be doing. . . where you run into something that looks like a brick wall. . . .I've sat down and had some really. . .wild creative sessions in figuring out how to overcome some of the problems. . .that we've encountered."

"Can-do" means productivity, but this engineer never loses sight of the safety factor. "You know, you go along most days thinking that your primary objective is to get production out to meet some tight delivery requirements. . .[and] to be delivering a product of good quality. And then. . .something comes up where you'd have to make a choice between safety and your production. . .issues. And it's always safety. The decision always swings toward safety. . .safety is Number One. That overrides everything else." Safety, quality, and productivity are touchstones for Leslie Krone-Speck, as they are for the other women who have transformed Merck in the years since Rosie left the factory.

*A sample Merck stock certificate.*

## FINANCE AND PLANNING

If senior vice president Francis H. Spiegel had to pick one program that would best illustrate the crucial role financial and planning services play in Merck's continued success, it would be the restructuring of the firm's assets in the mid-1980s. Following several decades of global expansion, Merck's extensive assets needed to be reevaluated, coordinated, and brought under tighter financial control. That job fell to financial services, whose responsibility includes questions involving capital structures and dividend policy. Financial services achieved this particular goal quietly and efficiently. There was, Spiegel says, "no fanfare, no publicity." The result? "All of our assets are now exceeding the cost of capital." Financial services had helped the company put its fiscal affairs in order for the next great surge of global expansion.

Restructuring along these lines would not have been possible if several of Spiegel's predecessors had not restructured financial services itself in the years after 1945. Ray Snyder and Phil Roy transformed the functions of accounting and fiscal reporting into dynamic managerial activities that added value to Merck's decision-making. Under their leadership, the company developed new techniques of financial analysis and planning. This was particularly important during the 1960s and 1970s

because Merck's overseas operations were experiencing rapid growth and currency fluctuations were exerting an increasing influence on earnings. Becoming adept at currency hedging, financial services helped Merck make a success of its strategy of overseas expansion.

More recently, under Spiegel's leadership, the organization has begun to contribute to decision-making in other important ways: by developing new means of setting company objectives and of measuring results; by fostering a competitive team approach to performance; and by facilitating resource allocation around the globe. Of special importance in the area of resource allocation is chief financial officer Judy C. Lewent's new planning models for Merck's all-important research and development operations.

The result of these fiscal innovations, Spiegel says, is enhanced shareholder value in a company that is the "leanest in the industry." It is also a corporation with outstanding capabilities in financial and planning services, one of the pillars of Merck's success in the past decade.

"We are a Christian family, and we just have a strong belief and give everything to the Lord," Granville Clark says. Born during the Great Depression of the 1930s, he grew up near the West Point, Pennsylvania plant where he has worked for 33 years. "Grannie" has strong roots in his community. He and his family attend the First Baptist Church in Darby, Pennsylvania—the same church he belonged to as a child. Stability and trust are important to Grannie and his wife, Dorothy, as are opportunities to be of

## A LIFE OF SERVICE WITH GRANVILLE CLARK

service to others. "We're mainly concerned about the older people," he says, "because. . .when you get old and sick and you can't get out, people sort of forget about you. So we have a Home Fellowship Ministry that we take to them. We call on them, take them food, and after we eat, then we fellowship." After graduating from Darby Senior High School in 1952, Grannie went into the U.S. Army as a cook and baker. He had been cooking for some years and recalls asking his mother to teach him how to bake one of her special cakes when he was in the tenth grade. "It took me a couple of times to get the hang of it," but when he did, his mother said, "The job's yours!" It continued to be his job during his two years in the service at Fort Hood, Texas.

Afterward he became a dental technician, but in 1957 he took a job at MSD at the suggestion of a friend who was employed at West Point. Grannie started out as a lab helper, which was "a Godsend": he and Dorothy had married in 1955 and in 1957 they had their first child. He wanted to remain in the health care industry, and at MSD there were plenty of opportunities to serve others, as part of the team, for example, making a vaccine. Later he worked in the narcotics division, where he became a process compounder, and today, in the Merck Pharmaceutical Manufacturing Division (MPMD), he compounds *Lacrisert* for dry eyes.

Over the years, Grannie has learned new skills and has had a variety of jobs with Merck. These changes appeal to him quite a bit. "I don't like to be in a routine. . .just doing one thing," he explains. At work as in his religious life, he wants a degree of stability and some new opportunities as well. Grannie has enjoyed learning new things at MPMD, and he also appreciates the economic security that has enabled him to put his three children through college. Stability, new opportunities to be of service. As Grannie explains, "You go. . .to help some one, and to bless them, but it really blesses you."

Ken Ryan and his ancestors have lived and worked in the "Vale of Honey" for many generations. Translated from Gaelic ("Cluain Meala"), the reference is to the picturesque valley where Ken's home town of Clonmel is nestled between lush, rolling hills. "Slievenamon," or the Mountain of Women, is the most prominent landmark in this Irish region where Merck's Ballydine plant is located.

Young Ryan grew up here, an only child, "nearly spoiled, but not quite." As a student, he had a strong interest in math and chemistry, and a secondary school teacher persuaded him to blend "the chemistry and math together by doing chemical engineering." In 1974 he joined Merck as a process engineer during the exciting start-up phase of the Ballydine plant. He began his career with a six-month induction period at Rahway, where he and his fellow Irish engineers shared vital information with their American counterparts. Ken and his colleagues studied production techniques by day and became instructors in social development by night at a local Irish pub.

When they returned to Ballydine, Ken says, "we were very strong as a team as a result of the induction period. . . .We were ready to challenge concepts and tear them apart as a team, without there being any friction that lasted outside the meeting." One of the challenges he and his cohorts enjoyed most was "taking new processes and finding ways to improve them."

After playing a major role in getting the Ballydine plant opera-

THE IRISH ENGINEER WITH
KEN RYAN

tional, he spent time in Puerto Rico, Switzerland, and France, where he helped guide new factories and product lines through their start-up. The operation at La Vallée, France, was particularly rewarding, because, "I. . .participated in the project right from the conceptual design. . . through the process demonstration." He took his family along, and they lived in a small village called Solignac-sur-Loire, "high up on the side of the mountain with a breathtaking view of the valley." They came to know just about everyone in town, and "the day we were leaving, we were toasted by the local grocer and the butcher and the baker."

Back at Ballydine, Ken—like Leslie Krone-Speck—became deeply involved in implementing safety initiatives. "There's such a tremendous focus of attention to protect the individual, that it gains everyone's attention," he says. He also worked for a time on the plant's environmental performance and its relationships with the surrounding community. "Explaining to people what you're doing," he said, "has taken away the whole 'black box' syndrome that would otherwise exist. . . . I guess our attitude has always been that we have nothing to hide."

Ken, who is currently a section manager in manufacturing, still finds time to follow sports. His favorite? "Hurling," of course, because this distinctively Irish brand of field hockey is "the best game in the world." The Ballydine plant is in County Tipperary, and, as Ryan is careful to note, "the Tipperary team are currently the all-Ireland hurling champions."

## BALLYDINE

In the early 1970s Merck's European operations were experiencing a major period of growth and needed production facilities for *Indocin* and other new drugs developed in the 1960s. One of the sites considered was in a verdant valley beside a fast-flowing river, in the peaceful countryside of County Tipperary, Ireland.

In a contest based on beauty, Ballydine was a clear winner. But of course there were other, less gentle considerations that prompted CEO Henry Gadsden to invest ninety million dollars in what would become Merck's largest bulk manufacturing facility in the European Community. There were talented people like Ken Ryan. A government interested in promoting enterprise. Access to markets and supplies. All were important to the decision that resulted in 1973 in the beginning of construction at Ballydine. Three years later, Ireland's Taoiseach (Prime Minister, that is) Liam Cosgrave and Merck's John Horan formally opened the plant.

In the years that followed, the fully automated Ballydine operation experienced steady growth. Three products became eight; a work force of 165 grew to 270. Ballydine had, after all, been designed for expansion: it was the first of Merck's new plants built on the modular principle to accommodate new products and processes with maximum efficiency. "The modular concept is like having a whole series of building blocks," Ken Ryan explains, "and being able to configure the plant in a particular way to make one or more drugs. And then being able to dismantle those blocks and reconfigure them in another way to make a different series of products." Innovation in manufacturing, a staff that thrives on change, and the "luck of the Irish" have made the Ballydine plant a success story. So perhaps we can excuse Henry Gadsden for making his decision on grounds other than the beauty of the Irish countryside.

*A view of the beautiful countryside surrounding the Merck plant in Ballydine, Ireland.*

# COMPUTER RESOURCES

When Chris Copeland makes a sales call on an Australian sheep rancher, he routinely takes along his portable laptop computer so that he can create on-the-spot, individualized parasite control programs. A pioneer in the use of portable PCs, Merck today uses its own software programs for every aspect of sales, from internal communications and order-tracking to developing up-to-date customer profiles. "Information systems excellence," Glen Rifkin (*Computerworld* magazine) says, "might be one of the best-kept secrets about Merck & Co."

How did Merck attain this degree of sophistication in computer technology? For most of its history, the company left questions of information flow and storage to individuals. Then, in 1956, CEO John Connor decided that this was another aspect of Merck management that had to be changed. Twenty-four Merck employees with the most experience in data processing were brought together in one new department. Electronic Data Processing studied emerging computer technology and ways to apply it to Merck's operations. Applications in R&D and in clinical data exchange, in pharmaceutical and in chemical manufacturing were found. By the mid-1970s, the department had become Management Information Systems (MIS), with five separate staffs and over 300 employees. Under the leadership of

Herbert H. Blevins and William Pater, Merck invested heavily in state-of-the-art equipment and top-notch personnel. Soon they had the company at the cutting edge of computer applications. MIS helped introduce the first computer-run pharmaceutical processing and manufacturing systems in the industry. Merck began to use computers to help calculate molecular structures. Later, MSDRL used computers to design and simulate animated molecules to fit key receptor sites in the body, facilitating the search for new drugs.

Today, Computer Resources has a staff of nearly 700. Under the leadership of Al Cinorre, they are exploring robotics and intelligent vision and voice recognition systems. Meanwhile, the company's data transference network between subsidiaries and divisions has become so effective it has dissolved geographical boundaries and put the firm on a realtime, global basis. With nearly fifty years of experience in computer technologies, Merck has become *Computerworld*'s choice as "the most effective user of. . .[information systems] in the pharmaceutical market."

*Robert N. Funk (left) and Herbert H. Blevins (center), Assistant Controller, discuss the use of a new IBM 650 computer to analyze data from* Decadron *clinical studies with Dr. Augustus Gibson (right), Executive Director for Medical Research, in Merck's Electronic Data Processing department, 1956.*

Dr. Theresa Williams grew up reading Isaac Asimov's science fiction novels and watching "Star Trek" on TV. Intrigued by the science dramas, she still never dreamed that one day she'd become a scientist, let alone a senior research chemist at Merck's West Point, Pennsylvania laboratories. In fact, she "really disliked chemistry" in high school and decided she was "going to major in *anything* in college except chemistry." But her experiences with science sans fiction, combined with some inspiring teachers at the University of Maryland, got her hooked on the scientific method. "I found in chemistry the perfect blend of hard science—which has predictive theories or conventions—and a certain amount of creativity. . .where you can sort of put your own personal stamp on ideas."

Since she joined Merck in 1985, Theresa has been encouraged to put her "stamp" on the research problems she and her colleagues have tackled. Her work is goal-oriented, and her "creativity has to be channeled in a certain direction." But Theresa feels she has a "tremendous amount of freedom. . .in terms of being able to solve the problems." The research team she is a part of has harnessed creative energy to develop a promising new compound—in the class known as carbonic anhydrase inhibitors—a product which lowers pressure in the eyes. Now in the early stages of clinical testing, this drug may prove to be an important step forward in the treatment of glaucoma.

Theresa was the first woman in her department to be hired at the Ph.D. level. But because she was the only woman majoring in

## HOOKED ON SCIENCE WITH THERESA AND PETER WILLIAMS

organic chemistry in her college class, she had grown accustomed to being the only female scientist "in a room full of men." Because there are very few female role models, and because of the tremendous amount of pressure she feels compelled to place on herself, she thinks there is a "certain disability" in being a woman in science. But at Merck "the opportunity is incredibly equal."

Theresa is well placed to compare those opportunities because she can discuss them at breakfast with her husband, Peter, also a senior research chemist at MSDRL. Dr. Peter Williams is currently working with a group of Merck scientists on the development of a new drug to prevent premature labor in pregnancy. Unlike his wife, Peter has been hooked on chemistry since high school. He recalls some fairly sophisticated experiments that he conducted in a makeshift lab in his parents' basement. Sometimes his experiments worked. Sometimes they didn't. And "there was more than one occasion when we had to evacuate the basement because it was filled up with white smoke."

These two budding scientists met while pursuing their doctorates at Michigan State University, and after graduation in 1982, Theresa married the "boy in the lab across the hall." They came to MSDRL together because "Merck does good science." As Theresa says, "I really take a lot of pride in what I do." She and Peter have thrived in an organization that gives them "tremendous freedom because we are left to solve the problems however we see fit." Teamwork and creativity—at home and in the lab.

When Dr. Kiyofumi Ishikawa was a boy, he suffered from a serious illness which nearly caused paralysis in one of his legs. Almost miraculously, a new medication was developed just in time to cure him. This firsthand experience with the healing power of drugs led Ishikawa to make a decision that would change the course of his life: he would become a scientist and would work for a pharmaceutical manufacturing firm—just like the one that had restored his health. "I wanted to do work which would contribute to the world," he said, to develop medical products which would be "extremely useful to humanity."

His dream has been realized. Today Dr. Ishikawa runs an organic chemistry laboratory at Merck's affiliate, the Banyu Pharmaceutical Co., in Japan, guiding 12 other scientists in the development of new compounds for treating diseases of the circulatory system. He began his career at Banyu in 1978, after completing his doctorate in chemistry. Five years later, Banyu and Merck consolidated their long-standing relationship, and in Ishikawa's view, the union "was extremely fortunate for me personally. Since this relationship with Merck developed, I was sent overseas [to Rahway], and was able to experience life in the U.S.A.

## THE BEST OF BOTH WORLDS WITH KIYOFUMI ISHIKAWA

firsthand." This experience, he thinks, broadened his "field of vision." His daughter was so taken with American culture that she is currently attending school in the United States. His on-the-job training at Rahway in the laboratory of Dr. Arthur A. Patchett (vice president, exploratory chemistry) was his first experience abroad. A bit nervous at first, far from his family and home, Kiyofumi thought his English was not as polished as it should have been. But the language of science is not culture-bound. He quickly came to appreciate "the high level of synthetic and medicinal chemistry. . ." at MSDRL. "I believe," he said, "by receiving guidance over there, I improved my own level of technical understanding."

Back in Japan, Dr. Ishikawa put his improved "technical understanding" to good use in his own laboratory. Now one of his primary goals is to help "skillfully unite" the best of both worlds: to combine the strengths of Banyu's 75 years of experience with those of its sister laboratories abroad. Together, he believes, they will build "a much stronger team," one that will "continue to grow," realizing synergy from the two cultures.

# Women and Minorities at Merck

Merck's Rahway facility hired Camille Connor, a black, college-educated school teacher from North Carolina, as a chemical operator during World War II. In 1944, *Merck War News* saluted her for performing the "heroic triple duty" of raising four children, keeping house, and "helping our fighting men" by filling one of the 500 vacancies in the Rahway factories. In that same year, the United Negro College Fund was founded, and Merck made a donation—one of the first companies to contribute to this cause.

While Merck has thus found a place on its workforce for women and minorities over the past century—indeed, from the 1890s on—their numbers were small and most filled subordinate positions in secretarial or production jobs. As late as the 1950s, management was still a white male preserve, as it was throughout American business. Neither the company's leaders nor its employees seriously questioned the conventions of that day, and in the Merck cafeteria, men and women sat at separate tables. Then the civil rights movement of the 1960s set the wheels in motion, bringing dramatic changes to the hiring practices of corporate America. Building on the civil rights legislation of that decade, the federal government required companies to take affirmative action to improve racial and gender balance in the workplace.

Running ahead of the pack, Merck responded to these governmental directives by establishing its Office of Minority Affairs (1968), under the direction of B. Lawrence Branch.

The company began to hire more women and minorities, to help them achieve parity in the workplace, and to give them a fair shot at higher job classifications through advanced training programs. But as late as the mid-1970s, a group of women at the company were dissatisfied enough to organize Women of Merck (WOM), and tell management that they were tired of still doing the "heroic triple job" without day care and promotions. Black Employees at Merck (BEAM) made their voices heard as well.

CEO John Horan listened. In the late 1970s, Horan began to require that all senior executives include affirmative action goals in their annual objectives—objectives which were tied to bonuses, stock options, ratings, and merit increases. As Branch recalls, Horan's initiative "firmly established affirmative action at Merck."

In the years that followed, Merck's Phase III affirmative action awareness program—designed to make employees more aware of racism, sexism, and other barriers to equality and advancement on the job—became an industry standard. The program was so successful that Merck made it available to other American companies and community groups, and even the federal government has used it to train some of its own employees. Merck was one of the first companies to support day care centers for employees' children and to use flex time to help its staff balance work and family life. With Roy Vagelos

building on Horan's initiatives, Merck now supports technology enrichment and summer internship programs for minority youths, as well as educational programs in minority communities. Albert W. Merck—son of George W. Merck—has long been a vigorous advocate for the company's affirmative action policies, as have other members of the board of directors.

The firm's programs have not gone unnoticed. The National Organization for Women (NOW) recently honored Merck for its "vigorous programs to recruit, develop and promote women and minorities." *Black Enterprise* and *Working Mother* magazines have identified Merck as one of the best places in America to work.

Are Merck's programs perfect? Of course not. But they are good enough to persuade chief financial officer Judy C. Lewent (one of the few women CFO's of major U.S. companies) that "I've never been impeded in anything I wanted to do." A peaceful revolution indeed, only a generation old, and still under way.

*Shown here in 1989 are Merck's Dr. Cecil Pickett (left) and Ibrahim Sharif (right), then president of the East Orange Parent-Teachers Association, with Carmen Restaino (second from right) and Gwendolyn Scott (second from left) of the East Orange, New Jersey, school district. They worked together on a project to improve science education.*

*A team of women from Sterile Packaging enjoy their lunch break, 1947.*

Mario Leone was destined to become a lawyer. Both he and his wife Rita come from a long line of lawyers—a line that stretches back to the seventeenth century. While Mario's father, Domenico, was a judge and later head of the Supreme Court in Italy, Mario chose the "defensive part" of law. He liked having "the chance to help somebody [rather] than sentence him to jail forever."

Mario was raised in Naples, a city "conquered by foreigners" over the centuries. This experience "left an image of the law being administered by foreigners. And therefore," he explains, "the lawyer was considered a bridge between the local society and the foreigners. . . .The lawyer was the champion" who had the opportunity to present "the case of the poorer man in a rural area."

Today, one of Mario Leone's chief responsibilities as legal advisor and external/social affairs director for MSD Italy, is to serve as a "bridge" between management and the trade unions. As chief negotiator, he has worked hard to gain their trust and respect. "Over the years . . .we were able to establish such a trustful relation[ship] with the trade

## A FAMILY TRADITION WITH MARIO LEONE

unions that we didn't have one strike in ten years' time!"

Mario joined MSD Italy in 1979. He had worked for a law firm in Naples, served as government representative for the province of Terni, and had been legal director for Gulf Oil in Italy. He was attracted to MSD Italy because it was still in its infancy. "After I joined," Mario recalls, the company "started flying like a rocket," and annual sales increased sharply. New products fueled this ascent, as did innovative joint ventures. One of the major projects Mario helped organize was the joint venture with Sigma Tau and the building of their new $60 million research facility in Pomezia.

Mario is proud of the fact that his two daughters, Alessandra and Tiziana, are following the family tradition, studying to become lawyers. He hopes some day to write a book on the lawyers of the Leone family. If he does, a major theme of the book will no doubt be the various kinds of bridges he has built: bridges between companies, between labor and management, between Italy and the United States.

# MSD ITALY

Gingerly. That best describes Merck's early efforts to supply the large Italian market with its innovative products. Turned away initially by an Italian patent law that would protect processes but not products, Merck management in the 1950s decided to license through a distributorship agreement two of its antibiotics—penicillin and streptomycin—to Farmitalia, a well-established Milan firm. Merck (North America) also marketed *Cortone* (the company's brand of cortisone) in Italy for a number of years.

In time, as the patent law evolved, Merck was able in 1961 to make a more substantial, longterm investment in Italy. Today, MSD Italy is a rapidly growing subsidiary, headquartered in Rome, with MCMD and MPMD production facilities in Milan and Pavia, and an exciting joint research venture (with the leading Italian pharmaceutical firm Sigma Tau) under way at Pomezia. The focus of research in this new laboratory will be on treatment for viral disease. With 1992 and the final integration of the European Community just around the corner, MSD Italy has every reason to look forward to further expansion in the years ahead.

*Merck Chairman and Chief Executive Officer P. Roy Vagelos, M.D. (left), and Claudio Cavazza, President of Sigma Tau, at the dedication of the new Istituto di Richerche di Biologia Molecolare (IRBM),*

*May 1990. The IRBM, a joint research facility in Pomezia, Italy, will eventually house up to 100 research and support staff engaged in the discovery of products to treat some of the most serious viral diseases of men and women, including cancer.*

# LEGAL SERVICES

From its birth as Merck & Co. to its centenary year, the company has always made use of expert legal advice. George Merck could not organize his company in 1891, nor could he buy his new site at Rahway in 1900, without legal assistance. His son, George W. Merck, had even more need for legal expertise when he consummated the mergers with Powers-Weightman-Rosengarten (1927) and then with Sharp & Dohme (1953). For the most part, however, the company's early leaders looked outside the firm for the legal counsel they needed.

They did, that is, until the 1950s, when Fred Bartenstein (who later became administrative vice president) began to recast the Legal Department. Instead of being dependent upon outside counsel, he wanted Merck to have an in-house law firm with the highest professional standards and capabilities. He expanded the department and assigned most of the staff directly to the operating divisions. "By being on the scene, you encourage consultation and become more intimately involved with the division's activities," Robert L. Banse explains. He was then assigned to MSDI, stationed in New York. Merck's lawyers could advise on a course of action before it was taken, helping the division achieve its objectives while complying with the law and Merck's corporate standards. The new structure was more economical. It gave Merck's lawyers an edge by dint of their superior knowledge of their divisional clients'

business. The Legal Department—like its financial counterpart—could add value to the decision-making process.

As the firm entered the age of increased regulation and new environmental concerns, this internal capacity became more and more significant. Under general counsel James M. Fulton after 1961, the Department continued to expand. Global operations greatly complicated the business of patent law, which was the primary means the company had to protect the fruits of its formidable research effort. New regulations made it all the more important that Merck apply one high standard throughout the world for the company's legal affairs.

By the 1980s Merck had clearly achieved its goals in the area of legal services. It was staffed across a wide variety of legal disciplines. The Legal Department—then under the direction of senior vice president and general counsel Robert L. Banse—had become a partner in decision-making "by advising management how best to do what they want to do." Many lawyers—including of course CEOs Connor and Horan—had gone into management. The Legal Department had succeeded because its leaders had nurtured within the organization the same high level of professional conduct and expertise that characterizes the nation's largest, independent law firms.

*Charles A. Darius was one of Merck's first lawyers. He began working for the company in the 1890s, at the age of 20, and retired in 1940 as head of the Patent Law and General Legal Departments. (top) Darius in 1896. (bottom) George W. Merck (right) congratulates Darius on celebrating 50 years of service, while H. S. Conrey (second from left), Gustave Bayer (center), and J. H. Ambler (second from right)—three fellow members of the Quarter Century Club—observe.*

Mary McDonald has also built some important bridges for Merck, but her roots reach back to a 500-acre dairy farm in upstate New York. There young Mary did chores, feeding the chickens and gathering eggs. She learned how to drive a tractor when she was ten years old. "It was a very healthy, very conservative environment," Mary says. She attended Catholic schools and had "a very religious upbringing." Her brother, Mark, is now a missionary in Bogotá, and Mary too has a strong sense of moral purpose.

## THE TEST WITH
## MARY M. McDONALD

Since high school, she knew she wanted to be a lawyer. She loved public speaking and debating and, like Mario Leone, she was drawn to the idea of "defending somebody's cause." After taking her law degree at Fordham University in 1969, Mary began her career with the Legal Aid Society in New York City. She provided legal services to the indigent, settled rent strikes, and tried to improve housing conditions in the South Bronx. For two years she worked for the Association of the Bar of New York City, investigating lawyers charged with misconduct.

In 1974, looking for a new opportunity to defend "somebody's cause," she learned that Merck needed a lawyer to work on matters of discrimination and labor relations. With her background in Legal Aid, she landed the job. New to the industry and to the company, she took to

heart some good advice from a colleague who said, "Look, when you advise somebody on something, and if they don't pay attention to you right away, don't think it's because you're a female. It's only because you haven't been here fifteen years." Merck continues to take great pride in the fact that many of its employees have served the company for decades. In a company like this, Mary knew it would take time "to get a certain amount of credibility."

Sixteen years later Mary McDonald has earned a great deal of credibility. She has been assistant general counsel of the firm and head of the international legal group. Now, as vice president and general counsel she sometimes prefaces her legal advice to people with the phrase, "In *all* my *twenty* years at the Bar. . . ." They listen, carefully.

Has she traded her sense of moral purpose for experience? No, she is proud to work for a company that sticks to "very ethical business practices." Whenever she's in doubt about the ethics of a particular issue, she applies the "Roy Vagelos Test." Concerned about the tenor of a proposed advertising campaign, for instance, she asked herself, "Would Roy Vagelos want such a thing circulating in the name of Merck?" The answer was no. The Roy Vagelos Test—or we could call it the Mary McDonald Test—worked, as it has so many times in her successful career.

The southern slopes of New South Wales, Australia, are home to one of the great fine-wool centers of the world. Chris Copeland is at home there in a land of rolling hills, sheep ranches, and kangaroos. He was raised in the country, in an old gold mining town in North Queensland. Until he was ten, he and his family lived in the schoolhouse where both his parents taught. Growing up in the Australian Bush was exciting— yet down to earth.

After his family moved to Sydney, Chris persevered in his education and evenually followed his parents into teaching. He taught agricultural science, math and music at Hillstown Central School, ''way out west'' in the Outback, in a small country town of 1,000 people. ''It was almost desert. . .and it was very, very flat. You could see as far as the curvature of the earth would let you without any landmark in view.'' There he became deeply involved in that tight-knit community. ''The local Catholic priest and I formed a concert band,'' he recalls, ''and we had farmers and townspeople and. . .primary school children in the band.'' Although he plays the piano and trumpet, he ended up being the conductor. Of course nearly the whole town would turn out to hear them play because 5% of the population was in the band and everybody had at least one relative or friend performing.

## HOME ON THE RANGE WITH CHRIS COPELAND

In 1988, Chris, who is 33, made a big decision. He decided to leave teaching and take a position with MSD AGVET. He had heard good things about Merck from one of the company's professional representatives, and he welcomed the opportunity to use his knowledge of agricultural science, of the countryside, and of the people. When he started on the job, he was happy to find that while the company gave him all of the training and preparation he needed, it didn't suffocate him with bureaucratic controls. From the beginning, he says, Merck ''encouraged me to use initiative, to carry out my responsibilities creatively . . .and I think I benefited from that very much.'' He calls it truly ''experiential learning.''

He picked a perfect time to join MSD AGVET, which was just launching its outstanding new antiparasitic, *Ivomec* Liquid for sheep. His territory, which is 260 miles long and 100 miles wide, includes 5 million sheep, 350,000 head of cattle, and 15,000 horses. It has been a Merck stronghold since the early 1960s, when the company first introduced the antiparasitic *TBZ* in Australia. Armed with a laptop computer which allows him to hand-tailor a specific parasite control program for each rancher, Chris finds that his clients quickly accept this new technology—just as they do the company's new products. In that sense, Chris has never left teaching. Nor has he left the beautiful Australian countryside that he learned to love as a child.

# MSD Australia

In 1953, when Merck and Sharp & Dohme joined forces in the United States, they did so as well Down Under. While Merck had been marketing its products through distributors, S&D had begun producing and selling its own pharmaceuticals in Fairfield, near Sydney. Through the late fifties, the combined enterprises steadily expanded their marketing efforts. Steady gave way to astonishing in the 1960s, however, when MSD Australia began to produce and sell *TBZ* (*Thibenzole*), its new anthelmintic for sheep and cattle. Actually, Australia helped save *TBZ* for Merck, at a time when Rahway seemed about to abandon the new product after some problems developed in the animal tests. Australia wired Huskel Ekaireb to the contrary: "It is the best we have ever seen." With *TBZ* leading the way, the subsidiary's sales to farmers were by the mid-sixties twice the sales for human health needs.

In subsequent years the balance at MSD Australia swung back toward human health drugs. Leading the way in the early seventies were *Aldomet*, a treatment for high blood pressure, and *Indocin*, an anti-inflammatory for arthritis sufferers. By 1975 when Douglas J. MacMaster, Jr. (later senior vice president at Merck) became managing director of the subsidiary, total sales had again increased by one-third, with human drug sales about twice the level of veterinary products. MacMaster, supported by excellent marketers like Ian Cook, was able to continue that record of progress, giving Merck a 10% share of the national market by the end of the decade.

New products—including *Vasotec* and the anti-parasitics *Ivomec* and *Eqvalan*—have kept MSD Australia marching forward at quick step through the eighties. This subsidiary has become a training ground for managers who master advanced techniques in production, planning, computer controls, and marketing before moving to positions of responsibility in Southeast Asia and in the United States. If Chris Copeland follows the path Doug MacMaster, Dewey Stallard, and others followed, he may someday find himself leaving the southern slopes of New South Wales and finding a new challenge overseas.

*The* Thibenzole *exhibit at the New South Wales Annual Sheep Show in Australia, June 1962.*

The Merck sales staff in January 1902. Standing, left to right: Samuel G. Livingston, Boyce Elliott, George B. Smith, William P. Mangdon de Camp, George P. Lehritter. Seated: William J. Whitman, William G. Hunter, Aaron W. Stewart, Charles E. Sutton, and Louis P. Barclay.

A cross the Pacific Ocean and deep in the heartland of the United States, in Galesburg, Illinois, Larry Clark has some time to reflect these days on what makes a good professional representative. Having just retired after 35 years with Merck Sharp & Dohme, Larry should know. You start with top quality products, he says, "and honesty. I was always very honest with all the doctors. I put the chips on the table as they were. And it was up to them to decide to pick them up and use them. And also enthusiasm and persistence," as well as creativity in your "detailing" to help your customer remember the products.

## THE ANATOMY OF A SALESMAN WITH LARRY CLARK

Larry and said, "Who the hell are you?" Larry replied, "I'm the new Merck Sharp & Dohme salesman, and you told me that you'd see me at one o'clock this morning." Tenacity was rewarded. The doctor grinned and said, "Well, get in here then." The two shared coffee, doughnuts, and information about MSD's new products. Larry was on his way.

Throughout his long career, Larry was sustained by knowing that Merck's products helped people and that he could promote these drugs "out in the field where the action is." He remembers a time when he was discussing *Aramine* (which is used to raise blood pressure in shock victims) with a doctor. The phone suddenly rang. The doctor was called off to the Emergency Room. When he returned, he said, "Larry, you just saved a life!" Larry laughed and asked, "What are you talking about?" The doctor replied, "I just used *Aramine* at the hospital and it saved the patient's life. If it hadn't been for the fact that you 'detailed' me right here and that information was right crisp in my mind, I'd have probably lost him."

He had to blend creativity with persistence just to get his foot in the door of one of his first customers. In 1954, a freshly minted "detail man," he heard from the other sales representatives that a particular doctor always refused to see them. Undaunted, Larry planted himself in the physician's waiting room, which was filled with patients. After a while, the doctor asked him, "Who are you?" Larry explained that he was a new representative from Merck. "I don't have any time for salesmen," the doctor grumbled. "Well, when *can* you see me?" Larry asked. "About one o'clock tomorrow morning," the doctor replied.

Refusing to take "no" for an answer, Larry went to dinner, finished his paperwork, and returned to the doctor's office at about 12:30 a.m. After finishing with his last patient, the doctor looked at

Combine those kinds of products with dynamic representatives like Larry Clark, and you have a first-class sales organization. Honesty, enthusiasm, dedication, and creativity make for success. As Larry will tell you, it also doesn't hurt to be a born salesman: "I've just had sales in my blood all my life." When he retired last year, he had led his region in sales for nearly 35 years.

"As far as my own people, the marketing people, the product managers, are concerned, that is my daily job: Listening to them. That I think is the most important thing. Listening to the people, having time for the people, coming to a conclusion, weighing the pros and cons of ideas and proposals, and giving the people the feeling that you are there for them." Klaus Hoerter is marketing director for human health products, MSD Sharp & Dohme, Germany, and he has spent a lifetime training to be a good listener.

## THE MAN WITH TWO GOOD EARS WITH KLAUS HOERTER

in Germany at the company's subsidiary, he decided to move to a larger firm with broader product lines. He joined MSD Sharp & Dohme GmBH as a manager of marketing planning, and then served as general manager of the company's newly established Frosst subsidiary in the 1980s. "I must say that was possibly the period I enjoyed the most." Why? "Well, I was relatively independent with a. . .broad scope of responsibility, with very sure ways of communication, quick decisions, and the challenge to establish something new, a new business unit, a new com-

Armed with an excellent education, he began his training in New York City in 1969. When he first arrived at JFK Airport, he didn't know "a single soul." He still remembers "the first night staying in a hotel and waking up the next morning with all the skyscrapers and the huge buildings which I was not used to at that time in Germany. . . . Being for the first time in the United States, you know, having heard so much about it, about America, in my youth—that was breathtaking."

He started in pharmaceuticals working on the east side of Manhattan for Richardson Merrell as a detailman, polishing his English and his knowledge of the industry. He broadened that knowledge considerably as assistant to the head of the firm's European operations. Back

pany, a new name. It was really very satisfying. . . ." Klaus met this challenge with a three-pronged attack: "You need the medical back-up:. . . everything we do for our products. You need people: the product manager who initiates the activities and makes the product breathe. And you need a sales force: that's the primary channel to implement marketing activities and to make a product a success."

This formula, plus a string of new, important products, helps explain why Klaus moved up to his present position. It also helps you understand why the firm's annual sales in Germany increased so rapidly during the 1980s. Klaus Hoerter and many other executives in Germany have clearly mastered the art of listening.

# MSD Sharp & Dohme, Germany

What a turn of fate! The Merck return to Germany, from which E. Merck had in 1891 launched the American firm as a distributor for its fine chemicals. By the mid-1960s, however, much had changed. Merck was a very large, very successful company, expanding its international operations and entering what was then one of the largest markets for pharmaceuticals in the world. Some things had not changed, of course, and that included the German reputation for advanced chemical research, for high quality manufacturing, and for aggressive marketing at home and abroad. When CEO Henry Gadsden visited the company's new manufacturing and packaging facilities in Germany in 1975, he was prepared to build on those traditions an enterprise that would blend the best of the American and German business and technical skills. "Let me emphasize," he said, "that we consider this plant to be a symbol both of what we have achieved and what we expect to achieve here."

Those expectations were more than met under his successors, John Horan and Roy Vagelos. The competition was and still is tough. But with talented employees like Klaus Hoerter, a finely tuned organization, and solid support from Rahway and West Point, MSD Sharp & Dohme GmBH has compiled an enviable record for growth. The new products coming out of MSDRL—especially *Mevacor*—have carried Merck forward in this, its land of origin.

*A color lithograph of E. Merck's manufacturing plant in Darmstadt, Germany, circa 1900. Courtesy William H. Helfand.*

*Production site at Bad Aibling, Germany, where MSD Sharp & Dohme began manufacturing in 1963.*

Since he was a boy, Ron McPeak has been obsessed with the ocean. Each underwater surveying dive through the "amber forest" of giant kelp off the coast of southern California is a magical experience for him. From underneath the waves, Ron sees "sun rays streaking down through the water and coming down through the kelp. . . .When you begin to look at the plants very closely, you find all kinds of creatures—little shrimp hiding, you may find abalone in the base of the plant—in the holdfast. . . .All the time having a

## THE FOREST BENEATH THE SEA WITH RON McPEAK

harmful effects of sea urchins. He also started surveying the kelp beds both from underwater and from the air to determine where to send the boats that harvest the tops of mature plants. "That's not something you get a degree in," Ron explains. "You learn by being out there."

Protecting the underwater environment is particularly important for Kelco. Kelp "is our life-blood. . .the reason that Kelco began," says Ron. There have always been regulations governing the depth at which you can cut these plants. Kelco harvesters cut only the

sense of a forest—of a terrestrial forest where you have a plant attached to the ground that grows up above and produces a canopy. Only this forest is gently moving and swaying with the swell."

He began diving in the coastal waters off his home in southern California when he was 8, joined the Sea Scouts at 13, and was certified for scuba diving by the time he was 16. He never lost his sense of wonder about the world beneath the sea. With his master's degree in biology from the University of Southern California, Ron took a job as a diving biologist with the California Department of Fish and Game in 1968. The next year he joined Kelco as a marine biologist and has been with them ever since.

Initially, McPeak helped run the kelp restoration program, designed to protect the giant kelp forests (*Macrocystis pyrifera*) from the

mature fronds that form canopies just below the surface of the water. The company works closely with the Department of Fish and Game and has helped develop programs to protect the kelp forests from harmful predators.

As Kelco's manager of marine resources, Ron enjoys talking to people about the necessity of protecting this important food resource. The kelp beds provide a home to over 800 different species of aquatic life, from microscopic plankton to sea otters. In order to share his love and understanding of kelp forest ecology with a larger audience, he recently co-authored a beautifully illustrated book, *The Amber Forest*. He enjoys photography and took many of the underwater pictures himself. If ever a Merck employee loved his work, it is Ron McPeak—"Mr. Kelp."

# "THE MERCK CULTURE"
## WITH THE ENTIRE CAST

From Ron McPeak in San Diego to Ricki Flower in England to Chris Copeland in Australia, all of these Merck people are distinctive individuals. They are as unique in the things they do and care about as we are. But they clearly share important values which are the essence of the culture: a strong sense of responsibility to society; loyalty to the company and a personal commitment to their work; a determination to produce and market high-quality products; an emphasis upon safety and protection for the environment; an intense interest in being creative in a coordinated team effort.

The company and society receive "value added" from a Merck culture that provides direction and cohesion to the 37,000 people who work for the firm. Drawing upon a global pool of talent, Merck can sustain innovation. Like different, brightly colored tiles in a mosaic, each of these Merck people is encouraged to be creative in his or her own way. Theresa and Peter Williams put their "personal stamp" on their research in West Point. Chris Copeland thrives on "experiential learning" in Australia. Kiyofumi Ishikawa raised his "level of technical understanding" by studying with Arthur Patchett in Rahway and now applies his knowledge at Banyu in Japan, developing new drugs to treat circulatory problems. Ricki Flower creates an ad hoc assembly line to get the job done on time. Ken Ryan captures the challenge of "taking new processes and finding ways to improve them."

Teamwork. One of the patterns in the corporate mosaic is the concept of team play. Klaus Hoerter, the good listener, is a team player, as is Mario Leone, who builds bridges that bring people together. Leslie Krone-Speck listens to her experienced co-workers, learns, and becomes a "very participative manager."

But what is the pay-back for loyalty and high performance? Grannie Clark is quick to tell you that the company's salaries and benefits are among the best in the industry. But there is a more subtle factor at play here—that is the knowledge that the products they develop, manufacture, and market serve the health needs of society. They prevent illness or relieve the suffering of the sick. They control parasites and infections in animals. They protect the environment by removing wastes from water and air. After his boyhood sickness and recovery, Kiyofumi Ishikawa takes great pride in creating products "extremely useful to humanity." Ron McPeak enthusiastically develops restoration programs for kelp beds, protecting over 800 different species of life. Larry Clark provides information that saves a life in the emergency room. All gain strength of purpose by working for a company whose products help others and whose practices pass the Mary McDonald Test.

Inside and outside the workplace, Merck people have a powerful sense of social responsibility and personal commitment. Bonded together by a culture that has been sustained and strengthened over a century of operations, they ensure that the firm's future will be as successful as its past.

When an organization and a culture thrive that long, you can usually assume that the institution has had effective leadership. For a better perspective on that aspect of Merck, we must now look to the history of the firm's three major functions: research, manufacturing, and marketing. In each we will meet some unusual leaders who have helped shape Merck's success during the past century.

RESEARCH & DEVELOPMENT

*A cross-section of the 1,200 people of the Merck Sharp & Dohme Research Laboratories staff outside of Building 50 in Rabway, 1963.*

# CHAPTER THREE

# RESEARCH: THE MERCK STYLE OF INNOVATION

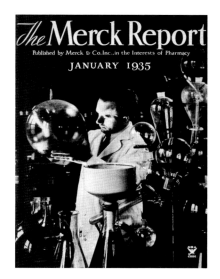

Strong traditions. Compelling values. And there seems as well to be a distinctive Merck career pattern. If the origins were not humble, they were certainly not from the elite: Gary Rasmusson or James J. Kerrigan. Hard work and a good education: John T. Connor and Henry W. Gadsden. High performance as a team player: All of the above. Not everyone at Merck has fitted the pattern of course. George Merck and George W. Merck were both born into the industrial aristocracy. But over the years a dominant pattern has emerged and there is no better example than Max Tishler, who would shape an entire era of Merck research.

*Dr. Max Tishler, circa 1963.*
*Tishler was President of*
*Merck Sharp & Dohme*
*Research Laboratories*
*from 1957 to 1969.*

His was in many ways the American immigrant story. His mother was from Germany, his father a Rumanian. Young Max was the fifth of six children living in Boston in the early 1900s in conditions of extreme hardship. He went to work at an early age selling newspapers and later working for a drugstore. He delivered medicine during the world flu epidemic of 1918 and remembered it years later. "I can still see the neighborhood and the people who were sick and dying. . . .It gave me a feeling that I might want to do something in the line of disease."

" *I used to come back at night and go to the pilot plant and help the operators and supervisors. They were very tolerant of me and I got my points across.*"

Tishler would have many opportunities "to do something in the line of disease," but first he had to master organic chemistry. He excelled in science in high school and at Tufts University, where he put himself through school working nights in the drugstore and grading lab papers. From Tufts he went to Harvard University's graduate program in organic chemistry. Armed with a Ph.D. and an outstanding record at a distinguished university, Tishler set out to look for a job in the midst of the Great Depression of the 1930s. Academia? He later recalled "there just weren't any jobs. One didn't have a chance to do a single interview. . . ." He did get an interview with a large chemical company, but the firm was apparently not ready to hire a Jewish chemist. One of

his professors at Tufts had warned him about this: "He said Jews have a hard job getting placed and you won't get anywhere." Now Tishler had reason to believe that prophecy might come true. He was good enough to stay on at Harvard for a few years, teaching in the lab and doing research. But his prospects seemed gloomy.

Then Randolph Major, who was heading the fledgling research effort in Rahway, changed Tishler's career and also the history of Merck & Co. In 1936 Major visited Harvard and discovered he might be able to hire the University's most outstanding young organic chemist, Max Tishler. The company's policy of encouraging its researchers to publish paid off at this crucial point. Tishler read a paper on vitamin $B_1$ written by some of the young scientists at Merck. "This excited me tremendously. Someone gave a seminar on the work at Harvard. And, gee, this was fabulous! I mean this was a place to which I wanted to go for an industrial job." He started at Merck the following year.

## RAHWAY RESEARCH: THE EARLY DECADES

When Tishler arrived in Rahway in 1937, the lab was humming, but as late as 1933 that had not been the case. Following George Merck's initial decision to launch a vigorous research effort, the company had jogged in place for a few years. The new work being done under Major's direction after 1930 had to be blended with the research operations already being conducted by Joseph Rosin—who had come to Merck with the PWR merger—and William Henry Engels. Engels had been at Merck since 1911. Trained in chemistry in Germany (again, the global tradition), he had started at Rahway as a so-called "production chemist." The title was apt. He and the company's other scientists were in charge of the production process. Each was a "trouble shooter," as well as a researcher, struggling to improve the firm's products, to adopt new processes, and to turn out high-quality bismuths, chloral hydrate, and other fine chemicals. They conducted research in conjunction with the firm's small pilot plant. They were the development side of what is today called Research and Development.

Even though the company had tried in 1916 to focus more attention on basic research in new products, the emphasis on development had persisted. From 1930 until 1933 it appeared that even Major's new research activities might not change the company's orientation. The labs were still scattered about the Rahway site, in a manner characteristic of firms that stressed the Engels style of process and manufacturing oriented development.

In 1933, however, Merck broke with that past. All of the research operations were gathered in one modern laboratory building that housed both basic research and applied development, as well as Dr. Hans Molitor's new Merck Institute of Therapeutic Research. Within a few years, Major was directing both research and development. He could now look to imaginative scientists like Dr. J. K. Cline and Dr. Karl Folkers for assistance. Folkers, who had earned his Ph.D. in organic chemistry from the University of Wisconsin, had worked for three years as a post-doctoral research fellow at Yale University's Sterling Chemistry Laboratory. He left the Ivy League in 1934 to try his hand at industrial research.

When Folkers arrived, Major had already guided the company into vitamin research. That work accelerated sharply after Dr. Robert R. Williams of Bell Labs telephoned to ask for assistance in his efforts to isolate vitamin $B_1$. The vitamin—thiamine—could prevent beriberi, a disease which still afflicted millions around the world, particularly in the Far East. Untreated, beriberi caused extreme fatigue, muscular weakness, and death in up to 50 percent of its victims. The disease responded quickly to $B_1$, and to continue his research on this vitamin Williams

*"Explorers Without Flags," 1939. This ad from* Chemical & Metallurgical Engineering *stressed Merck's commitment to research.*

*Dr. Randolph T. Major (left), Director of Research and Development, and Dr. William H. Engels (second from left), Associate Director, examine a sample of pantothenic acid with the team of chemists who synthesized it in 1940: (left to right) Dr. Karl Folkers, Assistant Director of Research, and Drs. J. Finkelstein, J. C. Keresztesy, and E. T. Stiller.*

*Dedication of Merck's new research facilities in Rahway, April 25, 1933.*

## The Merck Institute of Therapeutic Research

*A technician at the Merck Institute for Therapeutic Research mixes a chemically-pure synthetic diet for use in vitamin research, 1942.*

*Merck President James J. Kerrigan (second from right) and Dr. Hans Molitor (right) greet (from left) New Jersey Governor Alfred E. Driscoll and Dr. and Mrs.*

*Selman Waksman at the dedication of the new Merck Institute building, May 1953. Waksman received the 1952 Nobel Prize in Physiology or Medicine for his discovery of streptomycin.*

George W. Merck had two problems in 1931. He badly needed a talented pharmacologist to round out the new research organization he was creating in Rahway. He also needed an institution to conduct safety tests on the company's new products. Dr. A. N. Richards found the pharmacologist, Dr. Hans Molitor, in Vienna, and persuaded him to accept a position at Merck. Guided toward Rahway's "agreeable suburban places," Molitor came to the United States and to Merck & Co. in 1932, expecting however to return to Vienna in the near future.

The company organized for Molitor a separate entity, The Merck Institute of Therapeutic Research, with its own officers and board of directors. As director, Molitor initially had only two co-workers, but by 1938, he had a staff of twenty and was conducting fundamental as well as applied research. Some of the work was routine testing. But Molitor was too imaginative to concentrate wholly on assays to order; he and his colleagues launched wide-ranging studies, probing, for instance, the effect of pain on the circulatory system and the influence of anoxemia on liver functions. The Institute continued to perform this dual function, doing excellent work in pharmacology, pathology, biochemistry, and other biological sciences through the 1940s and 1950s. Even following the merger with Sharp & Dohme, the Institute (as of 1940, <u>for</u> Therapeutic Research) remained an active center for research and testing. It also served as a training school for young employees. Over the years, many went on to receive college degrees and graduate training, with financial help from Merck & Co. Hans Molitor—scientist, gourmet cook, and industrial diplomat—finally retired as director of the Institute in 1956. He served four more years as chairman of the organization's board and as director of MSDRL's scientific relations. Molitor died in his adopted country in 1970, never having found the occasion to return to academic life in Vienna.

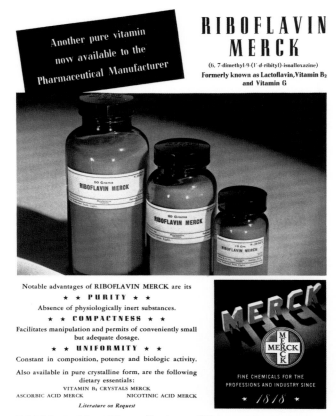

This 1939 ad announces the newest addition to Merck's vitamin line. His work on riboflavin introduced Max Tishler to development research.

In April 1946, Professors Leopold Ruzicka (Eidgenössische Technische Hochschule, Zurich, Switzerland) and Tadeus Reichstein (University of Basel) visited Rahway to confer with Merck chemists. Front, (L to R): Dr. Engels, Prof. Ruzicka, and Prof. Reichstein. Back, (L to R): Dr. Max Tishler, Dr. T. J. Webb.

needed to place his procedures on a pilot plant basis. He also wanted help in conducting clinical trials on the vitamin.

Major, with his new lab and the Institute running, was able to offer support on both fronts, and this research proved to have unexpectedly favorable results for the company. Merck produced the vitamin $B_1$ that was needed for further research and conducted the essential clinical tests. Merck chemist J. K. Cline shared with Williams the honor of developing in 1936 the first synthesis of vitamin $B_1$. The obvious results: a product that within a few years was accounting for sharp reductions in beriberi and was constituting over ten percent of Merck's sales. The less obvious result: first-rate science of the sort that excited Max Tishler, drawing him and others to Rahway.

The vitamin research was vital for other reasons. It opened a broad pathway for scientific innovation. As Major and Folkers recognized, there were other factors not yet isolated and fully understood in the B complex. Instead of a single shot, the $B_1$ breakthrough promised to produce a variety of major research efforts and valuable commercial products. This research also placed Merck "on the tip" of scientific discovery in the medical field in the United States. Major and the company's management decided, "We're going to isolate every vitamin. We're going to determine their structures if it hasn't already been done and synthesize them and make them available." The lab had a mission. It had the personnel it needed. It had the financial support and facilities necessary to carry forward first-rate research. This was the lab that Max Tishler joined in 1937.

While Folkers and others were working on a new project, vitamin $B_6$, Tishler started at Merck by trying to find a different method for synthesizing riboflavin (now called vitamin $B_2$). Swiss and German firms had already acquired patents on a synthesis and were unwilling to license Merck to manufacture it in the United States. As Tishler set out to devise a new approach, he quickly adapted to the team style of research. Soon he had a new synthesis in hand, and like a bulldog, Tishler would not let go of the innovation. He became heavily involved with the process of carrying the technique through pilot plant production and into large-scale, commercial operation. He had neither interest in nor respect for the eight-hour day. "I used to come back at night," he said, "and go to the pilot plant and help the operators and supervisors. They were very tolerant of me and I got my points across." Doing work that was as much chemical engineering as it was chemistry, Tishler saw the $5 million plant into production and along the way turned himself into an expert in developmental research.

While Tishler was injecting a new level of scientific expertise into process innovation, Karl Folkers was becoming the company's leader in basic research. Completing his successful project on $B_6$, he had begun to concentrate on the effort to isolate and synthesize a substance effective against pernicious anemia, a disease that had as late as the 1920s invariably been fatal. Scientists searched for this substance for more than two decades. It would take Folkers, his team, and several independent researchers almost nine years to complete the work of isolating vitamin $B_{12}$. While they would never succeed in developing a commercially viable synthesis of this complex molecule, $B_{12}$ was a successful product and the discovery drew the eyes of the world to the laboratory at Rahway.

These successes were not achieved by Merck alone. In all of the vitamin research there were important contributions by academic researchers in the United States and abroad. These were heady years for medicinal chemistry, which drew its support from many sources both private and public. The United States government was laying the foundation for its extensive efforts to promote medical research. In 1930 the government had reorganized the Public Health Service's Hygienic Laboratory as the National Institute of Health, an organization that

*This team of Merck chemists worked on the synthesis of hydrocortisone in 1950. (Left to right) Gino Sita, Dr. John Chemerda, Dr. Max Tishler, Dr. William Ruyle, Dr. Earl Chamberlin, and Dr. Evelyn Wilson.*

RED MAGIC
FOR
MILLIONS
- BY J. D. RATCLIFF

*Vitamin $B_{12}$ was introduced as a treatment for pernicious anemia in 1949.*

*(Opposite) A 1958 counter display for Merck animal health products:* VetStrep *and* DuoStrep *for ailments of both livestock and poultry;* S.Q. *to treat coccidiosis in poultry; and* HepZide, *introduced in August 1957 to combat blackhead and hexamitiasis in turkeys.*

would do much to foster the therapeutic revolution. From Europe in these years came the sulfa drugs, and for the first time in history, physicians could successfully treat bacterial infections. From Germany came a wave of talented scientists, driven out of that country by the Nazis, looking for a haven where they would have the freedom to work and the support they needed. The resulting marriage of European talent and American resources created a unique environment for medical research in this country. Riding this wave of scientific discovery, Merck's Rahway laboratories were drawn into research on sulfa compounds—an undertaking that would have paradoxical results for the company and the nation. Instead of a new antibacterial for human use, this research yielded a product that carried Merck into an entirely new market and helped the United States develop a new and profitable industry. All of this transpired while the company was producing large amounts of sulfanilamide under the patents of other companies.

Merck of course sought to develop its own patentable sulfas, and it turned the job over to Tishler and two of his colleagues. They found a new sulfa compound that they promptly gave to Molitor's Institute for testing. They hoped it would be useful against malaria. Alas, the Institute found that the drug was too toxic for human use, a common problem with the sulfa compounds. Failure? Not this time. It was discovered that the new compound—sulfaquinoxaline, *S.Q.*—was highly effective in preventing coccidiosis, a poultry disease. After extensive testing, Merck brought the product to market five years later. So effective was *S.Q.* that poultry breeders could now explore the mass production methods that would lead to the development of the modern broiler industry. *S.Q.* ushered Merck into the important animal health field.

Merck's new research capabilities and growing scientific reputation led to further alliances with academic research and significant contributions to the conquest of bacterial infections. One of the most fruitful of the cooperative ventures was with Professor Selman A.

*These three chicks demonstrate the growth effects of vitamin $B_{12}$ and penicillin. All three animals are three weeks old, yet their weights vary dramatically. The one on the left (126 grams) was fed a basal ration only; the one in the center (186 grams) received a basal ration supplemented with vitamin $B_{12}$; and the chick on the right (218 grams) received the basal ration with both $B_{12}$ and procaine penicillin.*

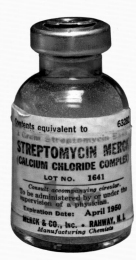

# WAKSMAN, MERCK AND STREPTOMYCIN

Today cooperation between businesses and universities is so widespread that it prompts very little discussion and even less controversy. Not so in the 1930s. The mood of the country was hostile to business. Most of the academic professions were unwilling to endanger their autonomy by working with the government, let alone business. "Pure" research was supposed to be just that, uncontaminated by concerns of power or profit. So it was unusual in 1938 and 1939 that Professor Selman A. Waksman and George W. Merck were able to strike a bargain. The outcome was for several reasons even more remarkable.

It all began in 1938 when Merck established a fellowship in fermentation studies in Waksman's laboratory. The Rutgers researcher had consulted with industrial concerns for years, had accepted such fellowships before, and was affiliated with the Experimental Station, an institution dedicated to practical applications of scientific knowledge. He was, moreover, in a new area of science, soil microbiology, which had yet to garner the respect of the established sciences or to receive substantial financial support. So Waksman badly needed Merck's assistance.

In 1939 as Waksman ventured further into what came to be called "antibiotics," the firm and the professor signed a formal agreement. He received support from Merck's outstanding chemists, the use of the extensive testing facilities at Hans Molitor's Merck Institute, and assurance that he would have available pilot plant facilities as promising substances were

discovered. For its part, Merck would receive the patents on any processes Waksman developed.

As Waksman later explained, "This agreement proved to be of the greatest importance in my work. Without it, most, if not all, of the antibiotics that we isolated would have remained bibliographic curiosities." Instead, Waksman and his colleague, Albert Schatz, discovered streptomycin, an extremely valuable and effective antibiotic.

Since the company played a crucial role in the research and had in force a legal contract, streptomycin should have been marketed in the 1940s under an exclusive Merck trademark. But it was not. Therein rests the final twist to the story. As the full implications of the new drug dawned on Waksman, he became concerned at "having turned over valuable public-health

*Packaging streptomycin in one-gram vials, 1946.*

processes to a single organization for commercial exploitation." He asked George W. Merck to be released from the contract. Short-term profit considerations said the answer should be "No!"

But Merck's president took the long-term view and said "Yes." The firm turned over the patents to a Rutgers foundation. All applicants were licensed to produce the drug. The company's relationships to the medical and university research communities were simply too important to place them at risk. George W. Merck was looking far into the future, past streptomycin, past next year's balance sheet. Even without an exclusive contract, Merck was able to profit from its sales of the new antibiotic and, in the meantime, the firm had laid a solid foundation for the excellent relations it has since maintained with foundation and academic research.

*Dr. Selman A. Waksman (left), plant manager J. H. Holcomb, Jr. (center), and E. J. Nolan, assistant to the director of manufacturing, discuss progress in the installation of one of the 15,000-gallon fermentors for streptomycin production at the Stonewall plant in Elkton, Virginia, December 1945.*

Waksman, a researcher at nearby Rutgers University. Waksman's work involved the search for antibiotics in soil samples. Under an agreement signed in 1939, the company provided Waksman with chemical assistance, experimental animals, and a guarantee of large-scale production if promising antibiotics were found. After five years of screening for active chemical substances, Waksman discovered streptomycin.

Waksman's discovery quickly became Merck's obsession. George W. Merck assigned a team of 50 scientists to help transform the new drug from an experimental finding into the world's first cure for tuberculosis. Both Folkers and Tishler applied their ample talents to the basic and applied research problems that still needed to be solved. Pilot plant operations yielded the information needed to produce the drug in commercial quantities while providing the clinicians with the samples they needed. Animal and human subjects were used to determine that the new drug was safe.

Then came the most daring roll of the dice: although the market was undefined and the competitive situation vague, Merck built a new factory to produce streptomycin at Elkton, Virginia, and a new finishing facility at Rahway. Construction was accelerated. Nine months after the plans were finished, the factory came into production—an award-winning accomplishment for Merck's chemical engineers. With streptomycin in the hands of physicians around the world, tuberculosis, the "white plague," was on the path to extinction in the Western world.

The same style of teamwork between industry and university scientists, between private and public institutions, was essential during the 1940s when Randolph Major became curious about the work being done in England on penicillin. At this time, the chief barrier to further testing and improvement of the drug was the inability to produce it even in pilot plant quantities. Since penicillin promised to be far more

*Dr. Randolph T. Major (center), Merck Vice President and Scientific Director, meets in 1949 with Dr. Selman A. Waksman (left), in whose Rutgers University laboratory streptomycin was discovered; and with Sir Alexander Fleming, Nobel laureate and discoverer of penicillin.*

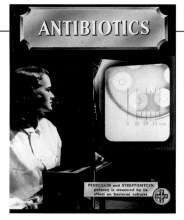

*One of a series of Merck posters distributed to pharmacists, emphasizing the benefits of scientific research, 1948.*

*Shipment of emergency antibiotics en route to Santiago, Chile, for victims of earthquake disaster, 1960.*

effective and have fewer side effects than the sulfas, Major set his research teams on the trail. But Merck's first efforts with the fermentation process failed. As Dr. H. Boyd Woodruff recalled, "They were just completely frustrated and Waksman, as a consultant, was frustrated trying to figure out what was going wrong." Waksman sent Woodruff to help, but the task was formidable even for a team that included Tishler and Folkers. "The mold is as temperamental as an opera singer," one drug manufacturer said, "the yields are low, the isolation is difficult, the extraction is murder, the purification invites disaster, and the assay is unsatisfactory." He was right on all counts.

With the United States at war after December of 1941, the pressure to rush into full-scale production in spite of these well-known problems was intense. Working in collaboration with erstwhile competitors Pfizer, Squibb, and Lederle—a union blessed by the federal government in the person of Dr. A. N. Richards, on wartime service—the Merck research team developed a submerged fermentation process that speeded the production in its new plant. The company was in full operation by 1943, when it turned out 4.18 billion units of penicillin, the first successful antibiotic. By June of 1945 the United States was producing 646 billion units per *month*, enough to take care of civilian demand and all of the casualties in American and British forces. Successes like those with penicillin and streptomycin were achieved because the three divisions of the Merck laboratories—basic research; developmental research; and the Merck Institute for Therapeutic Research, renamed as of 1940—were smoothly coordinated, staffed with confident, talented scientists, and attentive to the rapidly changing intellectual universe of medicinal science. The staff at the laboratories had increased from 35 in 1933 to over 500 by the end of the war. The budget had tripled between 1941 and 1945. The company had established a worldwide reputation and a durable network of academic

*Dr. Lewis H. Sarett (left),
Dr. Edward C. Kendall
(center), and George W.
Merck in Sarett's Rahway
laboratory, 1950.*

*Dr. Jacob van de Kamp.*

*The crippled hands of
modernist painter Raoul
Dufy, whose arthritic
condition was treated with
cortisone in 1950.*

*(Opposite) "The Regatta at
Henley," by Raoul Dufy. In
1952, in appreciation for
the benefits he received from
cortisone, Dufy gave Merck
& Co., Inc., reproduction
rights to five of his paintings
for distribution to the U. S.
medical community.*

ties. Merck had attracted new talent: Boyd Woodruff from Waksman's Rutgers laboratory; and an unusually imaginative organic chemist from Princeton University, Dr. Lewis H. Sarett.

Sarett was already urbane and polished when he completed his graduate work at Princeton University at the age of 24. He was already an accomplished scientist when he joined the research team at Merck two years later. In Rahway, he would start to work on steroids—prefiguring the careers of Glen Arth and Gary Rasmusson—following a research path created when Dr. Edward C. Kendall of the Mayo Clinic had turned to Merck for help. Like Waksman, Kendall needed to draw upon Merck's scientific resources. Kendall and others had isolated one of the cortical steroids, and they needed enough to test it on animals and human subjects.

They received more help than anyone could have anticipated. Their compound A failed in the clinical tests. But after two years of intensive research, Lewis Sarett met this challenge by synthesizing the closely related compound E, cortisone. His astonishing feat required over thirty separate chemical reactions conducted over a period of months. Even then, there was not enough cortisone to find out whether it would flop like compound A.

This was a problem for Tishler, aided by Dr. Jacob van de Kamp. It took two years for them to solve the developmental puzzles. But in 1948 with cortisone in pilot plant production, they were able to make amounts sufficient for the tests that established the drug as the first breakthrough in the treatment of rheumatoid arthritis. Patients who could hardly move could walk again. World-renowned artist Raoul Dufy was able to paint again. Lewis Sarett's brilliant accomplishment, one crucial part of an intricate web of scientific innovations, had the outcome George W. Merck sought: "medicine is for the people."

*Penicillin, streptomycin, vitamin B$_{12}$, cortisone, hydrocortisone—all breakthrough products of the 1940s and 1950s.*

Cross-section of some representative Sharp & Dohme products.

Distinguished Philadelphia Company
Pioneer in Pharmaceuticals
for More Than a Century

STOCKHOLDERS of Merck and of Sharp & Dohme, Incorporated soon will vote on a merger which will make it possible for both organizations to give greater service to employees, the professions, the public, and the many industries they serve.

First announcement of the approval of the merger by the Boards of Directors of the two companies was made last month.

The merger will unite with Merck one of the oldest and most distinguished pharmaceutical firms in the U. S. Sharp & Dohme had its origin more than 100 years ago when Alpheus Phineas Sharp, a Quaker, the first graduate of the Maryland College of Pharmacy, opened an apothecary shop in Baltimore, Maryland.

Seven years after Sharp opened his shop, a young man of 15 named Louis Dohme asked to be taken on as an apprentice. Louis proved an able assistant. He attended the Maryland College of Pharmacy, of which he was later to become president, and upon his graduation in 1857, Sharp appointed him senior clerk. In 1860, he was made a partner, and the firm was officially named Sharp & Dohme.

Some of the products which the company developed more than half a century ago still are in common use. These include Cascara Aromatic, S & D "Sedatole" cough medicine, and "La-

*From the* Merck Review, *March-April 1953.*

By the early 1950s, research and development at Merck had more than met the expectations of the company's president and his closest advisors. The company had contributed to two major projects that had produced Nobel Prizes—to Kendall and Dr. Philip S. Hench for cortisone and to Waksman for streptomycin—as well as profitable products. The elegance of the science was not always correlated with the size of the profits of course. And even those products which initially produced high revenues usually became less profitable as competition increased: in vitamins, for instance, profit margins had steadily shrunk and Merck had gradually withdrawn from the market. But most of the firm's income was nevertheless coming from new products developed in its own laboratories and pilot plant. Molitor's Institute for Therapeutic Research had thrived as well, gradually strengthening the pharmacological and biological input to Merck research. The marriage of chemistry and biology was not truly consummated, however, until after 1953 and the merger with Sharp & Dohme.

## TWO PLUS TWO EQUALS FIVE

When Merck joined hands with Sharp & Dohme, the job of combining the two labs looked impossible, like trying to harness a thoroughbred race horse with a trotter. The labs at Rahway had a sterling national reputation. In 1948, the medical news story of the year had been Folkers's isolation of vitamin $B_{12}$. If anything, the cortisone breakthrough and streptomycin, landmarks in medical science, had received even more attention. Sharp & Dohme's laboratories had scored their own successes over the years, but they were of lesser stature in scientific circles.

To understand what happened in the years that followed you first have to meet a new actor, Dr. Karl H. Beyer. He could have come out of the same mold that produced a Rasmusson or a Tishler. Beyer grew up in northern Kentucky, in Henderson, a town of about 12,000. "We, my two sisters and I, grew up in the church," he said. "Actually

*Chlorothiazide, discovered in 1957 and marketed as Diuril the following year, was an important advance in cardiovascular therapy. Dr. Karl H. Beyer, Jr., and Dr. James M. Sprague (molecular model in hand) directed the pharmacological and chemical research programs that led to chlorothiazide (illustrated on the blackboard).*

between the church and music, being taught to love flowers, the land and animals, and the social life of the town, it was a very pleasant environment in which to live." His father, a veterinarian who became a farmer, taught young Karl how to drive a team and how to work in the hay fields. These pleasures of the heartland gave way to science after his father gave him a 25-cent Chemcraft chemical set. Add to that a good chemistry teacher in high school, three years of training at Western Kentucky University, and you had a young man ready to go to Wisconsin to graduate school.

At Madison, Wisconsin, Beyer's instructor and the dean of the medical school decided he should have a degree in medicine along with his Ph.D. in medical physiology. As he recalls, "There was nothing dramatic about it. They just decided that Karl Beyer ought to have an M.D. as well as a Ph.D." By the time he left Madison he had both degrees and a good background in chemistry, biology, medicine, physiology, and pharmacology. Along the way, he had published enough research papers to earn a tenured appointment in many American universities.

But Beyer already had his eyes on industry. In 1943 he took a job at Sharp & Dohme where he knew he would have support in chemistry from the distinguished scientist Dr. James Sprague. At that point in his career he also came into contact with an outstanding renal (that is, kidney) physiologist, James Shannon, who would later have a dramatic impact upon American science as head of the National Institutes of Health. At Sharp & Dohme, Beyer started working on sulfa drugs—an area of research in which the firm had actually made much greater progress than Merck. S&D acquired a position of leadership in sulfonamide research, developing five of the most widely used of these antibacterials. The S&D laboratories synthesized sulfathiazole, and developed a new compound, sulfamerazine. Other successful sulfa drugs followed, and S&D also did some important work on formulations of penicillin.

When the merger with Merck took place in 1953, Beyer was particularly pleased. He knew he could take care of himself in biology, but now he would have even stronger and deeper support on the side of chemistry. He was right. The two organizations would quickly learn how to pull together—especially after S&D's first big success. The new West Point laboratories had been working in kidney research—remember the Shannon-Beyer contact—and Beyer and James Sprague were exploring diuretics. Starting from work done in the 1940s on the sulfa drugs, they got some research results that were "heretical so far as the physiologists were concerned." Beyer's reaction? "I didn't give a damn whether in theory you could or you couldn't, so long as you got it." Just what you would expect from a Kentucky farm boy. In this case, a very accomplished farm boy who pursued these "heretical" results with Sprague and came up with the first big post-merger drug: chlorothiazide, marketed by Merck Sharp & Dohme (MSD) as *Diuril* (1958), a drug which dramatically altered treatment of congestive heart failure and high blood pressure. The respect at Rahway for West Point research shot up when *Diuril* put Merck on the road to becoming the nation's leading cardiovascular company.

The next successful combination of biology and chemistry came in the development of new drugs for treating mental problems. The work started at West Point where the staff had been studying means of affecting behavior by action on the central nervous system. Merck chemists were able to modify a compound (originally discovered by Ciba-Geigy) so as to produce the effects for which West Point was looking. The result was *Elavil*, which was followed by *Triavil*, both successful anti-depressants.

By the time these drugs made it to market, the marriage between the two labs had been formalized as the Merck Sharp & Dohme

*MSDRL management reviewing plans for the expansion of research facilities, May 1964. (Left to right) Dr. Karl H. Beyer, Jr., Vice President for Life Sciences; Dr. Robert G. Denkewalter, Vice President for Exploratory Research; Dr. Karl Pfister, Executive Director of Developmental Research; Dr. Lewis H. Sarett, Executive Director of Fundamental Research; James E. McCabe; and Dr. Max Tishler, President.*

Research Laboratories (MSDRL). Major had retired. The tireless Max Tishler had become president of this joint operation, leaving developmental research in the capable hands of Dr. Robert G. Denkewalter. Tishler and his team had the full support of Merck's new CEO John Connor and of a distinguished science administrator, Dr. Vannevar Bush, who had been an active member of the company's board of directors since 1949, chairman since 1957.

With their backing, Tishler introduced his own style of research administration. He was involved, even intrusive. "I had to know what was going on. I mean I'd walk down to the laboratory and ask a person, 'How is it going today?' or 'What happened with that reaction?' or something like that." He also introduced more formal systems of reporting: short weekly reports and more detailed memoranda that were compiled in the "green book" and discussed at an annual conference at Absecon, near Atlantic City. The Absecon meeting produced a proposed research budget for the coming year (95 to 98% of which was normally approved by top management), as well as the kind of golf scores you would expect from a crew of scientists.

Under Tishler's vigorous leadership, MSDRL scored next with an important drug for treating arthritis. West Point biology and Rahway chemistry were again in harmony. At West Point Dr. Charles A. Winter developed a new and faster technique for screening compounds for anti-inflammatory effects. On the Rahway end was Dr. T. Y. Shen, who helped pinpoint the particular compound that would provide a non-steroid for treating arthritis. The working relationships, Shen said, were "informal and close. When the results were good, Charlie would be on the phone immediately. 'T.Y., you will be happy to know that the compound is very good.'"

With the help of about ninety other scientists and technicians, they found the best of the "very good" compounds, indomethacin,

*Leaders of the research team that discovered the new steroidal anti-inflammatory* Decadron *(dexamethasone) in 1958: (From left) Dr. Charles A. Winter, Dr. Lewis H. Sarett, Dr. Glen E. Arth, and Dr. Robert H. Silber.*

*Dr. T. Y. Shen, who played a key role in the discovery and development of* Indocin *(indomethacin), a potent new non-steroidal anti-inflammatory drug introduced in 1965.*

*(Opposite) New vitamins were among the first products of Merck research efforts in the 1930s. Vitamins and consumer health items like* Sucrets *and* S.T. 37 *were mainstays of the Merck and Sharp & Dohme lines during the 1940s and 1950s.*

which Merck introduced in the United States in 1965 as *Indocin*. In the years that followed *Indocin* was used world-wide to reduce the pain and inflammation of arthritis and is still prescribed extensively today. But for Charlie Winter one of the most important patients was one of the first, a colleague at West Point who had osteoarthritis of the hip: "He was in such bad shape he couldn't walk from the parking lot into the building. . . .When indomethacin was in the trial stage I told him about it. Well about two days later. . .here he was walking from the parking lot into the building. . . .'Oh Charlie,' he said, 'I tried your new drug and it's just wonderful.'"

During these same years, Merck was taking its second big step toward leadership in developing treatments for cardiovascular disease. Dr. Karl Pfister, who had come to Merck from M.I.T., had the original inspiration in 1951, but the initial tests on his compound, methyldopa, were disappointing. Convinced that he indeed had a substance effective against high blood pressure, Pfister pressed on: "He would go to meetings and when he saw a doctor that was interested. . .he would go and ask him would he like to try. . .it for the following reason."

Persistence was rewarded. In 1957 and 1958, two German laboratories found that the substance could prevent increases in blood pressure in animals. In January of 1959, the government awarded a patent, and that same month Pfister convinced two NIH researchers to conduct clinical studies of his compound. As Tishler knew, Pfister was more than a good chemist, he could "also get things done." The Merck-NIH collaboration got a great deal done, and the result was *Aldomet* (1963), which during its first decade would be used for 18 billion patient-days of therapy.

Along the way, Bob Denkewalter and the firm's chemical engineers did some brilliant work on the *Aldomet* production process, laying the cornerstone for a new era in chemical engineering at Merck.

*Dr. Karl Pfister III.*

*New Jersey Patent Award presented to Merck & Co., Inc., for the invention and development of* Aldomet, *November 1971.*

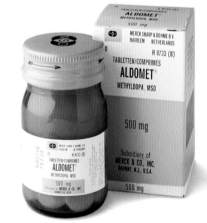

*The process research for* Aldomet *(methyldopa) earned well-deserved praise for Merck's chemical engineers.*

"My interest in the way the company functions," Bush told George W. Merck in 1950, "is, of course, by no means limited to the area of research and development." A new member of the board of directors, Bush had not wasted any time in reaching conclusions. What did he think of Merck's internal organization? It was "atrocious." The company's "lines of authority [were] blurred." There was more: "You now have a management committee. It is a contradiction of terms. A committee cannot manage." Merck restraint was tested. The company's president thanked Bush for his advice, set out to correct the problems, and asked for more criticism: "I hope we will have many [discussions] and that right soon." George W. Merck was determined to have an effective board of directors, with strong members from outside the company—a tradition that has continued to the present day. He was pleased to have the multi-talented New Englander on his board, pleased to have his peppery evaluations. They had become friends in Washington, D.C. during WWII, while Bush was in the middle of the third of his four careers.

The first career had been in engineering, which he studied at Tufts College (1913), as well as Harvard University and the Massachusetts Institute of Technology (1916). He then taught at M.I.T. for many years and served for a time as dean of its School of Engineering.

Bush also mastered administration, his second career. In addition to his deanship, he was a vice president at M.I.T. and

president (1938-55) of the Carnegie Institution in the nation's capitol. He looked forward to the day when the United States would have "an accepted aristocracy of management." They would be administrators "who have learned the technique of management, but have proceeded beyond this and learned the art."

He had clearly "learned the art" by the time he met George W. Merck in Washington. Bush was then in the heyday of his third career—in government. He had worked for the U.S. Navy in WWI, and during WWII he was serving as director of the Office of Scientific Research and Development. OSRD ran America's entire defense research establishment—just the assignment for a shrewd science-administrator who had designed one of the nation's first computers. In the final stages of this third career, Bush did the groundwork for one of America's leading postwar scientific institutions, the National Science Foundation.

As a member and then a chairman of Merck's Board, Vannevar Bush mastered his fourth career, in business. Writing to Dr. A. N. Richards in 1952, he said: "What we need are some free flowing views ahead, written by men who have vision, and also grasp. . . ." What better description of Bush himself? A man of vision and of grasp, he chaired the company's Board from 1957 to 1962 and died in 1974 at the age of eighty-four.

*Herbert Silcox (left) escorts William L. Dempsey (center) and Vannevar Bush of the Merck Board of Directors on a tour of the Stonewall plant, October 1957.*

VANNEVAR BUSH

*The joint announcement of the first synthesis of an enzyme, ribonuclease, by scientists from Merck and from The Rockefeller University was front page news in* The New York Times *on January 17, 1969. In front are the leaders of the Merck team: Dr. Ralph F. Hirschmann (left), MSDRL Director of Peptide Research, and Dr. Robert G. Denkewalter, MSDRL Vice President for Exploratory Research. The Rockefeller University scientists (standing) are Dr. R. Bruce Merrifield (right) and Dr. Bernd Gutte. NYT Pictures. Reprinted with permission.*

*Chemical engineers Rudy Cicchetti (center) and Richard Klophaus at the control panel of the* Thibenzole *plant in Rahway with operator James O'Brien, 1965.*

The earlier contributions of the chemical engineers to deep tank fermentation of penicillin and to the manufacturing process for cortisone had established their discipline's role on the development side of Merck's R&D. From then on, the company had achieved an unusual interdisciplinary intimacy between chemists and engineers. This new style of cooperation was evident in the swift transfer of laboratory and pilot plant results into manufacturing. It gave research management a set of options not found elsewhere in the industry. With *Aldomet*, their achievement—involving a direct, continuous method of selective crystallization of the desired isomer—was so ingenious that it garnered the 1965 Kirkpatrick Chemical Engineering Achievement Award. This innovation was one of a series by the engineers, who gained new respect for their ability to develop timely, cost-effective, capital-saving processes. They enabled the firm to cut production costs of *Aldomet* by 80 percent. The results: more patients were able to afford the drug, and as senior vice president Stanley J. Fidelman recalls, "After that, the engineers could for the first time yell at the chemists."

Good science and good science management had MSDRL on a roll. In 1968 Denkewalter and Ralph Hirschmann shared with Rockefeller University the honor of achieving the first total synthesis of an enzyme, ribonuclease—building the foundation for Merck's subsequent research in peptides. By that time, too, the effects could be seen in animal, as well as human health. The earlier work of Tishler and others (remember *S.Q.*) had already given Merck a strong position. Now the labs followed up with *Amprol* (1960) and later with *Thibenzole*, an anti parasitic for livestock. So successful was this line of business that in the 1970s Merck acquired Hubbard Farms, Spafas, Inc., and British United Turkeys Ltd. as a means of extending its business into poultry genetics and breeding stock.

Dr. William C. Campbell, 1987.

Growing microorganisms in petri dishes in a screening program to identify the activity of candidate drug compounds.

MSDRL's single most outstanding accomplishment in animal health came from a most improbable source and was achieved in a distinctly inelegant style. Let's have parasitologist Dr. William C. Campbell tell his own story: "It was not a neat event; it is not a 'gee whiz' story. No cerebral light bulb flashed the form and function of ivermectin on anybody's mental screen." Instead, Campbell led "a complicated and unglamorous" search, a multi-team effort, that finally found in soil sample No. OS3153 a microorganism that when fermented produced a broth potent against both internal and external parasites in animals. "Each step of the process was filled with suspense. . . ." Campbell said, and "the key to success from beginning to end" was "interdisciplinary research."

Microbiology was one of those disciplines. From the development of the original screening program, to the *in vivo* assay that identified an active substance, to the isolation and identification of the

## Ivermectin opened a new research pathway, just as the vitamins had in the 1930s and the diuretics in the 1950s.

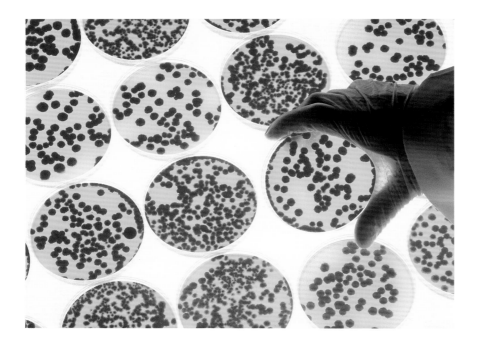

avermectin (the natural structure), the basic and developmental microbiologists were steering the research process. Dr. Edward O. Stapley and Dr. Jerome Birnbaum were at the helm, with a crew of nine, all dedicated to the kind of advanced microbiological techniques that would enable them to hand over an effective antiparasitic to the chemists, biologists, parasitologists, and veterinarians who would complete the discovery of ivermectin.

The reward for this kind of sustained team effort was an astonishing antiparasitic. Ivermectin opened a new research pathway, just as the vitamins had in the 1930s and the diuretics in the 1950s. As we saw, a human formulation became *Mectizan*, the first effective treatment for river blindness. *Heartgard-30* prevents heartworm disease in dogs. Meanwhile, MSDRL is still following the ivermectin path, developing

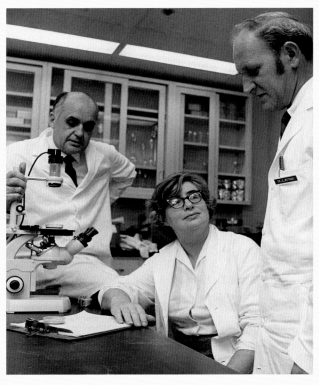

## Maurice R. Hilleman and the Vaccines

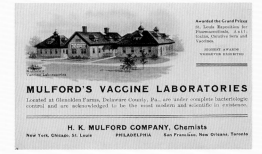

*Reviewing test results of the Marek's disease vaccine developed in the Merck Institute for Therapeutic Research, 1970. (Left to right) Dr. Maurice R. Hilleman, Executive Director of Virus and Cell Biology Research; Dr. Beverly Jean Neff, Senior Research Virologist; and Dr. Eugene B. Buynak, Director of Viral Immunology Research.*

*Early scenes from the Mulford Vaccine Laboratories in Glenolden, Pennsylvania. H. K. Mulford, acquired by Sharp & Dohme in 1929, pioneered in the use of diphtheria antitoxin in the 1890s.*

"Did you ever meet Maurice?" Max Tishler asked. "He can. . .swear like a trooper when he wants to. He was talking to some colonel and he said 'Colonel So and So. Get off your ___ and get out there and get some blood samples as quickly as possible. . . . Don't give me any excuses.' And he got them. And this impressed me a great deal," Tishler said. He shortly had persuaded this "terrific investigative scientist" to leave the Walter Reed Hospital and come to Merck & Co. (1956) to run its vaccine program. When Hilleman became director of virus and cell biology research in the Merck Institute, he brought to the company a rich fund of experience. After receiving his Ph.D. in bacteriology and parasitology from the University of Chicago (1944), he had worked for E. R. Squibb & Sons, becoming chief of their virus department. Next came his stint at Walter Reed, where he served as chief of the department of respiratory diseases. Dedicated and hard-driving, Hilleman would use his scientific and administrative (and linguistic) talents to make Merck Sharp & Dohme a leader in the field of vaccines.

Hilleman and his coworkers at West Point and Rahway developed new single and combined vaccines. One of the first of the combined variety was for measles and rubella, followed by a new triple vaccine (1971) for measles, mumps, and rubella. In 1978, Hilleman's team brought out *Pneumovax*, a pneumonia vaccine effective against fourteen strains of these

dangerous bacteria. The advances in vaccines continue today—in addition to *Recombivax HB*, Merck has recently developed *PedvaxHIB*, which prevents a number of diseases, including meningitis. But the climax of Hilleman's successful career was *Heptavax-B* (1982), a product of fourteen years of research. This plasma-derived vaccine was administered to millions and was the first major step toward the elimination of hepatitis B from the list of chronic and potentially fatal diseases.

When Maurice R. Hilleman retired in 1985 he could look back on a long and eminently successful career. He had made significant advances in the study of cancer etiology and immunology, of respiratory diseases, and of hepatitis. He had won many scientific awards and had helped prevent disease by developing a number of important vaccines. One of these was named for his daughter, Jeryl Lynn, who had conveniently contributed a mumps virus to her father's laboratory. Along the way, he had become an effective spokesman for research, prompting one of his colleagues to comment in amazement on Hilleman's "sweet and soft-spoken" presentations to the board of directors.

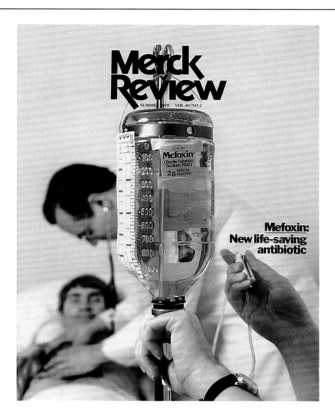

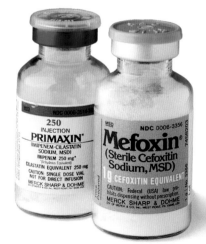

Mefoxin (cefoxitin) was first
introduced in Germany in
March 1978.

Jean and Fred Kahan, who
played leading roles in the
discovery and development
of the new antibiotic, Primaxin
(imipenem-cilastatin).

new formulations in this uniquely effective family of products. All of
this stemming from a single soil sample, OS3153, from a golf course
in Japan.

That soil sample would not have made it to Rahway if Merck
had not decided some years before to invest in screening programs.
They were, in a sense, the lineal descendants of Selman Waksman's dis-
covery of streptomycin. The facilities were in Spain at the Centro de
Investigación Básica España (formerly CEPA) and in Japan at the Kitasato
Institute. Sample No. OS3153 was one of the initial 4,000 microbial
cultures that Kitasato shipped to the United States: to find the needle,
Merck had bought an entire haystack.

The screening program also led to a series of new drugs in the antibiotic field. Actually Merck engages in double screening, operating a
system at Rahway that enables MSDRL to select from among the many
antibiotic samples produced in Spain and Japan those which have a particularly broad range of activity. In the 1970s this double screening procedure led Merck back into the antibiotic field. Fifteen years of effort
resulted in *Mefoxin* (1978), a particularly important new drug because
many types of bacteria had developed the ability to resist the standard
antibiotics that had been developed in previous decades. *Mefoxin* was
also safe enough to be used in life-threatening cases when a doctor
could not wait several days for a lab report.

Continuing its painstaking search for a super antibiotic, MSDRL's
microbiologists found a peculiar lavender-hued microorganism that set
in motion one of the most arduous research efforts in the company's
history. The substance was so unstable that researchers could not isolate
enough to study. Finally, in 1974 the research teams of Fred and Jean
Kahan produced a sample of the potent material pure enough to be
chemically analyzed. That enabled Merck's chemists to develop a stable
derivative and then to devise a totally synthetic process for manufac-

P. ROY VAGELOS, M.D.

You work hard and help your kids get an education. You won't make it to the top, but maybe they will. The American dream. Certainly the immigrant dream. And in the case of Roy Vagelos, the dream came true. His father and mother were immigrants who worked twenty hours a day during the Great Depression to make a living selling ice cream and candy. Roy, who spoke only Greek until he went to school, helped in the store: "I was paid 15 cents a day for sweeping out the shop and filling trays with chocolate." He made deliveries with his father across town, away from the railroad tracks, to the homes of the wealthy.

He began to think about getting ahead in life. A "cut-up" in grade school, he decided to bear down when he realized that the friends he respected were going to college. Working as a waiter—his family had a restaurant now—he was impressed by the customers who were professionals, including the chemists from a nearby pharmaceutical plant. "I was struck by the fact that these were nice, intelligent, fun people. They enjoyed their work enormously." Determined to join their ranks, he excelled in high school and at the University of Pennsylvania. A more confident young scholar, with a Phi Beta Kappa key and a B.A. degree, emerged from Philadelphia in 1950 and headed to the Columbia University School of Medicine. But as late as 1956, M.D. in hand and about to complete his internship, he was still uncertain where exactly he would make his mark.

Then he met Dr. Earl Stadtman. Professor at the University of Maryland and the top enzymologist at NIH, Stadtman made a convert of Vagelos: "I thought what he was doing was magical." Vagelos signed on to work half-time in the lab and half-time with the patients at NIH, but he quickly discovered a way to squeeze three halves out of the day by working nights as well. Stadtman converted others as well. A few years later there would be Dr. Bennett M. Shapiro (now in charge of MSDRL's worldwide basic research) and Nobel laureate Dr. Michael Brown. In 1959, too, Stadtman was making a convert of a hardworking graduate student, Alfred W. Alberts, who decided that year to accept a job at NIH, working for Vagelos. They clicked at once, and the team of Vagelos and Alberts, the analyst and the experimentalist, launched what would be the most exciting phase of their dual scientific careers.

Exploring the biosynthesis of lipids, they opened a new avenue of research that would win for Vagelos the Enzyme Chemistry Award (1967) and election (1972) to the American Academy of Arts and Sciences and the National Academy of Sciences. The research continued to gather momentum at Washington University in St. Louis, where Vagelos became (1966) chairman of the department of biological chemistry. He and Alberts discovered that cholesterol enabled animal cells to maintain their normal membrane structure and that a single enzyme defect could cause the cell to lose its viability. That enzyme was now the target, the substance that could stop the synthesis of the lipid.

In 1975, Vagelos found his next challenge at Merck in Rahway, New Jersey. He knew the city well and saw in MSDRL an opportunity to be a creative science administrator. "I didn't know entirely what I was going to get into," he recalls. "But I understood drugs. I understood disease." He also understood that while the labs had a great heritage, they had missed the turn into molecular age research. Starting at Merck in 1975, he became president of MSDRL a year later and had his chance to restructure the research. He quickly started to build from within, assisted again by Alberts. Some of the changes were painful. Most were expensive. But in a few years, he had in the research pipeline many of the products that would account for Merck's astonishing growth in the late 1980s.

That accomplishment and his manifest administrative ability won him the top post at Merck in 1985. It was fitting that he would share as CEO in the outstanding performance of the firm in the years 1985-1991. It was fitting too that as his company helicopter swept over Rahway, New Jersey, he could look over the city where he had swept floors and waited tables, where his father had sold ice cream and candy, where his own long journey to the top had begun. His journey tells us much about the society we live in and much about the American dream.

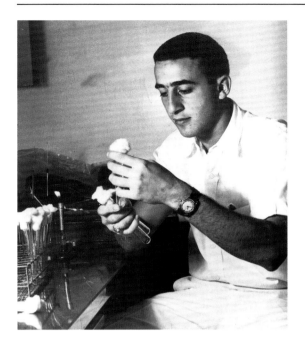

*Roy Vagelos as a summer intern at Merck's Rahway laboratories, 1951.*

*Massachusetts General Hospital intern class of July 1954-June 1955. Top row (left to right): Glenn A. Langer, Gerold L. Schiebler, Arthur R. Kravitz, P. Roy Vagelos, Ralph C. Williams, Jr. Center row (l to r): Katharine E. Spreng, William E. Lassiter, Edward Haley, Leonard Plotkin,*

*Beverly Orski. Front row (l to r): Frank K. Austen, Oscar E. Starobin, Jan Koch-Weser, Donald B. Martin, Gerald M. Edelman.*

turing the new drug, *Primaxin*. The process, Dr. Burton G. Christensen says, was "the first in Merck's history and the most complex total synthesis the industry has known." *Primaxin* is today the broadest spectrum antibiotic on the world market, a drug prescribed extensively in the United States and abroad, particularly in Japan.

## THE BIOLOGICAL REVOLUTION

From this account of discoveries, you may have concluded that MSDRL's history has been a straight line, sloping up toward a better today and tomorrow. Not so. There were plateaus, even valleys, to go with the peaks on the research frontier. In the mid-fifties, before Tishler took over, the labs hit a flat spot, leaving MSD and MSDI with the uncomfortable task of promoting a line of familiar products. The company persisted, with the favorable results that we have described. But again in the mid-1970s, the labs' output leveled off for a time.

In part this reflected a major transition that was taking place in the larger scientific world in which MSDRL lived. While the laboratories had been churning ahead, the world of scientific research had experienced a sea change. Biochemistry was now producing the major breakthroughs. Research at the molecular level was enabling scientists to pinpoint the sources of disease in animal and human subjects. The research focused on those enzymes that influence chemical reactions in the body's cells. By understanding how cells operate at the molecular level and how they change during disease, scientists were learning how to interfere with these changes.

Championing molecular targeting at MSDRL was a new team of leaders headed by Dr. P. Roy Vagelos. In 1969 the indefatigable Tishler had stepped up to a senior vice presidency, handing the presidency of the laboratories to Lew Sarett. In 1976, Sarett had followed a similar path, yielding to Vagelos, who would guide the labs into a position "on the tip" in the new style of molecular research.

*Al Alberts in his laboratory at the National Institutes of Health in the early 1960s.*

*The Vagelos group at Washington University, St. Louis, in the late 1960s. (Left to right) Alfred W. Alberts, Gayla Halbrecht, Dr. Vagelos, Dr. Allan R. Larrabee, Ginger Kelly, Dr. Nicole Baumann, Dr. Philip W. Majerus.*

As president of MSDRL, Vagelos implemented Merck's aggressive new strategy—increasing the research budget sharply, modernizing the labs' facilities, and recruiting a large number of talented scientists who could turn up the firm's "innovative energy." While the labs would continue to reap important benefits from large-scale screening programs, the main thrust of research under Vagelos would involve a different approach. As he explained, "In modern pharmaceutical research the emphasis is on the design of molecular structures that could lead to theoretically promising avenues. This is very far from random evaluation!" Nowhere was this more evident than in the cardiovascular field where Vagelos himself had made distinguished scientific contributions. At the National Institutes of Health from 1955 to 1966, Vagelos had conducted pathbreaking research on lipids and enzymes, tracking the body's mechanism for synthesizing cholesterol. He had benefited from the discovery by Karl Folkers and his Merck team (1956) of mevalonic acid, a crucial substance in cholesterol biosynthesis. At NIH, Vagelos also benefited from his discovery of an unusual research assistant. In 1959 Alfred W. Alberts was an "ABD"—that is, in his graduate program he had finished "All But [the] Dissertation." Today he is still an ABD, but he is also a Distinguished Senior Scientist at Merck, honored in 1989 with one of the firm's coveted Directors' Scientific Awards.

He got the award and his other honors because he caught fire for the first time in his life. He had always been a decent but indifferent student, less interested as a Brooklyn boy in studying than in walking to Ebbets Field to see Gil Hodges play baseball. Graduating in 1949 from Erasmus Hall High School—where the teachers ranged from "excellent to sadistic"—this self-confessed "dreamer" went to the best college he could afford within a trolley-ride of his home. At Brooklyn College he survived, actually learned some science, and graduated in 1953. A stint in the U.S. Army was followed by graduate school at the University of Maryland, where he found most of his courses dull stuff until he encountered Dr. Earl Stadtman and microbial physiology. That course provided the tinder. A job at NIH with a young "hot shot" named Vagelos lit the fire.

Bored by his dissertation, he was ecstatic about the research Vagelos was conducting. From his new boss he learned "an approach to science." He learned how to get "simple answers to complex problems." His excitement was converted into scientific progress: they published their first paper together (on the acyl carrier protein) in 1960; 17 more papers followed at NIH and 20 more after Alberts moved with Vagelos to Washington University's School of Medicine. Together, they joined MSDRL in 1975, moving the laboratories to the forefront of cholesterol research in one swoop.

*Dr. Arthur A. Patchett, MSDRL Vice President, Exploratory Chemistry.*

*Mevacor (lovastatin) was approved in the United States in 1987.*

*Julie S. Chen, who developed the screening program that identified the activity of lovastatin—later to be called* Mevacor—*as an inhibitor of the key enzyme necessary for cholesterol synthesis in the body.*

By 1978, Alberts and research associate Julie S. Chen had a microbial extract—provided by Dr. Arthur Patchett's new lead discovery department—that promised to inhibit cholesterol synthesis. One year later the Merck teams of chemists, spectroscopists, and microbiologists had isolated and crystallized the compound, which was patented in 1980. By then Alberts, the champion of *Mevacor*, was deploying about one-quarter of MSDRL's resources, and the drug was already in clinical studies. Then, Alberts and Vagelos received some shocking news: Japanese researchers were rumoured to have abandoned a similar compound because of its toxic effects. Vagelos abruptly called a halt to the clinical studies. He pushed *Mevacor* to a side burner.

To Alberts's relief, subsequent animal research and clinical programs demonstrated that the rumours had no relevance to Merck's new drug. *Mevacor* was indeed effective in reducing cholesterol and

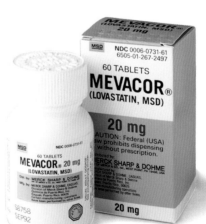

*This October 1987 profile of Merck appeared shortly after* Mevacor *received FDA approval. Reprinted from* Business Week *by special permission. © 1987 by McGraw-Hill, Inc.*

*A molecular model of enalapril, the active ingredient in* Vasotec.

Vasotec, *launched in the United States and Japan in 1986 and in other major markets in 1985, became Merck's best-selling product in 1987.*

had few side effects. In 1987, Mr. Alfred W. Alberts and the dozens of Ph.D.s with whom he worked could experience that final delicious moment ("You don't dream about it. You can't even imagine it.") when the FDA approves a new drug for use in the United States. Vagelos could celebrate too. He was now Merck's CEO, rewarded in July 1985 by the Board after having achieved his goal of successfully energizing innovation at MSDRL.

The laboratories at Merck were setting the pace for the industry. *Sinemet*, *Timoptic*, *Mevacor*, and *Recombivax HB* (described in Chapter I), had been followed by *Vasotec*, a drug so promising that one of the clinical trials was stopped so that the patients on placebos could be switched to the drug. *Vasotec* grew out of a major new movement in high blood pressure research—an effort to find a compound that would block the renin-angiotensin system. Renin is an enzyme produced by the kidneys. It helps insure that the body will maintain a proper level of blood pressure. High blood pressure is frequently accompanied by unusually high levels of renin. Merck researchers, led by Dr. Arthur A. Patchett, set out to find a drug that would inhibit renin development. The result of that work was *Vasotec*, the first of MSDRL's drugs to reach over a billion dollars in world-wide sales.

MSDRL—guided now by Dr. Edward M. Scolnick—is researching across a broad range of therapeutic categories, and the efforts that began almost a century ago with the "trouble shooters" at Rahway have become truly international. In addition to the Merck Frosst laboratories in Canada, the organization encompasses the Chibret Center in France, a new Italian lab (a joint venture with Sigma Tau) that will research antiviral therapies, the Neuroscience Research Centre in England, and in Japan a new Banyu laboratory which will emphasize research on cancer and on cardiovascular and infectious diseases. Linked by an effective

His name means "schoolboy" in Russian, but for his first four years in school in Dorchester, Massachusetts, Ed Scolnick didn't do anything distinguished. Then it happened. His fifth-grade teacher sensed his potential and pushed him ahead into the next grade. She persuaded his parents to transfer him to the prestigious Boston Latin School. There he set the kind of marks that get a few of the best schoolboys into Harvard University. To the joy of his parents, that's where this classic high-achiever went to continue his education in 1957. "I didn't know what I wanted to do," he said later, but then he heard Professor George Wald lecture on DNA, the newest marvel of the biological sciences. "That's how you really understand what life's about," he decided. "That's what I am going to do." Graduated summa cum laude in 1961, he continued his education at the Harvard Medical School (M.D. 1965).

After his internship and residency, he was still uncertain about his career. Lots of young people were uncertain about their future in the sixties. So he made a "non-linear move": to the National Heart Institute, where he researched protein synthesis. Here one of the basic patterns of his life could be seen: an initial period of doubt and difficulty; then a cycle of intense, focused effort; followed by a brilliant conclusion.

For Scolnick the intensity began when he met Dr. Marshall Nirenberg and talked genetics—"I was captivated." He joined the National Cancer Institute in 1970 and became involved in an "explosively exciting" project. A rush of scientific publications followed (he would write or co-author 176!), and his research interests carried him into animal virology and a position as chief of the Laboratory of Tumor Virus Genetics (1975). There he demonstrated the cellular origins of sarcoma virus oncogenes in mammals and identified specific genes involved in human malignancies.

His accomplishments were honored—the Arthur S. Flemming Award (1976) and the Eli Lilly Award in Microbiology (1980)—and new opportunities opened up for this intensely productive scientist. One was in Rahway, where Roy Vagelos was president of MSDRL. Impressed by the quality of the labs and the professionalism of the people, Scolnick joined in 1982. Again, the pattern; this time with Vagelos as mentor. Again, the intense effort to build up the research in cell biology and to master the art of conceptualizing not only his own field but the thirty or forty others being developed in MSDRL. Again, the triumph and in 1985 the presidency of MSDRL.

Now a senior vice president of Merck, he presides over a growing, successful institution. Are flat periods in research as intrinsic to industrial science as they are to the development of his favorite basketball team, the Celtics? "No!" Scolnick says. With the right kind of people, with a critical mass, and with intense, involved research administration to ensure that project cycles will be coordinated, he believes progress can be sustained. Ed Scolnick is determined to do his part, to continue to master those thirty to forty conceptual frameworks, to keep his fingers on the pulse of all of MSDRL's projects, to help drive the winners like *Mevacor* and *Proscar* across the finish line.

EDWARD M. SCOLNICK, M.D.

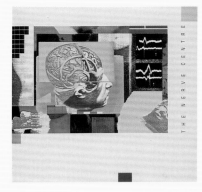

*A brochure on the Neuroscience Research Centre in Terlings Park, England, where Merck scientists investigate central nervous system disorders like Parkinson's disease and Alzheimer's disease.*

*Dr. Robert Young (left) and Dr. Cecil Pickett, both of the Merck Frosst Centre for*

## GLOBAL RESEARCH

*Therapeutic Research in Montreal, Canada, discuss ongoing research on an experimental leukotriene $D_4$ antagonist , 1989.*

MSDRL, once a Rahway and West Point combine, has become in recent years more of a global federation. One of its recent additions is the newly organized Neuroscience Research Centre in England, near Harlow, Essex. Dr. Leslie L. Iversen, former Director of the British Medical Research Council's Neurochemical Pharmacology Unit in Cambridge, heads a team of two hundred scientists and support staff. Their mission—on the "periphery of discovery"—is to explore the chemical message systems of the brain and the drugs that can influence them. The long-term objective is to find new drug treatments for mental illnesses such as schizophrenia and senile dementia, treatments that can only be developed as the Centre improves our basic understanding of the biochemistry of the central nervous system.

Across the Channel in France, MSDRL draws upon the research of the Chibret Laboratoires. Unlike the Centre, Chibret has a long history in research on the eye, ear, nose, and throat. The Laboratoires evolved out of a pharmacy founded in 1874 in Clermont-Ferrand by Ambroise Chibret.

Ambroise's brother, Paul Chibret, a specialist in eye diseases and co-founder of the French Ophthalmological Society in 1883, provided the pharmacy with ideas for ophthalmological ointments and solutions. In 1902 Henri Chibret established Chibret Laboratoires, which continued under family control into the 1960s. By the time Merck acquired a minority interest in Chibret (1964), it was the leading producer of ophthalmic products in France and North Africa. Since then Merck has fully integrated Chibret into MSDRL, reaping advantages in new ophthalmic products and formulations. The subsidiary MSD-Chibret also operated four plants, Clementel, Mirabel, Ferlux, and La Vallée—now under MPMD—marketing half of its products in eighty foreign countries.

In Canada—where Merck has long done a considerable business—the firm acquired Charles E. Frosst & Co., the largest Canadian pharmaceutical company, in 1965. Charles E. Frosst, a transplanted Virginian, had established his company in Montreal at the turn of the century. He began pharmaceutical research in 1927, and developed a substantial trade in analgesics, vitamins, sulfa drugs, penicillins, and hormones.

Two years after the acquisition, Merck Sharp & Dohme (Canada) and the Frosst subsidiary formed the Merck Frosst Laboratories. Its research center specializes in allergic and respiratory diseases, the use of radioactive isotopes in diagnosis, cardiovascular and central nervous system problems, and receptor

biochemistry. A Frosst research team led by Dr. Burton W. Wasson discovered the important Merck drug, *Blocadren* (1974). *Blocadren*, the first beta-adrenergic blocking agent discovered in Canada, relieves the symptoms of high blood pressure and has found important secondary uses in the treatment of glaucoma. Frosst science also contributed to the development of *Flexeril*, a muscle relaxant.

The latest international ventures are in Japan, where Banyu is creating a modern research facility at Tsukuba, and in Italy, where Merck is collaborating with Sigma Tau, that nation's top pharmaceutical firm, to develop drugs for viral diseases. If the past is a good guide to the future, MSDRL will in the years ahead further strengthen its commitment to global research as the best means of discovering new human and animal health products.

PAUL CHIBRET
1844~1911
FONDATEUR DE LA
SOCIETÉ FRANÇAISE D'OPHTALMOLOGIE

*Paul Chibret, whose ophthalmological research in the 1880s and 1890s helped lead to the establishment of Chibret Laboratoires in 1902.*

computer network, they can exchange data and research results on a real-time basis. They embody the global tradition.

How can we measure the results of this research effort? One can look at Merck's sales, which totaled $7.67 billion in 1990. Another measure is net income, which in that same year was about $1.78 billion. Science has clearly yielded substantial profits that have enabled the firm to sustain and recently to accelerate its research program.

But a third and perhaps the best way to measure what scientists like Tishler and Beyer, Folkers and Sarett, Vagelos and Scolnick have accomplished is to gauge the cumulative impact upon the reader of Merck's history of therapeutic breakthroughs. Your chances of dying from a stroke, infection, or cardiovascular disease have been sharply reduced. Your glaucoma or arthritis can now be treated. You will probably never suffer from tuberculosis or hepatitis B. Billions of people in the world have longer and fuller lives as a result of this research, and if MSDRL's current explorations succeed, there will be many more benefits to come.

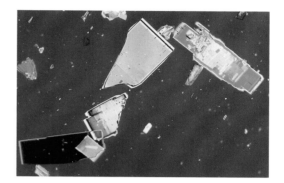

*Crystal photomicrograph of finasteride.*

*Discussing the effect of Proscar (finasteride) in reducing enlarged prostates and improving urine flow are (right) Elizabeth Stoner, M.D., Merck Director of Clinical Research in Endocrinology and Metabolism, and Reuben S. Mezrich, M.D., Ph.D., Director of Magnetic Resonance Imaging at the University of Medicine and Dentistry of New Jersey, 1988.*

*Chemical operators wear protective cotton hoods and goggles while working on sublimation process, circa 1940.*

# CHAPTER FOUR

# ON THE TECHNOLOGICAL EDGE: QUALITY AND EFFICIENCY IN MANUFACTURING

Research may get more headlines. Global marketing may seem more glamorous. But at Merck, manufacturing has always mattered. For almost half a century it was the dominant concern of the company. To be successful in business, Merck had to manufacture high quality chemicals and had to produce them at a level of efficiency that would enable the firm to turn a profit in a competitive industry. Methods of production mattered. The workforce mattered. As they still do today.

*View of Rahway plant circa 1915, looking north toward Building 10, the first manufacturing facility erected by Merck.*

*The St. Louis works of Merck & Co., Inc., 1938.*

*Materials handling at Rahway, circa 1935.*

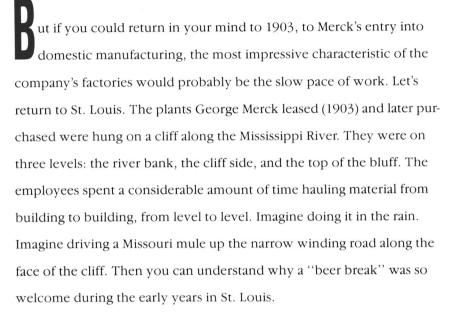

But if you could return in your mind to 1903, to Merck's entry into domestic manufacturing, the most impressive characteristic of the company's factories would probably be the slow pace of work. Let's return to St. Louis. The plants George Merck leased (1903) and later purchased were hung on a cliff along the Mississippi River. They were on three levels: the river bank, the cliff side, and the top of the bluff. The employees spent a considerable amount of time hauling material from building to building, from level to level. Imagine doing it in the rain. Imagine driving a Missouri mule up the narrow winding road along the face of the cliff. Then you can understand why a "beer break" was so welcome during the early years in St. Louis.

A branch of the local railroad brought supplies to the brick walled factory, which turned out iodides, bromides, salicylic acid, and various salts. These products were packaged by hand, using large scoops that were left in the open barrels lining the warehouse walls. When small deliveries had to be made, the company used either a wagon or a delivery boy. One of the boys, Charlie Drumm, also hand-delivered to the factory some of the chemicals that were shipped from the East Coast. When narcotics shipments came from Rahway, Charlie would take the streetcar up to Spruce Street where he would pay five cents to take the ferry across the Mississippi River to East St. Louis. There he would pick up four 50-ounce tins of morphine, which he would carry back over his shoulders on the ferry. Slow? Yes, it was. But even in the early 1900s the company was thinking about efficiency. If they had used a horse-drawn wagon instead of Charlie Drumm, they would have lost an extra day. Efficiency was also on George Merck's mind when he decided to consolidate all of the manufacturing at one site. A few years of experience producing at St. Louis and at the new plant in Rahway convinced him that he could achieve economies of scale at the ample (and flat!) site in New Jersey. He concentrated all of the manufacturing there and transformed St. Louis into a warehouse and distribution center. By that time, Charlie Drumm had graduated from errand boy to a job assembling orders in the warehouse. In 1917 he became warehouse superintendent, and when George Merck sent his son, George W., to St. Louis to learn the business, Charlie taught him the fundamentals of warehouse operation. Learning by doing was in those years the Merck way, regardless of what your last name was. Back east in New Jersey, beside the Pennsylvania Railroad, George Merck had started producing cocaine and morphine in 1903 and 1904. The red brick factory buildings were on the edge of a swamp that still belonged to the bullfrogs. For a time the company's president brought a flock of sheep to Rahway to use some of those acres he had yet to turn into factories, warehouses, and office buildings. During the next three years, he intruded on the swamp. He increased the plant's capacity, putting up new buildings for other alkaloids. Next came the production of iodides and bismuths, which were moved from St. Louis along with Dr. Henry Kippenberg who supervised that part of the manufacturing. Originally Kippenberg's building was designated with a "W" which stood for "wismuth," the German word for bismuth.

The bonds to Darmstadt were evident throughout the plant. Merck's processes, most of its research, its new products, and much of its machinery came from Germany. The narcotics production (regulated as of 1914 by the federal government) had been launched under the careful eye of Dr. Ernest Kauder, who had worked for two decades at E. Merck. Kauder introduced a synthetic codeine process that had been developed in Germany in the mid-1880s. Under his direction, Merck

*Building the chimney at Rahway, circa 1935.*

*Merck plant and offices in Rahway, 1942. Lithograph by Louis Lozowick. Courtesy Philadelphia Museum of Art, William H. Helfand Collection.*

*Early Merck chemical products.*

was also able to expand its output to include the narcotics ethylmorphine and acetylmorphine. Kauder, who became a vice president of the firm, stayed close to his work in every way, living in a cottage near the factory until 1913, when he returned to Germany. By the time he left, he was directing five "factory chemists" who had done much to adapt German processes to American conditions, improving efficiency and Merck's products.

In the decade before the First World War, Merck manufacturing grew in a steady, evolutionary style. Neither the sheep nor the bullfrogs were completely dispossessed. Output increased at about 8% a year. New buildings were constructed as new products were added, all under the watchful eye of George Merck, who visited Rahway from New York once a week.

When the war in Europe began in 1914, evolution gave way to revolutionary change in manufacturing. Of course revolution seen from the inside is often just a bad headache. Suddenly, without warning, Merck had to produce many of the materials it had imported—or lose orders. George Merck was not in business to lose orders. He looked to his factory chemists to find ways to make such products as hydroquinone, a photographic developer that had been imported. Within a year, Merck was manufacturing and selling this product. Others followed quickly, including synthetic benzene, phenol, and other coal-tar derivatives which could be made using benzene. No longer able to import the raw materials needed to make narcotics, Merck developed processes for manufacturing acetylchloride and the other necessary chemical reagents. In each case the machinery had to be produced in the United States. To get what the company needed, Merck's technicians worked closely with those equipment manufacturers new to the business. By 1918 the firm had greatly increased its total output and extended

*Process control in Rahway, circa 1935.*

*A 1930 advertisement for* Iodabs, *an alternative to tincture of iodine for treating minor cuts.*

Rahway's line of products. The headaches yielded to a sense of accomplishment and to a less traumatic era of growth in manufacturing.

In the prosperous 1920s the company continued to develop new products, largely using the technology and techniques first introduced during the war years. This was the case even during the late 1920s, when the founder's son, George W. Merck, guided his firm through the merger with Powers-Weightman-Rosengarten. As a result of this merger, Merck again expanded its product line. But the two companies produced a number of the same products: iodides and narcotics led Rahway's sales; narcotics and quinine topped the list at PWR. While the Philadelphia firm made a number of specialties—from mercury, for instance—which Merck did not produce, the combined enterprise acquired PWR's experienced workforce and managerial team, including chief chemist Joseph Rosin. They helped ease Merck through the merger and subsequent consolidation of the manufacturing operations.

George W. Merck estimated that he could reduce inventories by a million dollars and save an additional $150,000 or more in manufacturing costs by concentrating most of the production at one site. In the next two years he moved many of the PWR activities and employees to Rahway, eliminating duplication and realizing economies of scale. Where he could not improve the efficiency of the operations, however, he left PWR manufacturing in Philadelphia. Not until 1952 did he close the last Philadelphia factory. Through merger, George W. Merck had increased the size, complexity, and efficiency of his firm, but he had not really disrupted the balance that existed between manufacturing, research, and distribution. Rahway and the forces of production were still clearly dominant. The company's "factory chemists" served the needs of production, as did the sales and marketing representatives. Coordination was seldom a problem because the pace of change was relatively slow. From time to time the company introduced new products, but they were produced along traditional lines and sold through customary channels.

*Handling chemicals at Rahway, circa 1935.*

*Two-year-old Harry Trembley, Jr., sits on the fender of the truck his father drove for Merck, 1920.*

After the United States entered World War I in 1917, Federal Judge A. Mitchell Palmer sternly announced what would happen to the German-owned chemical companies in America: "They will be thoroughly Americanized." Since Palmer had just been appointed Alien Property Custodian—with authority to confiscate and sell such companies and all of their property—his statement sent a nervous tremor through boardrooms all over the country. When Palmer seized the Bayer Company two weeks later, the boardrooms quaked with concern. In rapid order Judge Palmer announced that the government was seizing the Perth Amboy Chemical Works, Rohm and Haas, the General Bakelite Company—and Merck & Co.

George Merck protested. He had already voluntarily turned over to Palmer 8,000 shares (of the total 10,000 shares) of his company's stock—that portion owned by the German members of the family. He had fully explained his firm's ties with E. Merck in Darmstadt. He, after all, was an American citizen, and he ran "the Company as if it were his own absolutely."

Several rounds of intense negotiations followed. Even though the government acknowledged that the company's president was "a thoroughly loyal and patriotic American citizen," the Custodian decided to sell the stock at public auction. Shocked, George Merck quickly mustered his forces to buy back his own company. Fortunately, he had the firm in solid financial condition and could call upon two leading investment banking companies, Goldman Sachs & Co. and Lehman Brothers, for support.

The auction started at 11:03 a.m. on May 9, 1919, in Merck's office at 45 Park Place, New York. There were five bidders, including the Merck representative. The bids started with Monsanto offering $2.4 million. American Aniline raised the bid to $2.5 million. Quickly the bidding mounted to $3 million, to $3.4, and American Aniline raised the figure to $3.58 million. Then came a final bid of $3.75 million, knocked down at 11:28 a.m. George Merck again had control of Merck & Co., which was certainly a more "Americanized" corporation after this exercise in nationalism and wartime control.

*George Merck, circa 1919.*

"THEY WILL BE THOROUGHLY AMERICANIZED"

*Operator using protective hood and respirator for iodine sublimation process, circa 1940.*

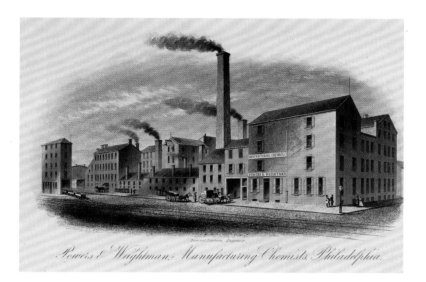

*A nineteenth-century engraving of the Powers & Weightman plant in Philadelphia.*

*This 1938 ad illustrates the range of fine chemicals Merck produced —in this case, cold remedies.*

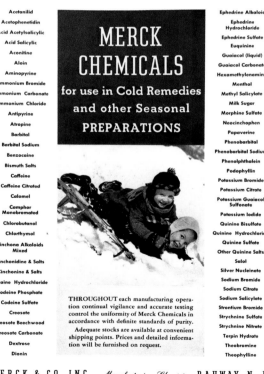

The factories made fine chemicals a batch at a time, using large-scale versions of relatively simple laboratory procedures. Iodine was heated in a large ceramic kettle. After the vapor was cooled and resolidified, a worker scraped off the purified product by hand. A similar pot and kettle operation yielded bismuth salts, and equally simple procedures were employed in the manufacture of narcotics. The factory chemists kept a close eye on the batches: the Mercks, father and son, were deadly serious about the firm's reputation for quality products. But William Henry Engels, Rudolph Gruber, and the other factory "trouble shooters" kept quality up and costs down for years using rule-of-thumb techniques.

## THE NEW ERA IN MANUFACTURING

All of that changed in the next two decades. George W. Merck led the firm along a new path, one that transformed manufacturing. As the process of change accelerated, manufacturing faced a series of challenges: the firm's reputation for quality could not be placed at risk; nor could Merck's employees or communities be endangered. But growth beckoned and that path called for the mastery of new processes and new means of achieving the efficiency that would enable the firm to remain competitive. Manufacturing at Merck after the early 1930s had to encourage innovation, increase productivity, sustain expansion at home and abroad, and maintain high safety and quality standards. No easy task.

The New Era changes began in research. As Randolph Major and Max Tishler got the labs cranked up, Merck began to introduce new products and processes at a much faster pace. Complex synthetic organic processes and fermentation procedures had to be developed, often from scratch. The 1953 merger with Sharp & Dohme further

increased the complexity, adding an entirely new line of finished products and introducing a different style of marketing. Change became a constant in manufacturing, quick corporate reflexes a necessity. The vitamins kicked off the new era. The synthesis of $B_1$ involved complicated organic reactions that could be done easily in a laboratory but had never been done in a factory. Merck had in fact started to extract $B_1$ from rice polishings, using huge wooden vats and the familiar pots and kettles. But it took a ton of polishings to get a fifth of an ounce of the vitamin. So in 1936 the company abandoned the vats and swallowed the loss as soon as synthesis became feasible.

Feasible. But far from easy. The company had to design equipment for low-temperature evaporation under a high vacuum. Corrosion forced the adoption of glass-lined vessels. Volatile solutions had to be filtered, raising new concerns about safety. Running on forced draft, the company was able to solve these problems in a matter of months and turn out 365 pounds of $B_1$ in 1937.

*Manufacturing at Merck after the early 1930s had to encourage innovation, increase productivity, sustain expansion at home and abroad, and maintain high safety and quality standards.*

*H. L. Coffey, a security guard at the Stonewall plant in Elkton, Virginia, searches the sky for enemy aircraft during World War II.*

*George W. Merck congratulates H. H. Wagner, first employee of the Stonewall plant, during the Army-Navy "E" Award ceremony, for excellence in production, February 6, 1943.*

**W**ith demand increasing, George W. Merck began to plan for a new factory. Rahway was getting crowded. The bullfrogs had lost out, and now there were over 75 buildings and more than 3,000 employees on the site. Without cutting into the tree-lined, campus-like research and administration area—dear to the heart of the president—the company could no longer expand in Rahway. The chosen land was Virginia, between the Blue Ridge and the south fork of the Shenandoah River. There Merck quickly constructed its "Stonewall" plant and brought it into production by 1941.

Fearful in 1940 that the United States might be drawn into the wars in Europe and the Far East, the government asked business to construct its new facilities at least two hundred miles inland where they would be relatively safe from attack. George W. Merck heeded that advice. He located an excellent site for a new plant in Virginia's Shenandoah Valley, in the shadow of the Massanutten Mountains. There, beside the south fork of the Shenandoah River, where Civil War General "Stonewall" Jackson had once encamped, the company bought a 312-acre tract with good rail and road connections and a bountiful mountain spring.

The Depression had been especially hard on the South. The Stonewall district needed a new industry, and the company was pleased to discover that it could hire most of the workers it needed locally. The new plant would employ about 300 men and women when it got into operation, and George W. Merck wanted that to be very soon.

The company, which had researched its way into the vitamin business, needed the Stonewall facilities to produce $B_1$, pantothenic acid, and $B_2$ (riboflavin). Groundbreaking quickly followed in the spring of 1941, and by December of that year Stonewall was already in production. After the United States entered WWII in December of 1941, the plant also made atabrine, a substitute for quinine in the treatment of malaria. But for years the chief products were still vitamins and this stretch of the Shenandoah came to be called "Vitamin Valley."

In the postwar era, Stonewall steadily added new products and more complex processes. Doubled in size by 1949, the plant was heavily involved in the complex fermentation procedures needed to make penicillin and streptomycin. Facilities for the animal health products *S.Q.* and *Amprol* were built at Stonewall, as were factories to make various steroids, *Sinemet*, and the company's new antibiotics, *Mefoxin* and *Primaxin*. In the 1970s—with over 500 people employed—Stonewall put into operation its first MSD production line, this one for *Aldomet*. It was the first fully automated, computer-operated facility in the United States and was able to produce 10 million tablets a day.

Today, there are over 800 Merck employees working at Stonewall, where the company is celebrating its fiftieth anniversary in the Shenandoah Valley. One of those employees is Sharon Davis, whose grandfather started working at Stonewall in 1943. Her father? He followed his father into the plant, as did four of his brothers and three of his brothers-in-law. "Merck's been good to my family," she said recently, "It really has. . . .You know, in this area, Merck is the place to work." Does she still like the Valley? She usually takes a trip every year, "But I have no desire to live anywhere else. . . .Of course," she says, "a lot of people in this area are like that. It's a beautiful place to live. . . ."

STONEWALL

*First shipment of strepto-mycin from Stonewall plant, 1946. (Left to right) H. N. Fiaccone, B. Olsen, F. Skrek, and Dr. Philip Colin.*

Economies of scale at Stonewall enabled Merck to cut the price of $B_1$ from $30 a gram in 1935 to 25 cents a gram by 1944. The company's other vitamins experienced the same transition from gram lots to tonnage output. With production of vitamin C up to 400 tons by 1944, the price had fallen slightly over 99%. The $B_2$ that launched Max Tishler's Merck career plummeted from $17 to under 50 cents a gram. What this meant to American consumers was that thiamine ($B_1$), niacin (nicotinic acid) and riboflavin ($B_2$) could be used to enrich flour, and ascorbic acid (C) could be widely available in tablets and prepared foods. From the 1940s on, increases in scale cut costs dramatically, increasing demand and transforming the market for medicinal chemicals.

While Merck was capitalizing on its effective process research and production in vitamins, the antibiotics and antibacterials were generating even more complex manufacturing puzzles to solve. Both penicillin and streptomycin were made by way of fermentation, a production process that was new to Merck in the 1940s. Only John C. Woodruff in research had any prior experience with fermentation, and as he discovered, the transition from spores in the laboratory to fermentation in a 15,000-gallon tank—a vessel large enough to be commercially viable for streptomycin—pushed Merck's research, development, and engineering teams to their limit.

*Inside a "G" fermentor at the Stonewall plant.*

*Madeline Anthony operating an automatic cartoning machine for streptomycin in the Sterile Techniques building at Rahway, 1946.*

Dr. H. Boyd Woodruff (no relation), who directed the early trials on penicillin, commented: "The very first one came out beautifully and right after that it was failure, failure. And the failures were all occurring during the time that Merck was planning to build a factory for penicillin." Contamination was a problem. As Woodruff recalled, the science in those days was vague, the engineering imprecise. Trial and error sufficed to get the firm into production in Rahway and later at its second new factory site, "Cherokee," near Danville, Pennsylvania. But not until

Until the 1940s, quality control in manufacturing at Merck had caused few headaches. After careful honing in Germany and the United States for a century, the techniques of chemical analysis were well understood. A happy balance existed between production and control—happy that is, until fermentation came along. As one experienced production man put it, with "fermentation you never knew what the bug was going to do." Fermentation was as old as alcohol consumption, but it had never been used in an industry with the stringent standards of pharmaceuticals. At Merck, fermentation strained the company's scientific and production resources, as well as the patience of its employees for several decades.

Merck & Co. had introduced two fermentation processes before penicillin. One (in making ephedrine) was a simple procedure "like baking bread" and the other (in vitamin C) was not much more complex. Penicillin was another ball game entirely. The first attempts were made using glass bottles in which the mold grew on the surface of the nutrient. But 10,000 bottles gave you 1,000 gallons of broth and only 100 vials of penicillin. So Merck put its teams to work in 1942 developing a new submerged fermentation process.

The wartime spirit of cooperation accelerated progress. Business and government worked together: the Department of Agriculture's Northern Regional Research Laboratory (NRRL) at Peoria, Illinois, made the vital discovery that a sticky gunk left after you take the starch out of corn (called corn steep liquor) was an excellent nutrient. NRRL also made several other major contributions to the successful commercial development of submerged fermentation. Business and business worked together too, and by 1943 Merck had the fermentation time in its 8,500-gallon plant down to one day.

Dr. H. Boyd Woodruff played a key role in improving the penicillin process, making certain the broth was properly aerated and agitated. "It was surely an art," he said. "In fact it remained an art until Per K. Frolich became the Research Director at Merck. . . . He was absolutely convinced that there was no reason under the sun why we should have such variable fermentations, why we shouldn't understand it." Frolich assembled a research team that put more science into the control: "It is mainly a matter of maintaining dissolved oxygen content and a measured degree of agitation."

By the early 1950s, Woodruff was head of Merck's microbiology department—with 70 to 100 persons working for him—and was the resident wizard of fermentation. Penicillin had been followed by streptomycin, also a product of fermentation. In subsequent years Woodruff and others developed similar processes for making vitamins $B_2$ and $B_{12}$, and more recently his successors have done the same for *Mefoxin* (an important antibiotic), ivermectin, and *Mevacor*. Over the years better science and engineering, joined with precise computer controls, have shifted the balance in fermentation from art to science. But even today, as an expert like Dr. James Gillin can attest, there is still a touch of art in this vital method of producing drugs.

# SCIENCE AND ART IN FERMENTATION

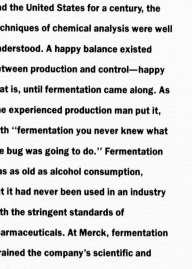

*Streptomycin fermentation vats at the Stonewall plant in Elkton, Virginia, circa 1946.*

In central Pennsylvania in the late 1940s, along the Susquehanna River near Riverside and Danville, the government had an unused plant site, left over from WWII. There were some left-over people too, unemployed or under-employed in the aftermath of the war. Merck put these two ingredients together by leasing (and then buying) the so-called "Cherokee" site in 1949 for its new plant. Breaking ground in 1950, the company had the plant producing $B_{12}$ and penicillin by the following year. Later, Merck built its *Cortone* production facilities here. There were miles of pipe, large fermentation tanks, and buildings for processing the formulations and pills—all tended by plant engineer Allen G. Hegarty and the 900 persons hired at Cherokee by 1954.

## The Cherokee Story

Cherokee's factories were all built in the age of bulk, large-scale production of low-potency drugs. These were dedicated facilities, efficient but inflexible. In the years that followed, the drug industry changed, and Merck added its new capacity at other sites in the United States and overseas. Although Cherokee had an excellent record for productivity growth, for low absenteeism, and for good labor-management relations, its plants had become outmoded, its taxes were relatively high, and its location not particularly advantageous. By 1987 Cherokee—down to slightly over 500 workers—was a good candidate to be closed. Off-shore production beckoned and the company launched a thorough study of where to locate its new facilities.

In 1989, Merck's Chemical Manufacturing Division (MCMD) came to an unusual and surprising conclusion. The Division recommended that the firm upgrade Cherokee instead of moving. As MCMD president David Conklin explained: "The value of the Cherokee employees, their past contributions, and the can-do attitude they showed to all challenges during these last two difficult years played a significant role in tipping the scales to keep the plant operating."

The company accepted this recommendation and decided to invest in the improvements Cherokee needed. "Most of us never gave up hope," lab technician Melinda Linn said. "We kept the faith that Merck would find a way to keep the plant operating." Forty years of success were rewarded in this case by the promise that Merck would continue to provide good jobs to another generation in the Susquehanna Valley.

*Moving MSG (monosodium glutamate) factory stock at the Cherokee plant in Danville, Pennsylvania, 1961.*

*Merck chemical tank car at the Cherokee plant, circa 1957.*

*J. H. MacDonald (left), superintendent of manufacturing at Merck's Cherokee plant in Danville, Pennsylvania, turns a valve to start the flow of raw materials to a giant fermentation tank used in large-scale production of vitamin $B_{12}$, 1951. Plant manager J. N. Millar (center) and Dr. Frank L. Cohen, Merck's director of production, observe the procedure.*

Dr. Per K. Frolich mounted a sustained team research effort did the company learn "scientifically how to control fermentations."

In all of these efforts, the pilot plant was the vital middleman between the laboratories and the factory. There the distinction between scientific research and scientific manufacturing blurred as the company learned how to jump from ounces to tons of output. There scientists like Tishler and Frolich created developmental research groups that worked elbow to elbow with the plant's director, Dr. Philip Colin, chemical engineer Dr. James Gillin, and teams from plant design and manufacturing. When Colin's pilot operation was successful, Merck's plants in Rahway, Virginia, Pennsylvania, and Georgia ("Flint River," as of 1952) could reach their expected yields at start-up. Given the novelty and complexity of the technologies, neither Colin nor his successor Gillin could always hit that mark. But they nevertheless made the pilot plant an effective partner in process and product innovation.

During the new era in manufacturing, there was increased pressure to bring innovations into production quickly. This was the case with penicillin and again with streptomycin. The heat was turned even higher with cortisone. With the 1949 announcement that a treatment for arthritis had been discovered, a wave of excitement swept through the medical world. The demand for the new product was broad and intense. In the next few years, Merck ran a series of races with its competitors to bring various cortisone products to market. After the 1953 merger, Merck Sharp & Dohme was particularly determined to bring out *Decadron*, a tablet form of anti-inflammatory, as quickly as possible. MSD's Joseph Fox was the point man, charged with coordinating Rahway's manufacturing and West Point's finishing operation. Instead of introducing each step of the manufacturing in order—the normal procedure—Fox and his coworkers started all of the steps simultaneously. Today this is called "concurrent production." In the late 1950s

*Inspection of new piping used in one of the many steps in the manufacture of* Cortone *at the Cherokee plant, circa 1952.*

when Fox was pressing for the new procedure, it aroused some stronger, shorter words at Rahway. Steps that would usually have taken several months to complete were all put on a rigid one-month schedule. When the tablets were ready to go, Fox allowed 24 hours to distribute them to MSD's customers. The race this time was successful. Manufacturing in overdrive was possible, without sacrificing the company's quality standards.

By the end of the 1950s, manufacturing had completed the transition to new era production. It was attuned to faster responses, more complex processes, and output on a scale that had seldom been achieved in medicinal chemicals in the United States. Domestic production—once concentrated in Rahway—was now carried on as well at West Point and three other sites. The management of manufacturing had become a far more demanding job. But Merck standards of quality had been protected, the company's efficiency had been improved, and the firm had achieved the fastest growth it had ever experienced. Manufacturing had met the first challenge of the new era.

## THE PRODUCTIVITY CAMPAIGN

But as CEO John Connor recognized, the company—now much larger and more innovative—was headed toward some difficult years in the 1960s. Manufacturing would again be challenged. Competition and government intervention in drug markets were squeezing profit margins on many of Merck's products. This situation was likely to get worse, not better. Meanwhile, the quickening pace of innovation and the increased potency of drugs were fundamentally altering the industry. Merck's chemical and pharmaceutical manufacturing operations had to become more flexible as well as more efficient. In 1964 the company handed this thorny problem to a task force headed by H. N. Fiaccone and Dr. Herbert Silcox.

Connor and his successor Henry Gadsden had the right people for this job. "Joe" Fiaccone was a chemical engineer who had a first-

After touring much of the South, "Joe" Fiaccone and D. H. McCondichie picked Albany, Georgia, in the southwest corner of the state, for Merck's new plant. Situated on the Flint River, the 704-acre site had good ground water, several rail connections, and an ample supply of labor. It was very hot in the summer, but as Fiaccone recalls, "It was a great place to live." He liked the schools and the people. "We still stay in touch with some of the people that we knew down there."

Fiaccone was the first plant manager at Flint River in 1952, and he supervised the installation to make sulfanilamide. Later Flint River produced *Benemid* (used to treat gout and to improve the effectiveness of penicillin), *Diuril*, and *Aldomet*. At Flint River Merck built a modular facility (1975), for the production of *Mefoxin*, the company's new antibiotic. Completely computer-controlled, the *Mefoxin* factory was Merck's state-of-the-art operation in this country.

As Merck, its products, and the industry evolved, MCMD's Flint River plant changed with the times. It now manufactures simvastatin for *Zocor*, one of the company's successful cholesterol-lowering agents, and tocainide for *Tonocard*, a treatment for heart arrhythmia. Operating 24 hours a day and seven days a week, Flint River is able to employ over 300 persons and to pay wages of more than $15 million a year. In this and other regards, Flint River has lived up to the expectations Fiaccone and McCondichie had in 1951. The plant's history is a case study in how productivity can be blended with safety and with sophisticated, high-quality products.

## FLINT RIVER

*Aerial view of chloro-thiazide production at the Flint River plant in Albany, Georgia, 1958.*

*Merck President James J. Kerrigan (left) and H. N. Fiaccone, Plant Manager, at the Flint River ground-breaking ceremony in 1952.*

hand knowledge of most of Merck's plants, several of which he had run. He had also served as secretary to the New Products Committee, the group charged with seeing that manufacturing, research, and marketing were all in step. Silcox too was an engineer with extensive experience. Together, they drafted a war plan for the company's chemical plants. They proposed and Gadsden approved a two-pronged attack: One part of the campaign involved automation of the production process, using computers to the greatest extent possible. The other involved the so-called "modular" concept of manufacturing. Modular equipment could be transformed from one product to another with relative ease. Merck could, Fiaccone and Silcox concluded, use modular equipment rather than a plant dedicated to only one product without reducing the company's efficiency.

Gadsden implemented both proposals. Easiest to handle was the modular concept because essentially it was a matter of plant construction and capital allocation. Merck's engineers introduced the modular plan in Factory 31 at Rahway. Next they built an entire plant along these new lines in Ballydine, Ireland, and later (1970), used modular design in Puerto Rico, at Barceloneta. The modular style of plant enabled Merck to shift from one product to another quickly, an advantage as drugs became more potent and product runs correspondingly shorter.

Computer control of manufacturing was a much bigger headache to introduce. The first "amateurish attempt" was, Fiaccone said, "an unmitigated disaster." Even though Merck's engineers had successfully introduced remote process control (for *TBZ* and niacin, for example) earlier in the decade, adding the computer did not at first subtract any problems. To the contrary, there were difficulties with both the software and the machinery. Indeed, the company and its supplier actually had to develop a new computer language for Merck. While they were pounding the bugs out of this system, the plant managers were trying

*Thomas Keenan, a pipe fitter at MCMD's Ballydine plant in Ireland, works on interconnections central to its modular, computer-controlled operations, 1976.*

to figure out how to transform the workforce from the old style of production to the new system of computer control. The transition for a worker accustomed to opening and closing valves and physically monitoring the process was substantial. Extensive training by Merck and flexible attitudes on the part of the employees finally got the job done. Gradually the company's engineers introduced computer controls in all of its chemical operations, and today the "unmitigated disaster" is a fading memory.

Automation, modular design, and continuous production operations dramatically improved the efficiency and flexibility of Merck's chemical plants, and David Conklin, president of the Merck Chemical Manufacturing Division, was determined to continue down that road. Recognizing that efficiency comes from the shop floor up, from people as well as machines, Conklin introduced a "Productivity Through Employee Participation" program (PTEP). The idea grew out of Merck's experience in manufacturing one of its new drugs of the late 1970s, the antibiotic *Mefoxin*. After substantial capital expenditures, Conklin and his coworkers were still unable to get production up to the necessary level. This was one of those exceptions to the pilot plant's rule. "We were dealing with a complex process," James Lago (vice president, process development) said, "involving a very fragile molecule that would decompose if there was the slightest deviation in operating procedures." It was, he noted, "an unforgiving process." At Flint River, however, they managed to bring this "unforgiving process" under control with suggestions from the shop floor, from at least half a dozen people including hourly employees. Conklin hit his target, and out of that experience came PTEP.

Pharmaceutical production at MSD—the counterpart of Merck's chemical division—also helped meet the productivity challenge of the 1960s and 1970s. In pharmaceuticals, Henry Gadsden had a team of energetic leaders: Robert Malcolmson (director of production); Charles

*David A. Conklin, President of the Merck Chemical Manufacturing Division, in 1983.*

*Russell Gibson monitors the control panel of the new* Aldomet *plant at Flint River, 1966.*

*Alfred H. Link (left) and Robert F. Hendrickson in the mid-1970s. Link succeeded*

*Hendrickson as MSD's Vice President for Operations in April 1980.*

Pike (vice president, operations); Dewey Stallard, Robert Hendrickson, and Alfred Link. Pike had recruited Hendrickson and Link—two high-performance team players—and he and Malcolmson guided their efforts as they sought to improve MSD's productivity.

Hendrickson was out of the mold that produced Tishler and Connor. Hendrickson's father was a policeman in Medford, Massachusetts. Education was as important to the family as hard work. Bob began his industrial odyssey as a sixteen-year-old janitor for a local doll factory. Was he discouraged by his low-status job? No, he was "enchanted with the idea of manufacturing." Hard work and intelligence got him to Harvard College and then to the Harvard Business School, where most of his peers had their eyes on Wall Street. Hendrickson's gaze never wandered. He was still "enchanted with the idea of manufacturing."

# *Extensive training by Merck and flexible attitudes on the part of the employees finally got the job done.*

*The Upper Merion High School Band leads the "Pride in Quality" parade in West Point, Pennsylvania, 1965.*

In the early 1960s, Hendrickson helped transform MSD production by introducing the kind of scheduling and planning that was best practice in American manufacturing. With solid support from Pike, Silcox, and CEO Henry Gadsden, he pushed computerization and automation, applied unit cost controls, standardized on the metric system, and clarified line and staff responsibilities. He integrated the planning process with day-to-day operations and was a vigorous advocate of MSD's new (1965) "Pride in Quality" program.

Dr. Paul Sinotte—director of quality control— kicked off "Pride in Quality" to the stirring music of The Upper Merion High School Band. The goal was "to prevent errors from happening, not just cutting down on the percentage of errors." As Charlie Pike, the first speaker, explained: "the idea of craftsmanship, Pride in Quality, [is] more important than it has ever been." He and Sinotte wanted MSD's employees to shoot for zero defects, to do it right "*the first time*." Motivation was

During Merck's German-American era, the company's leaders felt a strong personal attachment to their family of workers—many of whom were immigrants from Germany. Following the wave of German migration to America, Peter Lipp and his family came to Brooklyn in 1885 and because his father had worked for E. Merck in Germany, Peter landed a job as a porter with Merck & Co. in New York. Later, he set up and ran the receiving department at Rahway and retired after 43 years of service to the company. Merck honored him for exemplifying the "finest ideals in workmanship and loyalty, handling the Company's property and interests as though they were his own." The company expected—and received—total loyalty and dedication from this generation, and the workers expected—and received— the same sort of personal treatment from Merck.

But as the company grew larger, new government regulations were introduced, and labor unions became an accepted part of the industrial scene, the old style of personal relations inevitably gave way. During World War II the old paternalism yielded to the unions throughout manufacturing. By 1945, the AFL and the CIO each had six million members.

In that same year, the chemical workers of the Philadelphia-based pharmaceutical company, Sharp & Dohme, joined the United Gas, Coke and Chemical Workers of America (UGCCWA). Like other industrial workers across the country, these Sharp &

Dohme employees wanted a say in their working conditions, benefits, and wages. After Merck's merger with Sharp & Dohme in 1953, some of the West Point UGCCWA members went to Rahway to bring the chemical workers into their union. From these beginnings emerged the present-day unions at Merck's American production and distribution facilities. Today OCAW, the Oil, Chemical & Atomic Workers International Union (established in 1955), is the lineal descendant of the UGCCWA and is Merck's largest union.

Thirteen unions are now represented at Merck's plants in the United States. These unions have contributed a good deal since their inception, interacting with management on workplace issues and with the community on social issues and charity. "We're the oldest union here," says Bill Robbins, president of the 467-member Employees Organization (founded in 1937), which is proud to work with the company and other unions in contributing time and money to good causes.

Marvin Jones, the first black president of the ICWU (International Chemical Workers Union), is employed at Flint River in Albany, Georgia. He started working for Merck in 1964 when "blacks were very much in the minority." Since then he has seen their numbers grow with management and union support. As a union officer, he feels he has been given "the chance to develop my potential."

Working with management, the unions helped set up safety committees which improved working conditions at Merck's plants. The company established apprenticeship training programs in the

1950s to give employees the opportunity to learn a craft and to rise up through the ranks. As an example of the greater union-management cooperation over the years, Rahway has established a site Human Relations Committee, involving union representatives and staff from Labor Relations and Health Services, to help solve the personal problems of employees and their families.

The unions and management have not always agreed. There have been strikes at Merck—one just after the merger with Sharp & Dohme, another in 1969, and again in 1984. But labor leaders and management agree that both sides suffer from strikes and that cooperation benefits all. "We've come a long way together" since the organization of unions at Merck, says Guy Fleming, president of Merck's Inter-Union Council.

LABOR AT MERCK

*Members of the Grounds Department at Rahway, 1948.*

*Celebrating the first anniversary of the ''Pride in Quality'' program, 1966.*

*The U. S. Defense Supply Agency presented Merck with a Craftsmanship Award in November 1969 in recognition of the continued improvements in quality brought about by the Pride in Quality program. Accepting the ''Zero Defects'' flag on behalf of*

*West Point employees are (from right) John Lloyd Huck, MSD Vice President of Sales and Marketing; Charles W. Pike, MSDRL Vice President for Administration; and William E. Keppler, MSD Vice President of Operations. Presenting the*

*award for the DSA are Major General Daniel E. Riley, USAF (left) and U. S. Army Brigadier General William M. Mantz (second from left).*

crucial, hence the ''old-fashioned revival meeting'' to launch the effort. As designed by Pike and Sinotte, ''Pride in Quality'' (PQ) honored those employees most effective in getting it right ''*the first time*.'' Long before American automobile manufacturers had begun to realize their cars were slipping below world standards, the PQ idea had ''worked its way into the fabric'' of Merck Sharp & Dohme.

The drive to improve productivity often turned on seemingly insignificant changes, and Al Link was an expert in making small changes add up to big savings. He started at MSD (1961) by looking for ways to upgrade the company's warehousing. He was new on the job, new to pharmaceuticals, and only 31 years old. Every employee on his team had more than 31 years experience with the company! But Link wasn't intimidated and his workers didn't fight change.

Some of Link's improvements involved hardware, but they also incorporated a new attitude toward efficiency, especially toward making the best use of the company's capital. He found, for instance, that in the warehouse the space at the top of each of the aisles was left open. By using that space he increased the capacity of the racking system by 20%. Next Link worked on the packaging of pharmaceuticals, where he led a seven-year effort to mechanize the entire operation. He guided the transition from wooden to stainless steel equipment; new labeling techniques virtually eliminated errors; and a core control system improved coordination throughout the plant, reducing costs in materials management.

## GLOBAL MANUFACTURING

While these innovations in the pharmaceutical and chemical divisions were enabling Merck to increase the productivity and flexibility of its manufacturing operations, the firm's expansion continued to generate new challenges and opportunities. Diversification multiplied the complexity of manufacturing, as did the postwar drive to globalism. Both impulses were at work in the increasingly important field of animal health.

*Thibenzole underwent extensive testing prior to its national release in 1962. These sheep are being drenched with the wormer at a barn constructed at the Rahway plant for the testing program.*

*Inspecting chickens protected with the new coccidiostat nicarbazin at Merck's Branchburg Farm, 1955.*

The redoubtable Max Tishler (remember Chapter III) had edged Merck into this field when he and his colleagues discovered *S.Q.*, a sulfa treatment for coccidiosis in chickens. Developed in 1948, this product helped transform poultry production, first in the United States and then around the world. One of the chief barriers to large-scale poultry operations had been the diseases—especially coccidiosis—that chickens become vulnerable to when large numbers of them are raised together. With *S.Q.* in hand, the poultry entrepreneurs did for their business what Henry Ford had done with the assembly line for automobiles. Greater efficiency meant more and cheaper food.

That became possible because Merck was able to bring the price of *S.Q.* down sharply. The key here was the creative link that existed between the lab and manufacturing. Developmental research and effective pilot plant work lowered costs and enabled the company to get into large-scale production. So important was this market that in 1954 manufacturing returned to St. Louis. There, in the middle of America's agricultural heartland, Merck established a large blending plant for the formulation of micro-ingredient supplements for livestock and poultry feeds.

Well launched in this business, Merck steadily expanded its line of products, total output, and productivity. In the 1960s when the company brought out *TBZ*—a highly effective treatment for intestinal parasites in animals—it built a dedicated plant at Rahway with a capacity of a million kilos a year. Economies of scale helped to give Merck a strong competitive position in the U.S. market, and MSDI sought to duplicate that experience abroad. Two very large markets were in Australia and New Zealand, both of which had vast sheep-grazing areas. MSDI's Australian subsidiary built its own *TBZ* factory, as did the organizations in England, Holland, and Argentina. By 1964, MSDI had eleven overseas

*The Hagan Corporation (predecessor of Calgon) in Pittsburgh, Pennsylvania, 1918.*

*Signing of the merger agreement between Calgon Corporation and Merck & Co., Inc., December 7, 1967. Seated are William W. Hopwood (left), President of Calgon, and Merck President Henry W. Gadsden. Merck and Calgon*

## DIVERSIFICATION: THE CALGON STORY

*executives present included (standing left to right): Charles E. Childs, Jr., Daniel W. Byles, Hubert N. Fiaccone, Stuart Henshall, William Van Buren, Raymond E. Snyder, Owen Rice, Jess J. Tope, Carl M. Anderson, James K. Everhart, and James M. Fulton.*

Merck's experiences with diversification have ranged from very successful (Kelco) to extremely unsuccessful (ultra-pure silicon). Calgon Corporation has been a bit of both. Merck & Co. acquired Calgon in 1968, when CEO Henry W. Gadsden was worried about the future of the ethical drug industry. Public attacks on the drug manufacturers suggested to Gadsden that the industry faced increased regulation and narrower profit margins. What better recourse than to diversify, this time into a related industry involving water treatment chemicals that were likely to be in great demand as concern for the environment mounted. Calgon's tradition of chemical research, its service-oriented marketing, and its consumer products line seemed compatible with Merck. There was a promise of profitable synergies, and Merck seemed especially well positioned to assist Calgon's expansion overseas.

Actually, Calgon consisted of a number of related companies. Some of them had only recently been acquired, like Pittsburgh Activated Carbon in 1965, while others traced their history back to the original organization of the business (as the Hagan Corporation) in 1918. The Calgon name—"Calcium Gone"—had been transferred from a single product to the marketing division, and then to the entire firm (1963) after it sold its Controls Division and the Hagan name to Westinghouse. The business Merck acquired in 1968 had 1750 employees (compared with the parent firm's 15,800). That year Calgon made 14% of the net sales of the merged enterprise.

The high side of the Calgon venture was the water management technology business. Merck still owns and operates this portion of the company, which is part of the Specialty Chemicals Group. In 1986, in fact, it further strengthened Calgon by acquiring Vestal Laboratories (now Calgon Vestal Labs) to manufacture and market professional skin care products, disinfectants, and instrument germicides to hospitals and other healthcare institutions. That same year it acquired as well the water management technology business of the Hercules Company.

But other parts of Calgon did not "take" with Merck and have since been spun off. In 1977 CEO John Horan sold Calgon's consumer products divisions to Beecham. Then, in 1983 he put Calgon Carbon up for sale. By that time, Horan had Merck on a new strategic path, one emphasizing its core human and animal health business. That policy has continued to be followed until the present, centennial year of 1991.

factories manufacturing products just for the agricultural and animal health markets.

The same style of decentralized manufacturing was adopted in the human health field, as MSDI hit its stride in the late fifties and sixties. Between 1955 and 1962, the total assets in foreign manufacturing tripled, and by 1962 MSDI was running 20 plants in 19 countries around the world. By 1970, there were production facilities in 25 countries overseas.

Typical of these operations were the plants in Britain. At Hoddesdon, Merck Sharp & Dohme Limited operated a large pharmaceutical manufacturing plant. At Ponders End, the subsidiary produced chlorothiazide and hydrochlorothiazide for Merck's diuretics, *Diuril* and *Moduretic*. There too MSDI manufactured the sulfas and *Aldomet*, a treatment for high blood pressure. These manufacturing operations—like those of the other subsidiaries—were directed by the president of the U.K. organization during this early phase of global growth.

As Merck's CEO John J. Horan (1976-1985) realized, however, this sprawling array of plants could benefit from a higher degree of central control. The first structural expression of this goal was the Merck Chemical Manufacturing Division (MCMD), which now directs all of the firm's chemical production facilities around the world. In 1989 Horan's successor, Dr. Roy Vagelos, created the Merck Pharmaceutical Manufacturing Division (MPMD), which does the same job for the pharmaceutical side of the manufacturing operations.

Out of this reorganization drive came two successful strategies. One was a restructuring of the firm's assets, consolidating production in the most efficient units while eliminating or upgrading those plants which were no longer state-of-the-art or which served only small markets. In a sense, Merck had come full circle. This, as we saw, was the

*Dr. Piero Bellani (left), Senior Director, Italian Operations, MPMD, and Dr. Marco Res, Director, Quality Assurance, MPMD, examine facilities in Pavia, Italy, 1989.*

*Joseph W. Keating, MPMD President, in 1990.*

## GLOBAL PRODUCTION:
### PRIMAXIN

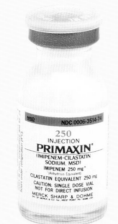

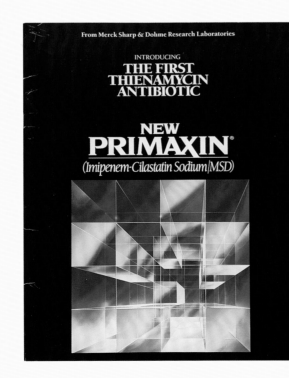

In 1986, Merck began to market *Primaxin*, its new broad-spectrum antibiotic, in the United States. It was already being sold in Germany, Austria, and Switzerland, and since then has been marketed extensively in Japan and throughout the world. It is, then, a global drug and a product that well illustrates the nature of manufacturing in today's pharmaceutical industry.

"There was challenge enough for all," said Dr. Seemon Pines (then MSDRL's vice president of process research and development), when Merck was bringing this new antibiotic into production. The product in this case was discovered and isolated by Merck's microbiologists; the firm's chemists then devised a stable derivative of the natural product. Still, the substance was extremely complex and chemically sensitive. The only feasible way to produce it was through chemical synthesis. As Burt Christensen of MSDRL noted, it was "the most complex total synthesis the industry has known." Eight of the reactions in the production sequence used chemistry that had only been developed in the last decade, and both chemical engineering and technical services had all that they could handle in the early stages of development. MCMD had to build an entirely new sterile facility (at Elkton, Virginia) for this single product. The facilities at Rahway and Cherokee were also altered extensively to play their roles in the manufacturing process.

*Primaxin, effective against a broad range of infections, combines the thienamycin antibiotic imipenem with cilastatin, a specific inhibitor of the renal enzyme dehydropeptidase-I.*

There were 16 steps—in four locations—in the manufacturing sequence. MCMD had to produce sterile imipenem, as well as cilastatin (an enzyme inhibitor), and a sterile buffer. The first steps took place in Switzerland; then, steps seven through thirteen were performed in Danville, Pennsylvania. The imipenem next went to Rahway for finishing and then to Elkton, Virginia, to be mixed with the cilastatin and buffer in sterile isolation. Finally, *Primaxin* could be packaged and shipped.

By using existing capacity where possible, MCMD and process development were able to chop the capital investment for manufacturing in half. At the same time, they doubled output over a two-year period. It helped to have at Elkton MSD's (and the world's) first completely computer-operated pharmaceutical manufacturing plant. *Primaxin* became a success story for Merck research, clinical studies, marketing—and particularly for manufacturing. The chemical engineering in this case was about as far removed from the pot and kettle operations of the 1930s as one can imagine. *Primaxin* production is on the front edge of a new age of scientific, global manufacturing.

*At the Elkton, Virginia, plant of the Merck Chemical Manufacturing Division (1988), Woody Johnson works with isolation equipment in the manufacture of imipenem, the active ingredient of* Primaxin.

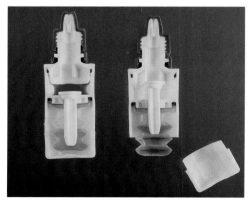

*An innovative package designed in 1989 by Merck Pharmaceutical Manufacturing Division engineers for* Timpilo, *a product for control of glaucoma.*

same strategy George Merck had implemented in 1903, when he successfully combined the St. Louis and Rahway operations, and his son adopted in the late 1920s after the merger with PWR.

The second and complementary strategy was that of creating a single Merck standard of excellence for all of its plants around the world. MCMD, headed by David Conklin, and MPMD, under president Joseph W. Keating, are attempting in all of their manufacturing operations to realize the same global standards of quality, efficiency, safety and environmental protection. As then senior vice president Douglas J. MacMaster Jr. explains, centralization hit some snags at first. But now, operations are more efficient: "It's doing the job." There is, MacMaster says, a new level of professionalism in the organization, "a new spirit."

In recent years worldwide interest in the environment has become intense. As early as the 1950s, Merck had begun to dedicate substantial resources to solving environmental problems such as those in waste disposal. By the 1980s, the company was spending more than $30 million a year to keep all of its production facilities well within the limits set in the United States by government regulations. "We've revised our environmental policy," Conklin says, "actually made it much tougher on ourselves—because we believe we can do better. As a company dedicated to manufacturing products that improve the quality of life. . .without doing harm to the environment, we simply must." Now, consistent with its new global strategy, Merck is implementing all of its programs worldwide, whether the local regulations require them or not. That is the essence of the new strategy.

In this, the centennial year of 1991, MCMD and MPMD are still in mid-course with the new strategy. Having met the challenges of a century of growth and innovation, both of Merck's manufacturing divisions are working hard to keep pace with the rapid changes taking place in the global pharmaceutical industry today.

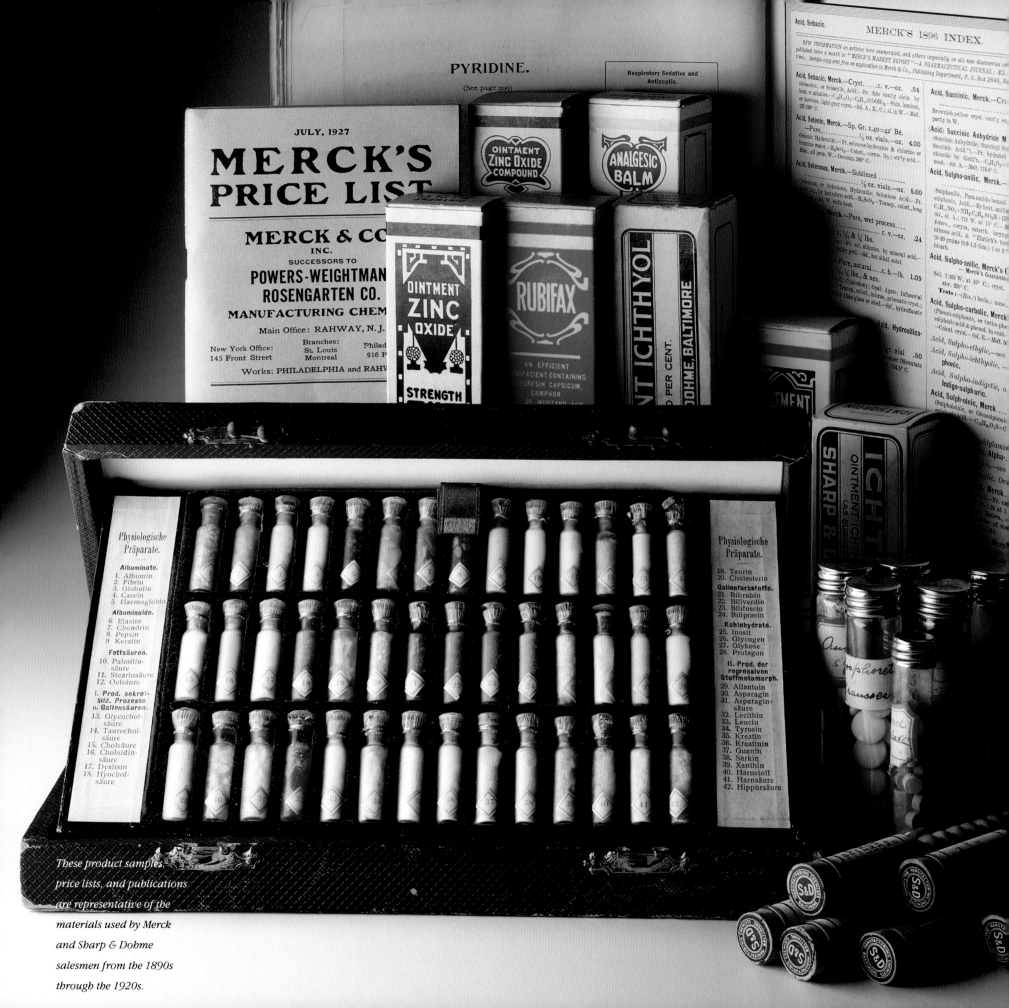

These product samples, price lists, and publications are representative of the materials used by Merck and Sharp & Dohme salesmen from the 1890s through the 1920s.

# CHAPTER FIVE

# GLOBAL MARKETING

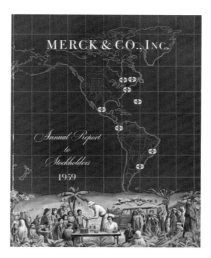

"The young graduate who wishes to combine language with an interest in international affairs should look into the possibility of export work." That was Merck's official advice to college graduates contemplating a career with the company. But who could have imagined that one of the recruits in 1949 would know Malayan, Bengali, French, and a bit of Urdu and Hindustani. But then Huskel Ekaireb didn't fit any pattern terribly well. Born in Penang, Malaysia, during the First World War, he had traveled with his father, a British export merchant who sold rubber and

*Huskel Ekaireb (l) and Dr. Antonie T. Knoppers (r) with Khasem Pangsrivongse, chairman of the B. L. H. Trading Company in Thailand. A joint venture with B. L. H., the Merck Sharp & Dohme (Thailand) Ltd. plant began operations in April 1960, producing vitamin B$_{12}$, diuretics, and steroids. It was the first pharmaceutical plant to be built in Thailand with U. S. technical assistance, and Merck's first integrated chemical and pharmaceutical plant on the Asian mainland.*

*Huskel Ekaireb as MSDI Vice President.*

tin, through China, Singapore, Europe, Australia, the Dutch East Indies, and India. Along the way young Huskel was educated at Goethal's Memorial School and College in Kurseong, India. What else but to become a sales representative for a British company during and after World War II? Concerned following Indian independence that his markets might disappear, Ekaireb contacted the Merck company about a job. President Kerrigan took a chance with this unusual young salesman. His territory? It included Asia, that is all of Asia, plus Australia, New Zealand, Africa, and the Middle East. His staff? No secretary and no assistants, he was flying solo. But what he did have to go with his easy smile was a remarkable knowledge of foreign cultures, a high level of energy, and an unusual sensitivity to the people with whom he was dealing. On his first tour, he wrote orders for $10 million. He was, in fact, almost too successful in what was once called the Third World. Merck had trouble supplying the products to fill all of his orders.

In the years that followed the company's capacity caught up with Ekaireb, and the master salesman churned out orders from several corners of the world. He was particularly effective after 1952 when he joined forces with Tonie Knoppers. Following the 1953 merger between Merck and Sharp & Dohme, Ekaireb launched the joint venture with Banyu in Japan and was responsible for establishing Merck Sharp & Dohme International (MSDI) subsidiaries in Australia, Pakistan, India, and Thailand. More attuned to marketing than the details of economic

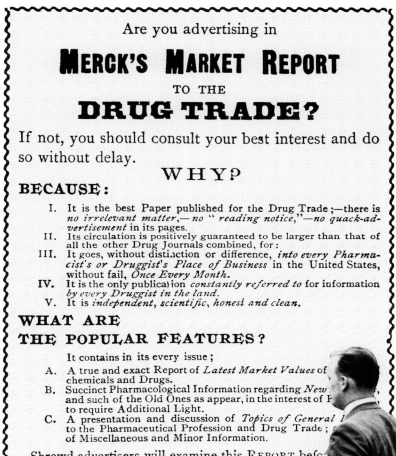

Are you advertising in

# MERCK'S MARKET REPORT

TO THE

# DRUG TRADE?

If not, you should consult your best interest and do so without delay.

### WHY?

**BECAUSE:**

I.   It is the best Paper published for the Drug Trade;—there is *no irrelevant matter,—no " reading notice,"—no quack-ad-vertisement* in its pages.
II.  Its circulation is positively guaranteed to be larger than that of all the other Drug Journals combined, for:
III. It goes, without distinction or difference, *into every Pharma-cist's or Druggist's Place of Business* in the United States, without fail, *Once Every Month.*
IV.  It is the only publication *constantly referred to* for information *by every Druggist in the land.*
V.   It is *independent, scientific, honest and clean.*

## WHAT ARE
## THE POPULAR FEATURES?

It contains in its every issue;

A. A true and exact Report of *Latest Market Values* of chemicals and Drugs.
B. Succinct Pharmacological Information regarding *New* and such of the Old Ones as appear, in the interest of to require Additional Light.
C. A presentation and discussion of *Topics of General* to the Pharmaceutical Profession and Drug Trade; of Miscellaneous and Minor Information.

Shrewd advertisers will examine this REPORT befo
their contracts.   A sample copy with terms to adver
be sent on application.         Address,

MERCK'S MARKET REP

**71** & **73** William St.,               NEW YOR

(2)

planning, Ekaireb was sometimes too optimistic. In Thailand, for instance, he guided MSDI into building a plant that lost money for five years. Eventually Thailand came up to Ekaireb's expectations, but meanwhile he had gone on to new deals in other corners of the world. As MSDI's commercial ambassador was fond of saying, "the nice thing about international business is that it's always Spring somewhere."

Wherever he went Ekaireb left behind a trail of friends and satisfied customers. The secret? Honesty, he said, and the ability to sense that your customer may not always want to do business when you want him to place an order. By the time he retired as executive vice president of Merck in 1982, the company was doing over $1 billion a year in overseas business, a tribute to Ekaireb and the other MSDI executives who drove the foreign business ahead in the years following World War II.

## THE TRANSFORMATION OF MARKETING

When Ekaireb joined Merck in 1949, the company already had a well-established tradition in marketing. From its earliest days in the United States, the firm had stressed the provision of complete and accurate information to its customers and to the trade in general. Adopting a policy that had been in practice in Germany for some years, George Merck began in 1891 to issue *Merck's Monthly Report to the Drug Trade*. This publication, later called *Merck's Report*, was directed at pharmacists, to whom it provided practical information, price lists, and essays on issues before the trade. Within a few years, it had become the leading journal in the business. Somber in appearance and moral in tone, the *Report* defended purity of products, fought adulteration, and proclaimed to druggists and doctors that "energy, invincible determination, with the right motive, are the levers that move the world."

In 1897 George Merck issued an edition of *The Merck Index*, an encyclopedia for pharmacists, doctors, dentists, veterinarians, and chemists. The *Index* quickly became—and still is today, in its eleventh edition—a standard reference work for technical information on the industry's products. Two years later he also brought out his first edition of *The Merck Manual of Materia Medica*, which listed therapies for everything from eczema to impotence.

George Merck knew his market. He had the company's energy focused primarily on the pharmacies that compounded most of the drugs of that day. The role of the doctor had yet to become dominant in health care. Most persons suffering an illness went directly to the pharmacy to buy either drugs (called "ethical drugs" at that time) or one of the numerous patent medicines that aroused the ire of the *Merck Report*. The *Report* prided itself on being an "effective weapon" against "Patent-Medicine Quackery," the "worst element in the business." The patent medicines were a "corruptive, malignant and contagious disease," the *Report* proclaimed, "that is slowly but surely poisoning the morality of the Profession. . . ."

*The prescription department of Merck's pharmacy in New York City, 1898.*

# The Merck Manual has been around now for ninety-two years, in fifteen editions....

In its advertising the company stressed quality as much as price. Pharmacists bought relatively small amounts of basic reagents and other fine chemicals to use in compounding remedies. They needed to be certain their ingredients were not adulterated in any way. But since their customers were price-conscious, so were the druggists, who were attentive to the price list featured in the *Report*. Frequently, too, they could make good use of the technical information that Merck provided them free. And since many of New York's pharmacies were run by recent immigrants from Europe, they could feel comfortable discussing these issues in their native language. Merck's tradition of using bilingual salesmen long predates Huskel Ekaireb. George Merck stayed close to his customers, whose letters the *Report* regularly published and whose sug-

## ADULTERATIONS

are more to be deplored in drugs than in foods. The druggist who is careless in selecting his drugs loses the confidence of both the customer and the physician. If confidence is once destroyed, trade soon diminishes.

The druggist who handles MERCK'S exclusively, knows where he stands. His prescription-work will always sustain the severest tests as to purity and excellence. MERCK'S goods are sold at current market prices and should be specified in all orders.

*December 1892 ad from Merck's Market Report.*

If an academic book sells 5,000 copies it is doing very well indeed. If your publisher sold 10,000 or 20,000 copies of the novel you've been planning to write, you could give yourself a pat on the billfold. So what can you say about a manual that is sold to 800,000 healthcare professionals who use it regularly, trust its contents, and respect its publisher and authors (all 270 of them for the last edition)? Yes, *The Merck Manual* has been around now for ninety-two years, in fifteen editions, and is a publisher's dream. If you thumbed through the first edition, you might wonder why it was an instant success. The treatments included bloodletting for acute bronchitis—arsenic, a big favorite, for impotence—and "tar" for eczema. More appealing to our taste are the suggested therapies for obesity, the "alkaline waters. . .

of Marienbad," and for diabetes, homely "almond bread." But our vision is warped by the therapeutic revolution. The 1899 edition of *The Merck Manual*, like all of the subsequent versions, recorded in condensed form the best available medical knowledge of that day. That is why it became "the Physician's Bible" of the twentieth century.

In the years since 1899, the Manual has grown with the profession. Its contents have become more sophisticated, its girth expanded, its tone more restrained. The current-day title is *The Merck Manual of Diagnosis and Therapy*. It now shares the bookshelf with a *Merck Veterinary Manual* (1955) and *The Merck Manual of Geriatrics* (1990). In addition to English, *The Merck Manual* appears in seven languages: Italian, French, Turkish, Spanish, Portuguese, Chinese, and German. The latter translation is particularly appropriate because George Merck's 1899 edition of the Manual was an English translation of E. Merck's German publication.

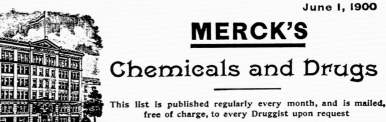

June 1, 1900

# MERCK'S
## Chemicals and Drugs

This list is published regularly every month, and is mailed, free of charge, to every Druggist upon request

### MERCK & CO., NEW YORK

Telephone Call: 1414 Spring          Post office, Branch O

*THE MERCK MANUAL*

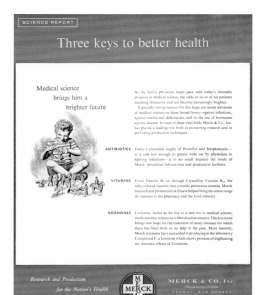

*Advertisements for Merck products marketed in the United States and Canada.* Merck Report, *1938.* Merck's Canadian Report & Price List, *1932. A Merck ad, March 1951.*

gestions the company acknowledged and heeded. Merck's products were distributed by two kinds of "jobbers": those wholesale druggists who bought in bulk and packaged and labeled the goods themselves; and those who sold original Merck packages. The latter group of jobbers ordered only those products the retail druggists, their customers, specified, and thus George Merck's efforts to reach out to the pharmacists were important. So too was the attention he gave to quality and promptness of service, both of which were selling points with his largest customers, the bulk jobbers and the manufacturers of medicinal and pharmaceutical products. By the 1920s, some of his largest accounts were with pharmaceutical and proprietary medicine manufacturers, firms such as Eli Lilly & Company and Sharp & Dohme.

After the founder's son, George W. Merck, became president, the company gradually organized a broader and more specialized marketing network. In the 1930s and 1940s, as the firm's new laboratories took hold and began to drive the business, Merck adopted new approaches to sales and marketing. The company took its first look at the medical profession as potential customers. Merck salesmen—and they were still all men—also began to bypass the wholesale drug jobbers, going directly to the pharmacist through a system of regional and local sales representatives. When new markets were opening up, as they were in dentistry, Merck gave advice to the pharmacists as to which products to use and what sales techniques to adopt for those particular customers. Separate departments in sales handled the druggists, industrial customers, and the very large accounts. As Merck & Co. became a larger and more complex business, its sales and marketing personnel became more specialized.

George W. Merck pushed the company out into foreign markets, first through the Powers-Weightman-Rosengarten export corporation, and then in 1947 by way of Merck North America and Merck Pan America. These subsidiaries worked through distributors and licensees in most of the countries they served. Many of the distributorships were exclusive, although in some of the smaller markets the company still operated through exporters. By the early 1950s exports (including licensee income) constituted about 20% of Merck's sales, with the international business divided equally between Europe and the Near East on one side and Latin America and the Far East on the other.

Huskel Ekaireb and his fellow salesmen overseas and in the United States were logging annual sales of over $100 million by the early 50s, but Merck & Co. was still essentially marketing in the traditional, chemical industry style. Its newest products—in particular penicillin, streptomycin, and cortisone—seemed to call for a different style of distribution, one that featured the physicians as customers. But Merck had yet to develop a sales and marketing establishment adequate to that task. Nor did it have a strategy for responding to the threat posed when some of its biggest customers began to produce for themselves the drugs and chemicals they had been buying from Merck.

I n 1953, however, George W. Merck and one of his former employees, John S. Zinsser, CEO of Sharp & Dohme, found a solution to both of those problems. By merging the two firms, Merck acquired a market for his major products and a nationwide network of salesmen accustomed to dealing with doctors as well as pharmacies. Zinsser, for his part, was able to strengthen significantly his organization's research and manufacturing capabilities. The new U.S. pharmaceutical division, Merck Sharp & Dohme (MSD, which they organized after the merger), could compete effectively with companies like Lilly, Squibb, and Upjohn, which had their own chemical manufacturing facilities.

Merck continued to sell chemicals, but after 1953 its primary products became finished drugs and its primary customers became hospitals and doctors. The company now had thousands of new customers. The doctors themselves did not buy the drugs. But they prescribed them, and thus every doctor was important to the company's future.

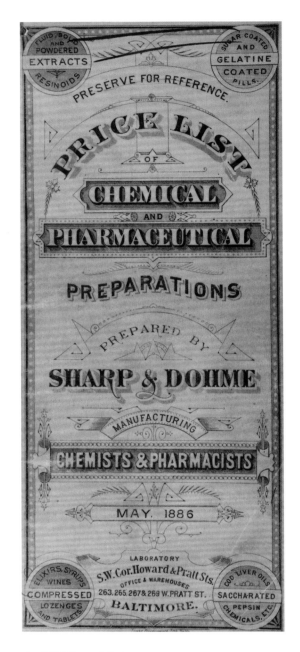

*An 1886 Sharp & Dohme price list.*

## JOHN LLOYD HUCK

He started in sales and marketing in Nutley, New Jersey. Twelve years old, John Huck set out to sell magazines, door-to-door, in the Great Depression. "I was sort of industrious in earning money," he said later. He sold *Collier's* and *American Magazine* ("a good one, a 25-cent magazine so you got more if you sold it") to his family's friends, to their friends, and to anyone else he could persuade to part with a dear quarter. He was successful: "I built up a pretty good route." But then his aunt intervened, giving his career a new twist.

She gave him a Chemcraft chemistry set (remember Karl Beyer's set?) and turned young John toward science. A hard worker in school, he did well in high school chemistry and biology, and after graduation headed to Pennsylvania State University to become a chemist. World War II interrupted his education—he served as a flight instructor and bomber pilot in the Air Corps—but in 1946 he returned to school and finished his B.S. in chemistry.

Sales and marketing seemed long forgotten during his first two years as a bench chemist at Hoffmann-La Roche. But the lab work began to seem "routine" and "narrow." Bored, he began to look for an opportunity to move to the business side of the company. Although he "didn't even know pharmaceutical companies had sales people," he ended up in Omaha, Nebraska, as a sales representative. Desperation bred innovation. Huck was shortly a successful salesman, good enough to become director of sales training and then an assistant general sales manager.

When he accepted an offer from Merck Sharp & Dohme in 1958, Huck thus had a solid grip on the fundamentals of sales and marketing in pharmaceuticals. He knew that sales people needed thorough training; that sales and marketing should be closely coordinated; that full disclosure of side effects was imperative; and that the provision of useful product information was the heart of the process. "There was no harm in sizzle, but if you didn't have any steak there. . .it didn't go over well with physicians." With solid support from John Horan, Huck was able to implement these ideas at MSD, where he became Horan's successor as president in 1973.

Two years later he moved up again, this time to Rahway as a senior vice president at Merck. During the next decade—as executive vice president (1977) and as president and chief operating officer (1978)—he helped CEO John Horan guide Merck toward the great expansion that would follow in the late 1980s. When he retired in 1986 as chairman of Merck's Board, he had the satisfaction of leaving behind a firm that was voted that year America's most admired company in *Fortune's* annual survey of senior executives and industry experts. Apparently, selling the steak instead of the sizzle is good business, as well as good ethics.

*A sample of the promotional literature distributed by Merck to inform the medical community about cortisone, 1950.*

*Eugene L. Kuryloski, MSD's Vice President for Sales during the 1960s.*

*An MSD professional representative presents his card to the nurse-receptionist during a visit to a doctor's office, 1960.*

Merck Sharp & Dohme's domestic sales and marketing operations became a vital center of innovation for the enterprise. Three of the leaders in this transition were John J. Horan, John Lloyd Huck, and John E. Lyons. As counsel for MSD in the 1950s, Horan recognized that the company had to improve the performance of its field representatives, the detail men who regularly met with doctors and hospital personnel. Instead of merely pushing MSD's products, the detail men should, he thought, give the healthcare professional a full and accurate description—including the side effects—of the drugs available for a particular treatment. What if a sale was lost? Fair balance in Merck's presentations was more important, Horan said, than making a sale. To implement the new approach, Horan had to revamp the company's sales training, strengthen its supporting clinical programs, and develop a new approach to the type of information released on all of its products. These goals were not achieved overnight. Nor were they achieved without some resistance. When Gene Kuryloski and John Huck started to "retrain" experienced detail men, they hit resistance from time to time. Some of the "little dukedoms" of the district managers had to be reconquered by headquarters before the new national standards could be realized.

Meanwhile, Huck was gradually introducing the "totally new concept" of marketing. He coordinated it with sales and advertising by working through a new cadre of product managers. Lawyers now carefully combed all of the information flowing from MSD to its customers, certifying that the data was accurate, full, and balanced. This practice led to the creation of medical-legal review boards—comprised of physicians and attorneys—to examine and sign off on every piece of advertising copy and training program used by the firm.

By 1960 MSD had over 700 men in the field dealing with or "detailing" the doctor and to a lesser extent contacting retail druggists, wholesalers, and hospitals. Ten years later another transformation had begun—the detail men became detail persons as women joined the force (today, more than half are women). By this time the division's training programs were in full swing, preparing the company's representatives to provide up-to-date and complete information, with dispatch. Many more of the representatives had medical or scientific training, as did John E. Lyons, who became vice president of sales that year.

Lyons had lived through the transition from detail men to detail persons to professional representatives. He had started in sales at a time when side effects were described "with a wink." But he realized early on that the best way to do well in this important industry was to "emphasize fundamentals," to build "trust." At MSD he taught his "professional communicators" how to "become infused with the duties and responsibilities of physicians, pharmacists, nurses [and] hospitals. . . ." They learned how to present information that was of value because it was "timely, accurate, balanced, solid." Lyons and Huck brought sales and marketing at MSD onto the same wave length because they were in basic agreement about the need to implement the Horan strategy of "fair balance."

As MSD settled into the new regime, other innovations followed. The professional representatives began, for example, to use computers to provide information to doctors and other healthcare providers. Using the computer, a representative who had the right kind of scientific background and knowledge of the field could offer printouts on areas of therapy of interest to the physician. MSD began as well to sponsor local meetings at which specialists presented information on

*A 1959 meeting of MSD district sales managers in Atlantic City, New Jersey, with members of the Philadelphia home office in the back row. From left, back row: F. Walton, E. J. Carroll, J. A. Wells, J. L. Huck, J. P. Feenane, E. J. Kuryloski, S. T. Henshall, J. G. Bill, J. J. Fee, L. P. Hudson, P. A. Nickerson, L. D. Roberts, and J. E. Lyons. Second row, from left: A. L. Barnum, L. J. Oden, L. C. Woods, W. C. Newberry, E. F. Schwab, H. M. Casey, W. C. Evans, J. L. Smith, and G. R. Klodt. Front row, from left: F. E. Hatfield, A. V. Ohlendorf, E. C. Schnaidt, W. N. Stebbins, G. E. Kessinger, H. H. Hill, and H. W. Parker.*

*Barry Wells, a professional representative with Merck Sharp & Dohme Limited in the United Kingdom, consults an extensive database on his laptop computer, 1989.*

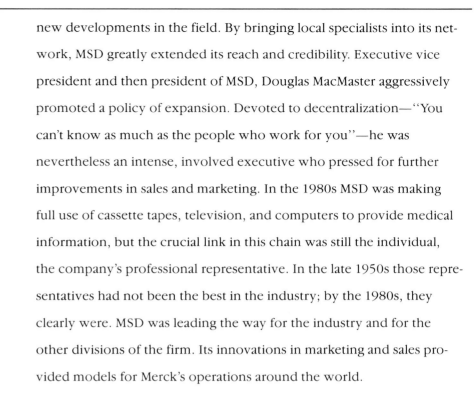

*Douglas J. MacMaster Jr. was President of Merck Sharp & Dohme from 1985 to 1988.*

*Warren J. Lambert (standing), Sales Training Coordinator at Merck Sharp & Dohme in West Point, Pennsylvania, shows Stephen J. Hulse, Associate Professional Representative, how to use an interactive video program designed to teach new sales representatives about the physiological processes of heart disease, 1989.*

*James H. Sharp, the first President of Merck Sharp & Dohme International.*

new developments in the field. By bringing local specialists into its network, MSD greatly extended its reach and credibility. Executive vice president and then president of MSD, Douglas MacMaster aggressively promoted a policy of expansion. Devoted to decentralization—"You can't know as much as the people who work for you"—he was nevertheless an intense, involved executive who pressed for further improvements in sales and marketing. In the 1980s MSD was making full use of cassette tapes, television, and computers to provide medical information, but the crucial link in this chain was still the individual, the company's professional representative. In the late 1950s those representatives had not been the best in the industry; by the 1980s, they clearly were. MSD was leading the way for the industry and for the other divisions of the firm. Its innovations in marketing and sales provided models for Merck's operations around the world.

## AROUND THE WORLD WITH MSDI

During these pivotal years, MSDI was rapidly increasing the firm's presence overseas. Before Ekaireb could go full blast, however, some groundwork had to be done. A crucial role in laying that foundation was played by James H. Sharp, MSDI's first president. A lawyer who in 1953 was heading Merck's international activities, he directed the initial integration of the two companies' foreign sales and marketing. Along with Sharp & Dohme came a foreign branch in Australia and export subsidiaries in England, Canada, the Philippines, Cuba, Brazil, and several other Latin American nations. S&D had 31 export distribution centers scattered around the world. It was Sharp's job to fold Merck North America and Pan America into the extensive S&D overseas marketing division, leaving the merged operations under MSDI. As he completed that task, Sharp turned over leadership to a new generation of international businessmen—the "Young Turks."

Commander of the "Young Turks" in MSDI was Tonie Knoppers, who was convinced that the world was Merck's "oyster."

## Merck in the United Kingdom

Merck's ties to the United Kingdom predate the company's founding in 1891. George Merck had prepped for his American venture by serving with E. Merck's London representatives, Mr. Fritz Böhm and Mr. Broicher, in 1887 and again in 1889. Completing his training for enterprise, he returned to Darmstadt and then made his fateful voyage to New York. After 1891, Merck & Co. developed commercial ties with the United Kingdom. It sold products in Britain through exporters and distributors and later licensed the processes for manufacturing penicillin and streptomycin to a British firm.

With the 1953 merger between Merck and Sharp & Dohme, however, the British connection became far more significant. S&D had acquired (with Mulford) a London sales branch and had begun small-scale manufacturing there (of Sucrets and other products) before World War II. Following 1945 it moved its operations about 20 miles north of London to Hoddesdon (Hertfordshire), and in the 1950s, MSDI was able to build on this foundation. MSDI acquired the long-established English firm of Thomas Morson & Son Ltd. in 1957, and subsequently expanded its manufacturing facilities at Ponders End and at Cramlington. At the latter site, Dewey Stallard guided the introduction of an automatic formulating and tableting operation which also implemented a modular approach to pharmaceutical production.

More recently, Merck has increased its stake in the United Kingdom. In the 1960s, it built a product development lab at Hoddesdon and added to that the Neuroscience Research Centre in 1985. It had earlier (1978) acquired one of the world's leading producers of turkey breeding stock, British United Turkeys Ltd., and in 1979 Alginate Industries Ltd. to complement Kelco's operations. Subsequently, Kelco began production of alginates in Scotland (Barcaldine) and of biogums at Knowsley, England (Kelco Biospecialties Ltd.). The most recent addition to the family is BritCair Ltd., a firm which produces an innovative wound dressing made from the alginate fiber Kelco produces from kelp. With extensive manufacturing, research, and marketing facilities in the United Kingdom, Merck was well positioned to share in the recent growth of the British economy and to prepare for the expansion that will follow the completion of the European Community in 1992.

*A 1952 issue of* Antigen, *the Sharp & Dohme employee publication in the United Kingdom.*

*A 1951 photograph of T. W. Rayner, Chairman and Managing Director of Merck Sharp & Dohme in the United Kingdom during the 1950s and 1960s.*

To transform that vision into reality, he set out to develop a new corporate style and a team of internationalists like Huskel Ekaireb. His strategic vision was to shift away from using licensees and distributors, stressing instead the development of subsidiaries. Working with strong support from CEO John T. Connor, Knoppers soon had MSDI producing and distributing throughout Latin America, Asia, and Europe.

*Sir John Marshall (left), the Prime Minister of New Zealand, congratulates Dr. Antonie Knoppers, President of Merck & Co., Inc., at the opening of MSD New Zealand's new Wiri headquarters, October 1971.*

Successful research catalyzed entrepreneurship in marketing—as it has so often in this firm. MSDI was able to ride new products like *Diuril* into a strong position in several overseas markets. Each subsidiary developed its own style, patterned on the personality of its local chief executive—some of whom "raised eyebrows" and a few hackles in Rahway. Knoppers later explained, "I had a knack of keeping controversial people together and letting them feel happy." In the next few years he led his happy team into an era of extensive expansion. Merck bought Thomas Morson & Son Ltd. so it could quickly get into production in England. Each country, however, required a somewhat different approach, and MSDI tailored its solutions to fit the various national settings.

In Latin America, Leo Fernandez called the shots. Knoppers gave him and his other subordinates substantial autonomy. He had every reason to have confidence in Fernandez, who had been with Merck since the Great Depression of the 1930s. He had joined the company shortly after graduating from high school a few miles up the Pennsylvania Railroad in Elizabeth, New Jersey. His first job was not elegant. He started working with Hans Molitor in the Merck Institute's animal clinic, cleaning cages and preparing special diets. But Fernandez, whose family was struggling through the depression, was delighted to have a job, even a dirty one.

Determined to move ahead, Fernandez continued his education in the evenings, taking a degree in electrical engineering (Newark

College of Engineering) and a masters in chemical engineering at Stevens Institute of Technology. The Merck Educational Assistance Program helped him pay his tuition, and the company quickly gave him a chance to parlay his engineering and his knowledge of Spanish into a new job. Merck sent him into the Amazon Valley to build a small plant that could recover an enzyme (ficin, a protein digestant) from a particular Peruvian forest tree. Successful in the Amazon, he returned to Rahway in the mid-1940s and worked for a time on penicillin. Later, he made a number of trips to Latin countries and helped develop the firm's new operations in Japan and then in Holland.

An experienced engineer and manager, Fernandez returned to Latin America for MSDI, serving as general manager for the development of manufacturing in the entire region. In these years the South and Central American countries wanted their own production facilities. Merck was more than willing to cooperate. Under Fernandez's direction MSDI built plants in Mexico, Peru, Argentina, Brazil, Venezuela, and Costa Rica. Fernandez—who would in 1968 succeed Knoppers as president of MSDI—also developed new marketing organizations, following the guidelines created by MSD in the United States. In each country he introduced extensive training programs and recruited a new cadre of representatives.

Although Latin America was well in hand by the late 1960s, Knoppers (now a senior vice president) was worried. He had guided the firm into a favorable position in his home country, the Netherlands, where it had been in production since 1957. But still, he thought, MSDI was missing opportunities in the very large and growing European market. MSDI's planning organization, under the direction of Dr. Irwin Goldman, pushed hard for a decisive shift in emphasis from Latin America to Europe. Goldman's first long-range plan stressed the great potential market in the European Economic Community. He called for

*Leo Fernandez in 1960, at the time he was MSDI Vice President for Latin America.*

*Processing cinchona bark (shown here in Colombia in 1945) to extract quinine was labor-intensive. Merck had established experimental quinine plantations in Guatemala and Costa Rica as early as 1932 to produce this treatment for malaria.*

*A. E. Cohen in the early 1970s, when he was MSDI Vice President for Europe.*

*Production crew celebrates the completion of batch #500 of* Amprolium, *in Haarlem, Holland, 1964.*

extensive investments and looked toward the point where international sales would equal those in the United States. ''The plan required a heavy ante,'' Knoppers recalled, but he and Connor accepted the proposal.

A new cadre of executives implemented MSDI's strategy for the 1970s. Ekaireb became president of the international division in 1970 when Fernandez retired. One of Ekaireb's key managers was the youthful, dynamic A. E. ''Barry'' Cohen, who had an ideal background for an MSDI executive: Born in Calcutta, he had been educated in India and Japan. During his first ten years at MSDI, he served in the Indian subsidiary and in Pakistan, before becoming regional director for all of South Asia.

In 1967 Cohen moved to Europe and began preparing for the expansion. ''You have to be an optimist,'' he said later. ''I think you have to be optimistic so you don't get burdened by all the good reasons why you can't succeed.'' There were plenty of ''good reasons'' in Europe. Two of them were named Hoechst and Bayer, tough competitors who could achieve economies of scale that Merck could not match.

In both human and animal products, the progress in Europe was uneven. Neither the Spanish subsidiary (after 1968) nor the one in Italy, where there were no patent laws to protect Merck products, did particularly well at first. Nor was MSDI able to penetrate the German market successfully. Because of its previous ties to E. Merck of Darmstadt—by now itself a pharmaceuticals producer—MSDI could not use the ''Merck'' name there. In Germany too the competition from very large and long-established firms was stiff. It would take many years of effort for Merck to get up to scale. While significant gains in market share have been achieved in recent years, further progress will be necessary to position the company among the very largest firms in that important market.

In each of the European countries, Merck & Co. had to build its reputation a step at a time. Neither the firm's products nor its research were well known in the academic or clinical communities. Physicians were not accustomed to prescribing Merck drugs. MSDI had to overcome these disadvantages gradually by implementing new programs on a country-by-country basis. Dr. Kalman Mezey set up extensive clinical plans and organized an international medical advisory council. "We created," Mezey said, "a network of clinical pharmacology experts, of medical research people of our own abroad. . . ." The role of the advisors was "to discuss. . .issues of immense relevance for medical science at large, not necessarily for Merck alone." But nevertheless these discussions helped the European medical communities see "how Merck research would fit in with the medicine of the future."

While organizing these programs, MSDI stepped up its sales and marketing efforts. Cohen became vice president for Europe in 1969, and as he knew, "professional good-quality marketing" was "critical" to the business. "And I'm obviously not talking about novelties and gimmicks," he said. "No matter how cleverly you can approach the doctor, if you are going to talk nonsense to him, he has no reason to listen and certainly no reason to respond." Training programs and extensive reference libraries helped ensure that MSDI's detail men and women didn't "talk nonsense."

MSDI and Cohen implemented a new strategy which emphasized the development of a critical mass in the leading countries, in each of which the Merck subsidiary became a "national asset." The way was eased by the firm's new products. *Diuril* had been followed by *Aldomet*, "a real original in the antihypertensive market," by the antidepressant *Elavil*, and by *Indocin*, a new (1965) arthritis drug. In the United Kingdom Merck became by mid-decade the leading firm in pharmaceuticals. Having long before acquired and consolidated the Thomas Morson & Son pharmaceutical company, MSDI was well

*Kalman Mezey, M. D.*

*A poster announcing a 1977 MSDI symposium in Italy to inform physicians of the latest scientific results in treating hypertension. Courtesy William H. Helfand.*

METHYLDOPA
IN HYPERTENSION
International Symposium
**Florence, 1/2/3 December 1977**

"I don't want this to be a successful company that was bypassed," CEO Horan said in 1982. He had been president of Merck since 1975, CEO since 1976. He had tripled the firm's research budget and imported "one of the world's outstanding scientists," Roy Vagelos, to lead MSDRL. "We felt our lab needed his kind of leadership," Horan said, in order to strengthen the company's resources in biology, "a breaking science."

Not a scientist himself, Horan had become "a patron of research" as he moved steadily up the executive ranks at Merck. This interest was catalyzed by his association in the early 1960s with MSDRL's Max Tishler. His own training was in law: after graduating (A.B., 1940) from Manhattan College at the age of 19, his career at Columbia University Law School had been interrupted by World War II. As an officer in the U.S. Navy, he was in combat for over two years in the invasions of North Africa, Sicily, Italy, and France. The war over, he completed his J.D. in 1946 and practiced law for six years. In 1952, however, he took a cut in pay to join a firm making great contributions to public health. Attracted by the company's pioneering work in the synthesis of cortisone, he accepted Merck's offer.

Quiet and low-keyed, Horan set to work on trademark problems and soon made his own mark. In Germany he helped negotiate the "E. Merck Treaty," which settled the differences between the American firm and Merck-Darmstadt (Emanuel Merck offene Handelsgesellschaft). The bone of contention was the Merck name, the trademark.

Both companies decided that a peaceful compromise was preferable to extended rounds of legal combat, and Horan, counsel for MSD, recommended a judicious settlement. The company's new CEO, John T. Connor, agreed. As Connor later noted: "John Horan performed so well on that occasion. . .that thereafter I looked for opportunities to pull him into management work where he continued to excel in one position after another." One of these assignments was to improve Merck's planning. The result: a new long-range strategic planning process still in use today. "He had good judgment," Connor said, "he was bright, he had integrity. . . ."

The integrity became evident in his work at MSD, where he served as counsel (1955-57), executive vice president for marketing (1963-67), and top executive (1967-72). He helped revamp the division's training, sales, and marketing programs, developing the goal of "fair balance." He went into the field to find out first-hand what the sales force was doing. By the time he left MSD, the transition from detail people to professional representatives was complete.

Two other transitions highlighted Horan's integrity. Working closely with Fred Bartenstein, he was a particularly effective

strategist for the company while the Kefauver hearings on drug prices and proposed regulatory legislation (1959-61) were frothing the waters in Washington, D.C. Horan could, it seems, practice the "fair balance" that he preached. Later, when issues of gender and race emerged, he placed Merck at the forefront of affirmative action. "I call upon you," he said to his human resources executives, "to make it clear to our own people that Merck's effort will continue without slackening—not only because we see it as good business, but because we see it is right."

In 1985—after thirty-three years of service to Merck—John J. Horan retired as chief executive officer. He left his firm well positioned, with new drugs to market, with several follow-up, human health products coming out, with the animal health business riding a steep growth curve. Reaffirming Merck's primary commitment to health research, he had expanded the U.S. laboratories and established new ones abroad, modernized the firm's manufacturing, and made Merck "the industry standard" in marketing. Turning leadership over to Roy Vagelos, Horan had ample reason to believe that his "successful company" would not soon be "bypassed" in the global pharmaceutical market.

JOHN J. HORAN, ESQ.

*Vannevar Bush (left), Merck Chairman of the Board, with a youthful John J. Horan, circa 1960.*

situated both for manufacturing and sales. It added to this base a new
$28 million chemical facility (at Ponders End) and a computer-controlled
pharmaceutical operation (at Cramlington). In Scandinavia Merck
became the leading U.S. firm in the drug industry.

In France, Ekaireb and Cohen could look to William H. Helfand
for leadership in the seventies. Helfand had helped draft MSDI's new
strategic plan before going to Paris to implement it. He effectively
smoothed out his subsidiary's relationships with Chibret, while leaving
operational decision-making to his French managers. This, the Cohen
style of decentralization, was extremely effective. Where American techniques were better, Helfand introduced them (in planning and in MSD's
style of sales training), but where French methods were superior, he was
happy ''to keep French ways. The last thing we want is to make this an
American company. Besides, they do some things better than we do.''
By the end of the decade, this approach had succeeded in France and
Merck had shot up from ground zero to a position among the top four
pharmaceutical firms.

By that time, too, Barry Cohen had become—in 1977, at the age
of 42!—the president of MSDI. He and Ekaireb, who became executive
vice president of Merck and then a member of the Board, had seen the
European strategy through to success. In 1978, the firm's foreign operations generated 47% of its total sales and Merck was the leading U.S.
company in pharmaceutical sales abroad.

By the 1980s, in fact, MSDI had done so well that ideas were
beginning to flow from overseas to Rahway and West Point. In the
United Kingdom, for example, the subsidiary had worked out new
kinds of evening programs that were so successful they were adopted by
MSD in the United States. French innovations in clinical trials were also
influential, as was the Belgian experience with audiocassettes. Merck
was thus becoming a truly international enterprise.

In the second largest market overseas, the Far East, MSDI used a
somewhat different strategy. There, Huskel Ekaireb was at home. His ties

*Main entrance to the
Institut Chibret complex,
opened in 1962, in
Clermont-Ferrand, France.
Chibret became a Merck
subsidiary in 1969.*

The symmetry was appealing. In the United States Merck was again selected as the nation's most admired corporation. Meanwhile, in France, the weekly business magazine *L'Expansion* ranked Laboratoires MSD-Chibret third among the nation's firms. It was, *L'Expansion* said, "the revelation of 1988." Only the most optimistic of MSDI's planners would have predicted that outcome when they were launching the firm's effort to expand its operations and sales in France. Through the 1960s the battle had been uphill. But in 1970, the American firm was determined to make its Euro-centered strategy a success, and A. E. "Barry" Cohen and William Helfand thought they had the right ally in France, where the ties with Chibret were all-important. What Chibret had going for it was solid expertise in a particular field of drug development: ophthamology. That, joined with Merck's new products and the network of clinical pharmacologists that the two organizations developed, enabled MSD to improve its market share steadily through the decade.

The next ten years brought even more rapid growth. In 1982, the subsidiary broke ground for a new MCMD plant—La Vallée—to produce enalapril maleate (*Renitec*, an enzyme inhibitor used in the treatment of hypertension) for the entire European market and Merck's other overseas subsidiaries. In addition to this operation and the extensive Chibret research facilities at Riom, MPMD has two other modern plants in France. This combination of production, research, and marketing facilities—like the amalgam of U.S. and French resources and ideas—has paid off here as it has in the rest of Europe. Merck subsidiaries like Laboratoires MSD-Chibret have truly become vital assets of their host nations—as they are of course of their parent firm.

## MERCK IN FRANCE

*The MCMD La Vallée plant began manufacturing operations in 1985.*

# BANYU AND THE IWADARES

Today the sun never sets on Japanese enterprise. But it was not always so, and the story of that nation's rise to industrial eminence is mirrored in the history of Banyu Pharmaceutical Co., Ltd. and the leadership provided to that firm by Dr. Toru Iwadare and his son, Koichi.

War plays a large role in that story. Toru Iwadare was a graduate student in organic chemistry (Tokyo University) when World War I began. Cut off from German supplies of drugs, the Japanese government asked Tokyo University to develop a synthesis of Salvarsan (for treating syphilis) and the University gave the job to Toru Iwadare. Successful, in 1915 he organized the Banyu Company to manufacture the drug.

Banyu gradually built up its product line and total sales in the years that followed, establishing along the way a substantial network of salesmen. The firm was a pioneer in supplying Japan with the best available medications. In addition to producing its own drugs—including sulfas—Banyu imported from the United States, sometimes buying Merck's products and those of Sharp & Dohme.

War again intruded in the 1940s, shortly before Koichi Iwadare received his doctorate in organic chemistry from Tokyo University. Koichi worked at Okazaki, 200 miles to the southwest of Tokyo, on Banyu's rudimentary penicillin process, directing all of the research and the developmental experiments as well. Although Banyu was still a relatively small firm at war's end, Koichi's efforts made it number one in antibiotics. Now Merck entered the story again, with streptomycin. Banyu imported Merck's product, and Toru Iwadare, as representative of the Japanese industry, visited Rahway to inspect the laboratories. The ties grew stronger in 1952 when Huskel Ekaireb contracted with Banyu to sell *Cortone*. He and the Iwadares then laid the groundwork for a joint venture, Nippon Merck-Banyu, first to manufacture cortisone and hydrocortisone in Japan.

There were problems. Japan was tight on foreign exchange and the government was nervous about any venture that would repatriate funds to the United States. Capital was hard to obtain. As Koichi Iwadare said, "It became very competitive." Like other Japanese firms of that day, "Banyu had to slash prices to protect its market share."

So long as Merck's flow of new products held up, however, the joint venture prospered. In 1963 Dr. Koichi Iwadare became president of Banyu, and by 1969 he had pushed total sales of Nippon Merck-Banyu up to almost 5 billion yen (about $40 million). The joint venture tripled that figure in the next decade. By the time the joint venture was integrated into Banyu in 1984, NMB's sales had doubled again. In that year, too, Banyu's total sales were 68.5 billion yen (about $540 million), a tribute to the effective leadership provided by two talented scientist-businessmen — the Iwadares, father and son.

萬有製薬株式会社

to Japan went back to his first job at Merck, when that nation was still under the authority of the Allied powers. In order to combat tuberculosis, the Supreme Command issued a directive ordering that streptomycin be manufactured in Japan as soon and on as large a scale as possible. Merck responded by cooperating with Japanese companies to introduce its highly effective antibiotic, working under a contract that Ekaireb helped negotiate.

So in 1952 Ekaireb had a sound strategic perspective on Japan and its potential. He was well prepared to do business when he met Dr. Koichi Iwadare, whose father was the founder and chief executive of the Banyu Pharmaceutical Company. At Rahway, Iwadare "was very much impressed." A chemist himself, he was interested in the laboratories and pleased too by Ekaireb's hospitality. Banyu was a young enterprise, only 37 years old at that time, but it was nevertheless one of Japan's major drug makers. So it was important to both companies when Iwadare and Ekaireb were quickly able to strike a deal: Banyu would import Merck's cortisone.

Out of that initial contract grew an unusually successful joint venture. Iwadare and his father, "delighted then" to have an opportunity to sell Merck's "effective drugs," made a big push for sales. When that effort succeeded, the two parties first signed a distributorship agreement and then, a year later (1954), an unusual contract that enabled Banyu to manufacture Merck's drugs. The joint endeavor, Nippon Merck-Banyu Company Ltd. (NMB), came into production in 1955 with *Cortone* and *Hydrocortone*. Within a few years, NMB was manufacturing Merck's other anti-inflammatory steroids as well as its diuretics.

During the next three decades, the joint venture prospered, finding innovative ways to manufacture and sell Merck's new products through Banyu's extensive distribution network. Iwadare and his father

*(From right) Dr. Koichi Iwadare and Huskel Ekaireb at the dedication of Nippon Merck-Banyu's Okazaki plant, 1955. Courtesy Dr. Koichi Iwadare.*

*Participating in a Shinto ceremony at the 1990 groundbreaking for a new research facility in Tsukuba Science City, Japan, were (front row, from left) Dr. Nobuo Tanaka, Senior Executive Director, Banyu R&D; Noriyuki Toyama, President of Banyu; A. E. Cohen, Merck Senior Vice President; and Dr. Koichi Iwadare, Chairman of Banyu.*

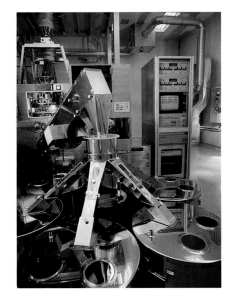

*A completely automated, self-adjusting, tablet-compressing machine located at the Menuma plant of the Banyu Pharmaceutical Co., Ltd., Merck's affiliate in Japan.*

*Professional Representative Jun Yoneyama (left) discusses* Primaxin *with Dr. Kaoru Shimada, Professor of Infectious Diseases and Applied Immunology at the Institute of Medical Science, University of Tokyo, in 1987.*

arranged "meetings with physicians and asked the leading professors to make lectures to the. . .physicians." NMB used a special advisory council of distinguished medical researchers to ensure that its products and research were attuned to "the medicine of the future" and to Japan's very demanding market. The joint venture increased its sales force of detail men, and in the 1970s built an entirely new, $50 million facility in Menuma, northwest of Tokyo. This state-of-the-art, computer-controlled plant later produced the company's new antibiotics (*Mefoxin* and *Primaxin)* and a drug for high blood pressure, *Vasotec,* which has become extremely successful in Japan.

In the 1980s the joint venture, NMB, matured into a revolutionary new relationship between the U.S. and Japanese firms. Now, Iwadare was the chief executive at Banyu, Horan was CEO at Merck, and Cohen was president of MSDI. They began to probe the possibility of turning the venture into a "fully integrated" company with its own research, manufacturing, product line, exports, and management. To achieve this goal, Merck would buy a majority of the stock of Banyu—the first such agreement involving a first-tier company on the Tokyo stock exchange. Several years of delicate negotiations produced a consensus in 1981 and the "fully integrated" firm became a reality in 1983.

Since the consolidation, Banyu—still under Japanese management, of course—has smoothly absorbed the joint venture's sales force and other personnel, while expanding its own research, manufacturing, and marketing operations. The new firm, Iwadare says, has "absorbed good things from Merck." And he has never been "hesitant to explain the Japanese way of thinking or the Japanese way" to the American company. Merck management has been receptive to these suggestions and optimistic about Banyu. "We remain firmly committed," Vagelos recently said, "to even greater penetration of the Japanese pharmaceutical market, the second largest national market in the world."

In the Far East and in other global markets, some of Merck's most successful products in the past decade have been in the animal health field. This is not an outcome that even the best corporate planner would have predicted in the late 1940s when the company—in the person of Max Tishler, as we saw—stumbled onto *S.Q.* for treating coccidiosis in poultry. Since coccidiosis, a parasitic disease, normally had wiped out about ten per cent of the nation's chickens each year, Merck's marketing division found a ready demand for the drug among pharmaceutical and feed manufacturers throughout the United States.

Encouraged, Merck researchers pushed ahead in this field. They developed *Nicrazin* and *Amprol* (both also for poultry) in the 1950s and 1960s, followed by *Thibenzole* (*TBZ*, 1962), which could be used to eliminate worms in sheep, cattle, and horses. Later, a new formulation of *TBZ* was employed to prevent fungal diseases in grain, fruit, and vegetable crops. What did it mean to world food supplies when MSD and MSDI were able to distribute this new, low-priced product? One example will suffice. In Europe, where 90% of the potatoes were treated with *TBZ*, significant inroads were made in a disease that formerly destroyed about 20% of the crop in storage. Similar results were achieved in horticulture at home and abroad.

During these years, new drugs and breeding techniques were responsible for a worldwide revolution in agricultural productivity, and Merck was able to play an important role in this transformation. MSD and MSDI gradually developed new sales and marketing teams to handle these special products, as the business continued to grow, becoming ever more complex. In the 1970s, Merck acquired Hubbard Farms (1974), Spafas, Inc. (1976), and British United Turkeys (1978). These subsidiaries moved the firm into the business of supplying superior breeding stock and, in the case of Spafas, eggs and poultry free of specific pathogens.

*Marketing display and label for different formulations of thiabendazole, a new Merck product (1962) to eliminate worms in sheep, cattle, and horses.*

*Demonstrating the use of TBZ, 1974.*

*Baby chicks at Hubbard Farms, a leader in poultry genetics, acquired by Merck in 1974.*

## DR. JAMES GILLIN AND MSD AGVET

"I had just started to work [in 1949] when I came back from my honeymoon...," Gillin said. "About two weeks later, I got shipped off to Stonewall, Virginia. In those days when you went off on one of these plant trips,...you stayed down there....That was a great way to start a marriage." It was in part his wife's fault. He had completed most of his work for a doctorate in chemical engineering at Cornell, and she had wanted to move near her family in Roselle Park, New Jersey. That helped persuade Gillin to accept Merck's offer.

It didn't all go smoothly at first. At Stonewall, working on isolating $B_{12}$, his crew made a million-dollar mistake. They broke a glass jar containing all of the vitamin they had isolated. The floor ran red, and you can imagine what color the boss's face was when he saw what had happened: rumour has it that when he saw the mess, he said, "That had better be blood."

Gillin, now a more careful young engineer, survived that incident and went on to the pilot plant at Rahway, where he became a supervising operator. Working for Phil Colin, a "stickler for accurate report writing," he continued his practical education and steady advancement. He became manager and then director of the pilot plant, directing all of the firm's chemical engineering activities in the late 1950s and 1960s. He was a shirt-sleeves manager: "I wasn't going to ask anyone to do something I wasn't perfectly willing to do myself."

During these years, engineering came into its own at Merck. The turning point came, Gillin believes, when *TBZ* and *Aldomet* (both 1962) were being nursed up to full-scale output. The production process for *TBZ* won chemical engineering some new respect, and *Aldomet*—"a bit of a beast" to bring into production—finished the job. Merck's pilot plant was by this time a leader in the pharmaceutical industry, in part because developmental research, engineering, and manufacturing were so well coordinated. Gillin's success led to a position heading new drug development and then—a first for engineering—a vice presidency (1971) in development.

His experience with animal health products—including the new ones in the research pipeline—helped persuade John Horan to make Gillin the first president (1979) of MSD AGVET. Here too, he survived some shaky moments to guide the division to a position of leadership in the U.S. market. When he retired at Merck in 1987, he could look back on a long series of jobs done uncommonly well, on a profession, engineering, that had earned its spurs, and on a marriage that had survived a long, post-honeymoon plant trip to Stonewall.

*Dr. James Gillin (right), Executive Director of Chemical Engineering Research, discusses the modernization of the Building 50B pilot plant in Rahway with Henry W. Gadsden (left), Merck Executive Vice President, and John T. Connor, Merck President, December 24, 1963.*

Among MSDI's subsidiaries, the operations in Australia and New Zealand were particularly important markets for animal health products. The livestock industry "Down Under" was large and growing. In 1964 there were about 12 million people and 148 million sheep in Australia, 3.3 million people and 60 million sheep in New Zealand. Little wonder that Merck Sharp & Dohme (Australia) sold twice as much to wholesalers and retailers of animal health products as it did that year to pharmacists. Nor was it surprising that the Australian subsidiary (MSDA) built its own *TBZ* plant the following year. By the late 1970s MSDA had doubled its animal health sales, even though Merck had not introduced any new products in this field for several years.

Merck's CEO John Horan had by that time come to two conclusions about animal health: First, the business was likely to grow. Second, his firm's sales and marketing efforts in animal health products needed

## "Innovation has always been central to our growth and profitability."

to be improved. He turned to Dr. James Gillin, an experienced research administrator, for a study of the domestic and international operations of Merck and other companies. Gillin and Horan agreed: the company needed a single worldwide animal health division. Horan asked, "If we set it up, will you run it?" Gillin accepted the challenge, becoming in 1979 the first president of MSD AGVET.

As Gillin knew, MSDRL had some exciting products in the pipeline, but he had first to build an effective organization that would enable his division to capitalize on these opportunities. That took some "pounding on the desk." He and his right-hand man, vice president for marketing Anthony Viscusi, had to convince the "barons" heading MSDI's subsidiaries to support their efforts while surrendering control of the animal health business. Fortunately, Viscusi and Gillin had a strong

*Merck Representative Pierre Odoul (left) demonstrates the* Ivomec *injection technique to French farmer Jean-Marie Boutet, 1988.* Ivomec Injection for cattle *is one of the many formulations of ivermectin, MSD AGVET's broad-spectrum anti-parasitic.*

*The Merck experimental farm in Springdale, Arkansas—one of ten worldwide—focuses on research in poultry feeds.*

MERCK FARMS INC.

ally in Huskel Ekaireb, who told the subsidiaries to let Gillin "sink or swim but let him have his way."

They did, and the organization was soon humming—but for a few years it appeared that Gillin still might "sink." One of his two "exciting" products collapsed. U.S. agriculture slumped. Competition intensified and profits in animal health sagged. Gillin said he was "absolutely convinced MSD AGVET would make it, but I wasn't convinced I would make it as head. . . ."

Then, in 1983, his fledgling division turned the corner. The other exciting product was ivermectin, which would in various formulations become the world's leading animal health product during the second half of the 1980s. By that time the division had honed its marketing units, cut costs, and improved returns across the board. MSD AGVET found new ways to reach veterinarians, farm store dealers, and agrarian cooperative outlets. It began to use sales representatives more extensively and developed a specialized network to sell large animal products. It organized large-scale demonstrations, using both television and field shows in the United States and abroad.

*At a sheep station in Australia, this dog—whose health is protected from heartworm disease by the once-a-month tablet* Heartgard-30 —*keeps the sheep in line.* Ivomec Liquid *for sheep, an orally administered formulation of ivermectin, was introduced in Australia in 1988.*

*MSD AGVET's ivermectin formulations and selected other animal health products.*

This global marketing system was brought into full play with ivermectin. Armed with several formulations of this highly effective drug, the division racked up sharp increases in worldwide sales and income. By the end of the decade, MSD AGVET was making an extremely important contribution to Merck's total increase in income as well as sales. As worldwide distribution was developed for the new ivermectin formulations, including the new heartworm treatment for dogs, *Heartgard-30*, the prospects were for even more rapid expansion in the years ahead.

By 1987, when Gillin retired and Eugene McCabe became president, MSD AGVET had become a vital part of Merck's global business. Its

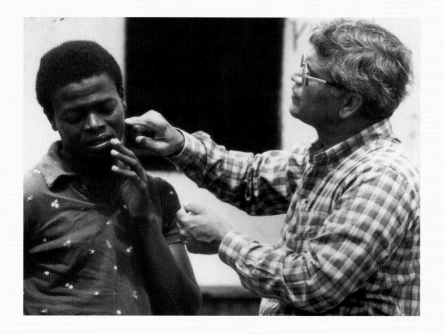

## *MECTIZAN* AND
## DR. MOHAMMED A. AZIZ

*Dr. Mohammed Aziz (right), then Senior Director for Clinical Research, MSDRL, examines a 14-year-old boy in West Africa who has been blinded by onchocerciasis, 1984.*

Dr. Mohammed A. Aziz was not a salesman and the product he relentlessly developed will never make any money for Merck. But the late Dr. Aziz is one of the heroes of the company.

This native of Bangladesh attended Presidency College in Calcutta, India, and then Dacca Medical College, receiving the equivalent of a U.S. medical degree in 1954. He continued his studies at the University of Minnesota (Ph.D. in clinical pathology, 1962), at the Johns Hopkins School of Hygiene and Public Health (1962), and at the London School of Hygiene and Tropical Medicine (1970, Diploma in Clinical Medicine of the Tropics).

Academic life beckoned, as did public service. He taught and conducted research at the University of Maryland (1962-73) and served for a time as coordinator for the World Health Organization in Sierra Leone, West Africa (1975-76).

Following his service in Africa, Aziz decided to accept a position at Merck—a decision that would prove to be much to the advantage of mankind. Aziz joined the company in 1976 as a director in domestic clinical research and by 1981 was a senior director of the firm's international clinical research. It was in this capacity that he played his leading role in the development of *Mectizan*, a drug that treats and prevents the dread river blindness disease (onchocerciasis).

Aziz was the first to establish that an appropriate formulation of MSD's antiparasitic ivermectin was effective against the disease. As Roy Vagelos explained, "It was Dr. Aziz's drive and organizational ability that set in motion a worldwide series of multi-clinic studies comparing *Mectizan* with the standard therapy then available."

In this extended effort, Aziz found what he had sought at Merck: "opportunity to do what I most want to do—research to help mankind." He was the champion of a drug that was not in demand in the wealthy nations of the world. This drug was not a subject of the "crisis" or "war" mentality that periodically sweeps through the American population and medical communities. But Aziz persisted, and in 1987 his seven-year clinical program ended with success. Suffering from cancer, Aziz was honored with Merck's coveted Scientific Award of the Board of Directors. He died that year at the age of 58 shortly before the first free mass-treatment program for *Mectizan* was set in motion. The program was a fitting memorial to Aziz's long battle against one of the world's most devastating tropical diseases.

strategy now was to develop species-specific formulations, while diversifying Merck's operations across a broader range of species. By the end of the decade, MSD AGVET was the number one company in the animal health market for pharmaceuticals, biologicals, and medicated feed additives in the United States and throughout the world.

## THE GLOBAL OUTLOOK

Indeed, the prospects seemed good in all of Merck's traditional markets and in some that it had failed thus far to penetrate. As CEO Roy Vagelos commented, "Our long-standing key strategy for outpacing competitors is unchanged. . . .We will strive to keep on introducing new and better human and animal health products that will provide the income needed to maintain our high-performance effort. Innovation has always been central to our growth and profitability."

Innovative leadership has enabled Merck to renew itself several times during the past century. The founder, George Merck, built a successful fine chemicals business. His son, George W. Merck, transformed the firm into a fully integrated, research-driven pharmaceutical company. CEO John T. Connor launched Merck's international expansion, a drive that Henry W. Gadsden and John J. Horan carried to fruition. Today, Roy Vagelos is renewing the company again, refocusing its research, broadening its mission, centralizing operations, and grooming a new generation of leaders.

The company's past and current leaders have succeeded because they revitalized the company's mission while capitalizing on Merck's powerful culture and traditions. They reaffirmed the company's values: creativity, quality, personal commitment, efficiency, safety, and a strong sense of social responsibility. They built upon the traditions of global enterprise, of innovation, and of service to the health needs of society. It remains to be seen, of course, how well these traditions and values will serve the company during the renewals of the next century. What is clear in 1991 is the fact that they have served Merck and society uncommonly well through the past one hundred years.

*A bearded George Merck in 1896. Courtesy Albert W. Merck.*

*This August 18, 1952,* Time *cover story highlights Merck's commitment to innovation and George W. Merck's credo that "medicine is for the people,...not for the profits." Copyright 1952 Time Warner Inc. Reprinted by permission.*

# Part II

# VISIONS

# THE NEW BIOLOGY:
## NEW TARGETS FOR THE NEW MEDICINE

*Michael S. Brown, M.D., and Joseph L. Goldstein, M.D.*

A reductionist revolution has transformed biology in our lifetime, and soon it will expose new targets for prevention and therapy of disease. The reductionist principle states that all life processes, no matter how complex, can be reduced ultimately to chemistry. This concept originated long ago with the discovery of the cell and the isolation of the first organic molecules. Progress was slow until the middle part of this century when dazzling technical and conceptual advances, occurring with cumulative speed, propelled biology into a new dimension.

The great product of this revolution was the discovery of the simple structure of DNA and the stunning realization that it provided a chemical explanation for the rules of heredity that had been delineated over the previous half-century. The vision of DNA as an ordinary chemical led to recombinant DNA technology and all of the insights into gene structure, function, and regulation that followed. When the genetic code was deciphered, gene structure could be translated directly into protein chemistry.

By purifying and sequencing proteins and determining their 3-dimensional structures, we learned how proteins fulfill their two major functions: recognition and catalysis. The understanding of recognition went hand in hand with the unraveling

*Michael S. Brown, M.D.*

*Joseph L. Goldstein, M.D.*

of the antibody molecule and the development of monoclonal antibodies. The understanding of catalysis led to a roadmap of intermediary metabolism and the pinpointing of roadblocks created by mutation. These advances were facilitated by the development of radioactive tracers that allow us to follow single molecules as they maneuver through the maze of metabolic pathways of a living organism.

We learned that complex organs such as the kidney and brain are ordered arrangements of specialized cells. This knowledge led to the discovery of the hormones and receptors by which cells communicate. It reduced developmental biology to a study of the ways in which specialized cells differentiate and find their proper positions in space and time. Further reduction became possible when we appreciated that cells themselves are ordered arrangements of membrane-bound organelles that can be isolated and studied biochemically in test tubes. The problem of cellular development became the problem of understanding organelle development and deciphering the sorting code that targets proteins to functional sites.

The new biology will have a profound impact upon the ways in which we comprehend, diagnose, and treat human disease. Medical research will proceed with a level of precision unimaginable two decades ago. New targets for disease prevention and treatment will come into sharp focus. Our skill at molecular and chemical engineering will be the laser that guides us to those targets.

## TARGETS FOR DISEASE PREVENTION

All diseases result from interactions between factors that are exogenous to the individual and those that are endogenous, namely, the individual's genetic makeup. Diseases caused predominantly by exogenous agents, such as toxins and bacteria, were the first to be solved. Soon the purely endogenous diseases, i.e., those caused by single-gene mutations, will also be elucidated. We will be left with an enormous number of diseases that have more complex etiologies involving both exogenous and endogenous factors. These include all of the common degenerative diseases of adults (heart disease, cancer, dementia, arthritis, and the like) and most birth defects (hydrocephaly, congenital heart disease, spina bifida, etc.). These diseases are not inherited as Mendelian single-gene traits. Rather, they are caused by multiple predisposing genes acting in concert with environmental insults in a manner that is termed polygenic or multifactorial.

Over the next few decades we will pinpoint the exogenous and endogenous agents that conspire to cause multifactorial diseases. The Rosetta Stone will be genetics. Rare varieties of these diseases are transmitted as single-gene Mendelian traits. Examples include familial hypercholesterolemia, a single-gene cause of heart disease, and hereditary retinoblastoma, a single-gene cause of cancer. Through the power of molecular genetics, scientists have discerned the genes responsible for these two diseases. Through study of families with affected individuals, it is now possible to identify other genes and environmental agents that modify the severity of these diseases. When these factors are identified, we can examine people with the garden-variety multifactorial forms of these diseases to determine which of the predisposing genes they possess. By screening the population we will identify individuals who possess versions of these genes that render them disease-susceptible. Then, by modifying their environments, we will remove the exogenous component and so prevent the disease. To be successful, this approach requires a high-resolution map of the human genome. Such a map is currently being compiled by the Human Genome Initiative, a multi-institutional effort sponsored by the National Institutes of Health. The map will allow scientists to pinpoint the genes that predispose to complex multi-factorial diseases.

## TARGETS FOR DISEASE TREATMENT

**Protein Targets.** The new biology will profoundly affect the ways in which we design and use drugs. Inspection of the crystallographic structures of enzymes and regulatory proteins will reveal the geometry of the active sites. New techniques of nuclear magnetic resonance will allow us to visualize these active sites as they bind effective molecules in solution. We can then design our own molecules that bind to these sites and influence the proteins in desirable ways. But X-ray crystallography is too slow for widespread application, even with recent technical refinements. Crystallization of proteins remains a hit-or-miss affair that can take years to achieve. Progress would be speeded if we could predict the 3-dimensional structure from the amino acid sequence of a protein, which we can infer rapidly from the DNA sequence of the gene. Such predictions have not been possible up to now because any short sequence of amino acids can assume a nearly infinite number of conformations depending on interactions with other amino acids in the protein.

A potential solution is beginning to emerge from the observation that highly related sequences of amino acids often recur in different proteins, owing to the fact that they derived from a common ancestor. The shared sequences are encoded on discrete segments of DNA called exons. Proteins evolve by reduplication and shuffling of these exons from one gene to another. A shared amino acid sequence often, but not always, has the same 3-dimensional structure in each protein in which it appears. If we learn the shape of this sequence in one protein, we can predict it for all proteins that share the sequence. Soon crystallographers will have a library of exon-encoded sequences, and then it should be possible to design drugs based on the class of sequence that forms the active site of the target protein.

Progress in structural analysis of proteins will put great pressure on chemists to use this information to design molecules that bind with high affinity to defined 3-dimensional targets. Ideally, we would like a series of backbone chemicals that can be altered to any 3-dimensional shape by varying substituents, much as nature has built upon the peptide backbone chemicals to form 3-dimensional proteins. The shape of a protein is determined by multiple noncovalent interactions between amino acids, a requirement that can only be fulfilled in a large molecule. To be useful therapeutically, chemically engineered molecules should be much smaller than proteins so that they can be orally absorbed and can penetrate readily into cells. Such a small molecule can maintain a stable 3-dimensional shape only if it has precisely oriented covalent bonds, a phenomenon known as chirality. We need general methods to synthesize chiral molecules, a challenge that will be met only if we recruit the most talented synthetic chemists into this emerging field.

Among the most attractive targets for the new chemicals are cell surface receptors that bind protein hormones and thereby regulate cell growth and behavior. Through recombinant DNA technology, genes for many hormones and receptors have been cloned. An example is erythropoietin, which stimulates the growth of red blood cells, and is used in the treatment of anemia. With the cloned genes we can manufacture the proteins by genetic engineering and thereby use them for therapy. This is obviously a great advance, but it is not perfect. Proteins cannot be given orally. Moreover, we often do not desire to mimic the action of the protein hormone, but rather to inhibit it. In the future we must learn to synthesize small molecules that mimic the protein hormones and others that bind to receptors and antagonize the hormone's action. When the structures of the hormones and their receptors are determined, we may divine the general mechanisms by which hormones trigger intracellular events. We can then develop a general strategy for the synthesis of inhibitors that would apply to many hormone-receptor systems. For example, many hormones act by inducing the receptors to cluster together in aggregates. Designing a chemical that will bind to the receptor but not allow aggregation should produce an effective inhibitor of the hormone's action.

**Transcription Factors**. Attractive targets for the new chemicals will be the transcription factors that regulate the rates at which genes are transcribed into messenger RNA and ultimately into proteins.

*By screening the population we will identify individuals who possess versions of these genes that render them disease-susceptible. Then, by modifying their environments we will remove the exogenous component and so prevent the disease.*

Transcription factors are proteins that bind to short segments of DNA and recruit sites for RNA polymerases. Certain transcription factors are regulated by small molecules such as steroid hormones. It should be possible to make molecular mimics of these regulatory molecules and thereby alter the activity of transcription factors at will.

The isolation of transcription factors is a major accomplishment of the past decade of biology, and it has created new opportunities for pharmacology. We have learned that a single regulatory molecule such as thyroid hormone binds to different transcription factors in different tissues. When we learn the 3-dimensional structures of these transcription factors, we will be able to synthesize mimics of these regulatory agents that bind to transcription factors in one tissue but not in another. This will endow nuclear regulatory molecules with the same type of tissue specificity that was achieved long ago for molecules such as histamine analogues that interact with cell surface receptors. The most widely used inhibitors of gastric acid secretion are histamine analogues that bind specifically to histamine receptors on the surface of acid-secreting cells in the stomach and not to histamine receptors in other tissues, such as the salivary gland and brain. The tissue-specific antihistamines do not cause dry mouth or drowsiness, two major side effects of earlier histamine antagonists.

This same type of tissue specificity should shortly be available for analogues of hormones that act in the nucleus, thus allowing us to influence gene transcription in one tissue but not another. For

example, thyroid hormone is an effective cholesterol-lowering agent through its actions in the liver. It cannot be used for this purpose, however, because it also stimulates the heart, producing abnormal rhythms. If the thyroid hormone-responsive transcription factor in the liver nucleus differs from the one in the heart, we should be able to design a thyroid analogue that acts only in the liver, eliminating the cardiac side effects.

In manipulating gene expression, it is not necessary to hit the transcription factor directly. We can influence these factors indirectly with drugs that inhibit enzymes in the cell, and therefore cause the buildup or depletion of a substance that regulates a transcription factor. An example is the drug lovastatin, a powerful cholesterol-lowering agent. This drug inhibits the activity of an enzyme required for the synthesis of cholesterol. The subsequent fall in intracellular cholesterol levels activates a transcription factor that causes the cells to take up additional cholesterol from the blood, thereby lowering the level of blood cholesterol. The design of such "indirect gene therapy" requires an intimate knowledge of the normal regulatory pathways in a cell —a goal that is achievable with modern techniques of cell culture and molecular biology.

**Genes**. Transcription factors are not the only nuclear targets of the new pharmacology: we can also target the nucleic acids themselves. It should be possible to synthesize chemicals that will enter the cell nucleus and attach to specific sequences of base pairs in the DNA. The first such chemicals might prevent the attachment of transcription factors, thereby inhibiting expression of the gene. Subsequently, it may be possible to configure the chemicals so that they substitute for transcription factors, recruiting polymerases and turning on genes. As with the protein targets, hitting the gene targets will require a new precision in synthetic organic chemistry. We need some type of backbone on which to hang substituents whose shape will guarantee binding to a unique sequence of base pairs in the double helix of DNA. Through crystallographic analysis of transcription factors, we have learned how proteins accomplish this task. Now we must design chemicals that mimic the structures of the proteins' DNA recognition sites. The task is complicated by the constraint that these molecules must be small enough to penetrate into cells and reach the nucleus. In the next section we present possible solutions to this problem.

## TARGETING MECHANISMS

**Targeting Macromolecules to Intracellular Targets**. In order to be useful, the new pharmaceutical agents must enter cells, and this poses a problem. How can we induce a cell to take up a large molecule (a macromolecule) that we have designed to hit an intracellular target? Advances in the field of cell biology have taught us that the plasma membrane which surrounds the cell is not as inviolable as we once thought. True, the membrane prevents large molecules from diffusing randomly into the cell. But it also has a mechanism for taking up certain macromolecules that the cell wishes to incorporate, and this creates an opportunity for pharmacology. This mechanism is called receptor-mediated endocytosis. The receptors are proteins that are embedded in the plasma membranes of body cells. The receptors bind extracellular macromolecules and incorporate them into membrane-bound vesicles that migrate through the cells and eventually fuse with lysosomes where the macromolecules are broken down into their component parts. These

*In a research culture driven by the energy of youth, growth is imperative. We must grow in order to make room for the bright young minds that dream up the freshest ideas.*

leave the lysosome and enter the cytoplasm where they can be used for metabolic purposes.

We can take advantage of receptor-mediated endocytosis by designing macromolecules that bind to receptors and are thereby carried into the cell. Receptor binding can be achieved by coupling the therapeutic macromolecule to a protein that binds to a receptor. The protein can be the normal ligand for the receptor, or it can be an antibody directed against the receptor. The latter approach has been followed in the coupling of a plant toxin, ricin, to an antibody that recognizes a receptor on the surface of blood lymphocytes. The lymphocyte is killed when the antibody-ricin conjugate enters the cell. This approach shows promise in treating certain lymphocytic tumors.

After a macromolecule enters a cell by receptor-mediated endocytosis, it must still cross the membrane of its enclosing vesicle in order to reach the cytoplasm. The antibody-ricin conjugate is effective because ricin has a special ability to penetrate such a membrane, but this is not general to all drugs. A more general approach makes use of another toxin, the exotoxin of the bacteria *Pseudomonas*. After it enters cells in a membrane-bound vesicle, *Pseudomonas* exotoxin dissolves the membrane of the vesicle and thereby reaches the cytoplasm. If any other macromolecule enters the same vesicle with the toxin, it too is released. In principle, it may be possible to couple therapeutic macromolecules with *Pseudomonas* exotoxin and a receptor-binding ligand to produce a molecule that enters cells bound to a receptor and is released into the cytoplasm.

It may not be necessary to use specific receptors for cell entry. Recently, surprising success has been achieved in the delivery of short segments of DNA (oligonucleotides) into cells. Oligonucleotides can be designed to be complementary to stretches of a specific messenger RNA and thereby to inhibit the synthesis of a specific protein. Very little is known about the way in which these oligonucleotides actually penetrate the cells, nor do we have accurate measurements of the amounts that enter. Nevertheless, the observed uptake suggests that it may be possible to deliver nucleic acid-binding molecules to cells in amounts sufficient to influence gene expression.

These uptake mechanisms should be a major focus of future research. We must understand more about the structure of the plasma membrane and the proteins that have learned how to penetrate these membranes. It would be tragic if powerful new drugs were useless simply because we could not deliver them to their targets within cells.

**Targeting Proteins to Animals.** Through the new biology we will not only synthesize novel therapeutic chemicals, but we will also make better use of natural molecules in the form of genes and proteins. Recombinant DNA technology already allows us to isolate any gene and to use it as a blueprint to produce a therapeutic protein in bacteria or animal cells. Classic examples include human insulin, growth hormone, tissue plasminogen activator, and erythropoietin. In the future it will be possible to place the gene directly into a patient's own cells, which thereafter will synthesize the protein within the patient's body. For this purpose scientists have already used blood cells that are removed from the body and induced to take up a particular gene. Other candidate cells include the epithelial cells of the skin and the endothelial cells that line the vascular system. The major unsolved problem relates to regulation. How do we adjust the production of the

protein so that it is sufficient, but not excessive? One possible approach involves placement of the gene under the control of a regulatory sequence (promoter) that we already know how to influence. If we are successful at making small molecules that regulate transcription factors, we can place a therapeutic gene under control of a promoter that responds to a transcription factor that we can regulate by the oral administration of a small molecule. By monitoring the level of the secreted protein in blood, we should be able to adjust the dose of the regulatory molecule to achieve the desired level.

WHO WILL HIT THE TARGETS? The revolution that led to the new biology was led by scientists in the United States, where biomedical research has flourished on an unprecedented scale. The success of the U.S. effort is largely attributable to the farsighted development of the National Institutes of Health (NIH) as a centralized, peer-reviewed funding agency that supports decentralized, investigator-initiated research at universities. Despite the health missions of the Institutes, the focus was always on *untargeted* research. NIH funding permitted the universities to develop modern facilities for biomedical research and this helped to lure the brightest young people into the field. Equipment was supplied, salaries were paid, and formal teaching duties were lightened so that the most promising scientists could devote the bulk of their time to research. Throughout, the emphasis was on youth. In addition to training its own young scientists, the United States became a magnet for students from around the world who came for graduate or postdoctoral training. Working alongside their American counterparts, these young enthusiasts contributed immeasurably to this success, and then they went home, spreading the new technology around the world.

The university effort was intertwined with an industrial effort in a mutually reinforcing double helix. The universities trained scientists who moved into industry and developed practical applications for fundamental discoveries. The industries, in turn, produced chemicals and equipment that allowed the basic scientists to advance. No longer was it necessary for university chemists to blow their own glassware or to prepare their own radioisotopically labeled compounds. Companies did it for them, and this allowed scientists to devote all of their attention to the actual research problem, and to perform many-fold more experiments than were ever thought possible. The result was knowledge gathered at a dizzying pace. Powerful new drugs were developed, and entire classes of disease were eradicated or ameliorated.

Recent events in the United States raise doubts as to whether this progress will continue. Limits on funding at the National Institutes of Health and the National Science Foundation have halted the growth of the research effort. In a research culture driven by the energy of youth, growth is imperative. We must grow in order to make room for the bright young minds that dream up the freshest ideas. Funding cutbacks have hit particularly hard at the training programs and first-time research grants that allow new scientists to enter the system. Competition for funding forces young scientists to follow safe, conservative research strategies that are likely to provide definite, but marginal, progress. No longer can a young scientist gamble on a brilliant idea that may fail.

The new biology has identified new targets for the new medicine. We have the tools to hit these targets and to change the way in which the human species faces disease. The great tragedy would be to fail because we lack the will to use these tools.

# MERCK'S SECOND CENTURY

*P. Roy Vagelos, M.D.*

*Chairman and Chief Executive Officer*

*Merck & Co., Inc.*

If we consider the nature and scope of change during Merck's first hundred years and try to envision what our Company will do in the twenty-first century — what a challenge to our imaginations! Our long-range strategic planning finds it hard to project ten years out, let alone thirty or forty years hence. However, admitting that any reader may do a better job of forecasting, let me offer my vision of our Company's future.

One thing of which I *am* very confident is that Merck will continue to be a driving force in our industry. I believe we are strongly positioned to achieve breakthroughs in science that will result in major victories against the most difficult and harmful diseases. In ways that we can now only dream of, we will help people everywhere and improve the quality of their lives.

## CHANGING ENVIRONMENT, UNCHANGING MISSION

While Merck will undoubtedly change in structure and in global strategies to meet new challenges, I do not foresee a change in our corporate *mission*. I hope and believe that we will continue to concentrate primarily on using advanced biomedical research to create superior, innovative products that improve and protect human and animal health. This will be the best way, I am convinced, to provide investors with superior returns and employees with superior opportunities.

As competition continues to intensify, we will see an acceleration of today's market trends — that is,

more companies will either fall by the wayside or be forced to merge in order to survive. In addition, companies will have to expand their marketing reach — selling products on a global scale — in order to fund increasingly expensive research projects. Based on this "global necessity" and our own ambitious goals, Merck should double or triple its share of the world pharmaceutical market.

## RESEARCH OF ENORMOUS MAGNITUDE

The foundation of this growth will be a strong stream of new products. Thus, we will have to conduct research and development of enormous magnitude — much greater than anything our industry has ever known.

We will continue the progress of the last fifteen or twenty years — away from drug discovery based on live animal experiments. It used to be that to discover nonsteroidal anti-inflammatory drugs, animals were injected with a substance to cause a small inflammation. They were then fed various chemicals to identify one that would reduce the inflammation. Early antidepressants, anti-anxiety drugs, drugs for infectious diseases, peptic ulcers, pain relief and others were based on these kinds of experiments where chemicals were tested in live animal models of human disease.

By contrast, in the last fifteen years, our focus has been on *mechanisms*, at the molecular level, that might be involved in the disease process. This targeted *rational* approach involves experiments with enzymes and cellular receptors to seek chemicals, through screening, that would modify the activity of these molecules. Such chemicals would be optimized by chemists to enhance their potency and specificity, and only then would they be tested in animals. Animal studies must always be done prior to human testing to verify safety and efficacy. Examples of drugs invented with this approach at Merck include *Vasotec* and *Prinivil*, *Primaxin*, *Mevacor* and *Zocor*, and most recently *Proscar* for treating benign prostatic enlargement.

The next development in drug discovery will be a refinement of the molecular approach. Target molecules that might be involved in a disease process will be characterized so that their structures will be known in three dimensions — at the atomic level. Instead of screening for chemical or natural product leads, it should be possible to design a chemical that will modify an enzyme or receptor molecule's activity. Such *ab initio* design has not been accomplished yet — but might be possible in this decade and certainly in the next century.

By mapping the human genome, scientists will be better able to identify molecules that are involved in disease processes. Their structures will be determined, and drugs will be designed to affect these molecules. This should bring a huge benefit both in finding new drugs and in speeding the discovery process.

What does all this mean in practical terms? It means that the progress Merck has made in its first hundred years will be surpassed in the next twenty.

## SEARCH FOR CURES INSTEAD OF TREATMENT

As our research becomes more precisely targeted, its scope will clearly broaden. Today, there are many chronic diseases that can only be treated symptomatically. As we understand more about disease, we will develop drugs that will eliminate the *cause* of the disease rather than simply treat its effects.

An example would be high blood pressure. Today high blood pressure is treated by numerous drugs to reduce the pressure, but we still don't know exactly what *causes* high blood pressure. It is very likely that high blood pressure is a symptom of an abnormality somewhere in the body. One can imagine correcting that abnormality and thereby curing or even preventing the high blood pressure — permanently.

Our scientists will work on other diseases that have not even been identified simply because we don't have the proper diagnostic tools. Some aspects of aging, for instance, may prove to have components that are actually disease processes, which may be stopped or delayed.

## DRUG DEVELOPMENT — WORLDWIDE AND SIMULTANEOUS

Once a new drug is discovered through research, its development becomes the enormous and costly challenge. And this process will be different by the year 2000, partly because of the changing political scene in Europe. It is probable that review and approval of new drugs will be carried out for Europe as a whole, instead of today's country-by-country approval process.

In any case, we will have development strategies designed specifically for various parts of the world, and the process will move forward everywhere simultaneously. We will have well-established laboratories in many of these places so that our scientists will be able to interact effectively with government scientists who regulate the approval and use of drugs. Understanding their needs and knowing how to work with them, we will provide the reliable scientific background they will need to evaluate our products.

## CONCENTRATION OF PRODUCTION PLANTS

While Merck research will spread out around the world, I expect our chemical production and pharmaceutical manufacturing to become more concentrated. Today, we have facilities in more countries than we should, mainly because of government requirements regarding access to specific markets and the pricing of our products.

This kind of duplicated effort has been imposed on many pharmaceutical companies during the last twenty-five years, but it is indefensible economically. I believe far-sighted political leaders will bring it to an end — particularly after 1992, when formation of the European Community will permit an unimpeded flow of products across national boundaries. Ultimately, to conserve resources, Merck will consolidate: we will have fewer chemical plants outside of North America and we will have fewer pharmaceutical manufacturing centers in Europe, the Far East, and elsewhere in the world. In any case, the quality of our products will continue to be the highest attainable.

## LEADERSHIP IN PROTECTING THE ENVIRONMENT

Our worldwide commitment to conduct operations in a manner that protects the environment will continue to be important — not only to the health of Merck employees, but also to people living in communities around our facilities. It will also be important competitively. We have taken action that, by the end of 1995, will result in a 90% reduction in our releases of toxic chemicals into the environment, a leadership goal in industry.

Eventually, a considerable and steadily increasing degree of environmental protection will be *required* of all companies in all countries. When that happens, Merck will have an enormous advantage by reason of what we have already achieved. At the turn of the century, many other companies — in developing areas, as well as in numerous European countries — will just be starting this monumentally expensive task.

## SAFETY A TOP PRIORITY

We will also have an advantage regarding safety around the world. We very recently reviewed all of Merck's chemical and pharmaceutical processes to be sure that they are as safe as possible. As new processes emerge in the next century, we will continue to be uncompromising in our pursuit of safety. We do this because we care about Merck people, and because it is vital for a global company like ours to demonstrate that we are a positive contributor to society wherever we operate.

## NEED FOR LOW-COST PRODUCTION

Global economic and competitive realities will have a great impact on what we expect of our manufacturing people. On the marketing side of the business, we will face unrelenting pressure on drug prices. So, Merck *must* remain a low-cost producer.

It may seem that in the next century we will be asking our manufacturing people to do superhuman work: to be best in product quality, best in the environment, best in safety. And they will have to do those things at the lowest possible cost — low enough for us to compete even with companies that may not worry about those things as much as we do. I fully expect that Merck people can meet these requirements, but I know it won't be easy!

## GLOBAL SCOPE OF MARKETING AND SALES

Our marketing and sales efforts will be major in scale and global in scope. They will have to be, to support our research. I'm confident that we will continue to be leaders in the major markets of North America,

*As we understand more about disease, we will develop drugs that will eliminate the cause of the disease rather than simply treat its effects.*

Europe, and Japan. In addition, however, we should be strongly established in *potentially* huge markets such as Latin America, China and other nations of the Pacific Rim, Russia, and ultimately Africa as well. Clearly, fifty years from now these should be increasingly important markets for Merck products. We already have the greatest number of important products in the largest number of therapeutic fields. However, to make optimal use of our marketing and sales groups, we must provide them with products in *every* therapeutic area. Today, we are not represented in some very important fields. For example, we have no important modern drugs for treating cancer, cataracts, or serious mental disorders. If we are to maintain our global leadership, we must change that.

## STRATEGIC ALLIANCES WITH OTHER COMPANIES

As we enter new fields, we will look first to Merck's own remarkable research organization for major contributions. However, as biomedical knowledge grows explosively around the world, there is a limit to how fast we can effectively expand our scientific staff. So, we must supplement Merck's intramural research with an *external* strategy. We will continue to acquire or license-in new products from other companies. We will enter fresh markets by co-marketing or co-promoting drugs in different therapeutic areas. We will enter more joint ventures and other collaborative arrangements.

Choosing the right partner will continue to be the key to

success. We will follow good examples, such as our 1982 agreement with AB Astra, from which we expect our joint venture to obtain U.S. marketing rights to all new products of Astra's research. Our equity participation in the business of Banyu Pharmaceutical Co., initiated in 1983, opened the important Japanese market to us. Our 1989 joint venture with Johnson & Johnson marked our entry into the over-the-counter drug business. Our 1990 joint venture with Du Pont formed an independent, research-driven, world-wide pharmaceutical company.

As a result of such innovative arrangements, Merck will enjoy greatly improved access to first-rate research, fast-growing markets, and high-quality new products. Surely, Merck will make many more strategic alliances in the century ahead.

## CHANGING PHARMACEUTICAL MARKETPLACE

As the pharmaceutical marketplace changes very rapidly, our marketing and sales groups will have to anticipate such changes — and even help them move in the right direction. The United States and countries everywhere will see a continuing drive to control healthcare costs. Fee-for-service medical practice will continue to decline, while managed-care systems of various kinds will grow.

As a result, in the United States, our marketing people will be dealing more and more with "mega-buyers," large-scale purchasers of pharmaceuticals who represent hospitals and hospital groups, health maintenance and preferred provider organizations. And, as has been the case with our international subsidiaries for many years, national and state governments will continue to grow as prime customers. It may be that instead of talking separately with fifty different doctors in a community, we will hold a symposium where all of them can hear and receive literature about a new drug, after which a single person will make the purchasing decision for the group or the hospital involved.

## UNPARALLELED SERVICE TO CUSTOMERS

We may need to approach customers in the United States in ways that differ from our approach to customers in Europe, or China, or any other country. Their respective healthcare systems may be evolving at different rates and in different directions. But our goal always will be to determine what our customers need, and then to service them better than anyone else in the world.

Even now, Merck marketing and sales organizations are shifting emphasis and developing strategies to optimize the promotion of our products to different countries and buying groups. Ultimately, this is just one more major challenge, and — as this Centennial History shows — challenge traditionally brings out the best in Merck people.

## EXPANDING OPPORTUNITIES IN ANIMAL HEALTH

Merck is already the world leader in animal pharmaceuticals and medicated feed additives, and we have a growing business in crop protection. Thus, we are well positioned to benefit dramatically as opportunities expand to meet the world's need for food and clothing in the twenty-first century. Biomedical science will open doors for Merck researchers to invent new compounds for controlling the parasites and pests that adversely affect livestock and crops. At the same time, improved products that we can develop for the well-being of dogs, cats, and other companion animals should also find a very receptive market.

## ANIMAL HEALTH R&D — FOUNDATION OF PROGRESS

I believe future generations of Merck scientists can look forward to research breakthroughs as important as Merck's introduction in 1948 of sulfaquinoxaline, which was the first effective weapon against coccidiosis, a parasitic disease of poultry. That invention made possible the large-scale production that has brought costs down so far that chicken is now a staple of the modern diet rather than the Sunday treat it used to be. More importantly, our success stimulated further research aimed at drugs specifically designed to improve agricultural productivity, and the resulting discoveries have brought enormous benefits to the farm economy and to consumers around the world.

Today, our revolutionary antiparasitic, ivermectin, is the best-selling product in the history of the animal health industry. I expect this, and other Merck products, will make increasingly important contributions in developing economies.

People in the next century may still face the paradox of a shortage of high-quality protein in countries where it is needed most, while in many developed countries there will be excess production. I believe Merck scientists will help solve this problem by developing products that permit more economical and efficient production everywhere in the world.

## HUMAN HEALTH ALSO BENEFITS

Human health also benefits from this kind of research. For example, as this Merck history has described, ivermectin is on the way to saving millions of people in many tropical countries from the scourge known as "river blindness."

## POTENTIAL IMPORTANCE OF CROP PROTECTION

Merck should also achieve significant growth in the field of crop protection, where our present position with abamectin products is small but very promising. Our scientists, partly as a natural outgrowth of our research in human health, will certainly succeed in developing new fungicides and insecticides that are both effective and environmentally safe. With our proven marketing ability in crop protection, I'm sure we will quickly build sales for such products.

Overall, this portion of our business will serve society by making agriculture more productive and profitable for farmers and ranchers, while providing an abundance of safe, high-quality food at reasonable cost to consumers.

## SPECIALTY CHEMICALS

This segment of our business will continue to expand rapidly through stronger marketing and the introduction of new products. These will offer technological advantages that provide added value for customers in a wide range of industries, from water treatment and oil exploration to construction and food processing.

## MANAGING ASSETS TO IMPROVE PROFITABILITY

Turning to Merck's internal functions and staffs, which are critically involved in shaping our future, our financial group will remain close to the heart of the Merck enterprise. This area will focus continually on improving profits — which make it possible for the Company to go on serving patients and serving society.

As decades pass, Merck's financial people will have to develop new answers to major strategic questions — such as "How can Company resources be allocated most effectively to meet expenses and to invest in research and capital projects? How can we balance strategic needs and continue to give stockholders a solid return on their investments? How can we give Merck a competitive advantage through better

economic evaluations of the projects and potential investments that are continually brought forward?"

In addition to grappling with these questions, the financial organization will help to shape Merck's next century through innovation in such key areas as foreign exchange, global tax management, and competitive analysis. This group will expand its recently established studies concentrating on the economic dynamics of our industry. Such studies will be increasingly important to us internally, and in our work with governments as they formulate health-care policies.

## RECRUITING TOP PEOPLE — EVERY MANAGER'S MISSION

If Merck continues to grow in the next century as rapidly as I expect, the Company's progress will reflect continued success in attracting and developing the highest quality people. I see every manager, with assistance from Human Resources, personally involved in recruiting as an increasingly important mission. The better each manager does at recruiting and developing people, the better his or her own performance evaluation will be. So, the quality of people entering and moving through the Company — even though that quality is already excellent — must continue to improve. Top candidates will be eager to join us — if we show them that working at Merck is a great way to serve society and a great career choice. People entering Merck should learn quickly that they can go as far as their talents and energies permit. I should stress that point because — just like today — much will be demanded of Merck people. With the competition we face now and in the next century, our people will have to work both harder and smarter than everybody else.

## MERCK PEOPLE WILL REFLECT OUR GLOBAL BUSINESS

We will know that Merck is truly global when our top executives properly reflect the ethnic and national backgrounds of all our employees around the world.

To broaden the experience of up-and-coming executives, we will transfer them between functional specialties and from one country to another more than we do today. When they are transferred geographically — for example, from the United States to Germany — I would expect them to maximize the experience by learning all they can about the culture, sending their children to local public schools, and learning to speak the language.

## LEGAL COUNSEL

As our business continues to grow, our lawyers — like other Merck professionals — will have more complex issues to deal with than ever before. This function will grow ever more important as companies such as Merck look to legal counsel to gain a clear competitive advantage. I expect our lawyers to continue to serve management on critical issues such as improving access to new products by helping us develop and execute innovative strategies for acquisitions, joint ventures, and licensing. The legal staff will also be challenged to protect Merck inventions around the world by asserting and then defending our patent rights — as well as other intellectual property — against all challengers. In addition, our legal staff will need strong capabilities to deal with emerging fields of law, such as those relating to the environment and the European Community.

*But no matter what changes might have occurred in the Company, I know we would find one thing had remained the same — and that's the thing that matters most: the innovative, enterprising spirit of Merck people.*

## PRESERVING MERCK'S RECORD OF HIGH QUALITY AND FAIR PRESENTATION

Commercial laws in all countries where we do business probably won't get any easier to understand. As for the rules for testing new drugs and getting them approved, and then manufacturing and promoting them — those rules are likely to become more complex, just like the medicines themselves. So, the Legal Department will have to educate our people at all levels about such complexities. That's another challenge our lawyers must meet if the Company is to preserve its record of high quality and fair presentation with regard to our products and indeed to everything we do and say.

## HIGH PROFESSIONAL REPUTATION AND LITTLE PUBLIC RECOGNITION — EMERGING CHALLENGES FOR PUBLIC AFFAIRS

For close to a century, Merck has enjoyed an excellent reputation in the worlds of chemistry, medicine, and pharmacy. In recent years, we have reached a unique position of leadership in the pharmaceutical industry and achieved broad recognition in the financial community. Surprisingly, however, the average ''person on the street'' has never heard of Merck & Co., Inc. In the years to come, I'm sure that will change. Whether or not we are still the largest in our industry, the Company will be much better known to the general public in the middle of the next century than it is today.

## DUAL VALUE TO SOCIETY

This increased recognition will be based, first, on our growth — as a major player in the global economy, and as a major contributor to world health. Fame, however, brings with it the mixed blessing of greater recognition and greater scrutiny of our business. As

Merck emerges from anonymity, some of the toughest challenges will be faced by our Public Affairs group. They must relate effectively to people, governments, and healthcare purchasers around the world to instill an appreciation of the full value, and the *dual value*, that our enterprise brings to society. Public Affairs must help to make it clear that modern drugs not only save lives, but also save money in the long run by avoiding and managing disease, by shortening hospital stays, and by enabling patients to return more promptly to productive work. Public awareness of these facts should reduce temptations to hold down healthcare costs through arbitrary restrictions on either the pricing of pharmaceuticals or the access of patients to medicines.

## MANAGING THE PUBLIC POLICY ENVIRONMENT

Our Public Affairs representatives will also have to work unceasingly to manage effectively the complex societal, political, and economic policy environments that affect our continued research, manufacturing, and marketing successes. For example, they will collaborate with legislators and government regulators in shaping policy regarding the protection of patents, control of toxic emissions, and pricing. They must also continue to tell the Merck story effectively — to the news media, the financial community, and general public — giving an accurate picture of Merck's contributions to society. I believe they will be able to do that more broadly and persuasively than ever before by increased use of communications technologies, some of which I am sure we cannot yet imagine.

## MERCK PEOPLE A CENTURY FROM NOW

Just to complete my vision of Merck's future, let me ask Merck employees and retirees to imagine that all of us were suddenly transported to the year 2091. Much of what I have said on these pages would have already been changed by developments we cannot anticipate. But no matter what changes might have occurred in the Company, I know we would find one thing had remained the same — and that's the thing that matters most: the innovative, enterprising spirit of Merck people.

A century from now, I believe we would feel the same esprit de corps among Merck people that we see throughout the Company in this Centennial year. In years hence, I envision Merck employees who are skilled, loyal, and unbelievably hard-working — just as they are today.

I believe this, above all, because Merck's dedication to fighting disease, relieving suffering, and helping people is a righteous cause — one that inspires people to dream of doing great things. It is a timeless cause, and it will lead Merck people to great achievements during the next hundred years. That is why I am confident that, in the year 2091, there will be good reason to prepare another Merck history — that one celebrating *two* centuries of growth, success, and fantastic achievements.

*Roy Vagelos*

# Appendix

The Merck Board of Directors, February 1991. Seated (left to right): Jacques Genest, M.D., Albert W. Merck, P. Roy Vagelos, M.D., John E. Lyons, Marian S. Heiskell, John J. Horan. Standing (left to right): Lloyd C. Elam, M.D., Ruben F. Mettler, Ph.D., Paul G. Rogers, Richard S. Ross, M.D., William G. Bowen, Ph.D., Dennis Weatherstone, Charles E. Exley, Jr., H. Brewster Atwater, Jr., Carolyne K. Davis, Ph.D., Frank T. Cary.

# BOARD OF DIRECTORS, 1908-1991

| DIRECTOR | YEARS OF SERVICE |
|---|---|
| CARL M. ANDERSON | 1969-1970 |
| H. BREWSTER ATWATER, JR. | 1988- |
| WILLIAM G. BOWEN | 1986- |
| VANNEVAR BUSH | 1949-1962 |
| HARTWELL CABELL | 1918-1919 |
| FRANK T. CARY | 1979-1991 |
| WADDILL CATCHINGS | 1919-1930 |
| F. N. B. CLOSE | 1918-1919 |
| JOHN T. CONNOR | 1955-1965, 1981-1987 |
| FRANK L. CROCKER | 1919-1930 |
| GEORGE S. CURRIE | 1951-1956 |
| HENRY D. DAKIN | 1938-1950 |
| CAROLYNE K. DAVIS | 1989- |
| WILLIAM L. DEMPSEY | 1953-1960 |
| CHARLES D. DICKEY | 1953-1966 |
| RICHARD E. DWIGHT | 1927-1937 |
| HUSKEL EKAIREB | 1978-1982 |
| LLOYD C. ELAM | 1973- |
| CHARLES E. EXLEY, JR. | 1988- |
| HENRY W. GADSDEN | 1955-1980 |
| CHARLES S. GARLAND | 1953-1971 |
| JACQUES GENEST | 1972- |
| BEN S. GILMER | 1965-1977 |
| EDWARD H. GREEN | 1919-1962 |
| DIRECTOR EMERITUS | 1962 |
| RUDOLF E. GRUBER | 1925-1934 |
| J. GEORGE HARRAR | 1971-1979 |
| MARIAN S. HEISKELL | 1973-1991 |
| ROBERT C. HILL | 1962-1969 |
| HENRY L. HILLMAN | 1968-1970 |
| WILLIAM W. HOPWOOD | 1968-1969 |
| JOHN J. HORAN | 1975- |
| JOHN L. HUCK | 1977-1986 |
| ALFRED JARETZKI | 1918-1925 |
| ALFRED JARETZKI, JR. | 1919, 1925-1934 |
| HENRY W. JOHNSTONE | 1945-1959 |
| REGINALD H. JONES | 1981-1988 |
| ERNEST KAUDER | 1908-1913 |
| CHESTER S. KEEFER | 1960-1970 |
| JAMES J. KERRIGAN | 1925-1934, 1945-1956 |
| ANTONIE T. KNOPPERS | 1970-1975 |
| PHILIP LEHMAN | 1919-1934 |
| JOHN E. LYONS | 1988-1991 |
| COLIN M. MacLEOD | 1969-1972 |
| JOHN K. McKINLEY | 1982-1990 |
| ALBERT W. MERCK | 1961- |
| GEORGE MERCK | 1908-1926 |
| GEORGE W. MERCK | 1916-1957 |
| RUBEN F. METTLER | 1976- |
| WILLIAM B. MURPHY | 1959-1980 |
| HARRY R. NEILSON | 1929-1949 |
| WALTER H. PAGE | 1966-1979 |
| JOHN W. PARRY | 1914-1918 |
| GEORGE W. PERKINS | 1927-1949, 1957-1960 |
| HENRY H. PIERCE | 1911-1914 |
| GLENN S. POUND | 1971-1986 |
| EDWARD REYNOLDS | 1947-1964 |
| ALFRED NEWTON RICHARDS | 1948-1959 |
| PAUL G. ROGERS | 1979- |
| ADOLPH G. ROSENGARTEN | 1927-1946 |
| ADOLPH G. ROSENGARTEN, JR. | 1934-1942, 1946-1974 |
| DIRECTOR EMERITUS | 1974-1990 |
| FREDERIC ROSENGARTEN | 1927-1955 |
| GEORGE D. ROSENGARTEN | 1927-1929 |
| JOSEPH G. ROSENGARTEN, JR. | 1927-1934, 1942-1946 |
| RICHARD S. ROSS | 1984- |
| WALTER E. SACHS | 1930-1959 |
| ORVILLE H. SCHELL, JR. | 1957-1981 |
| HENRY SCHENCK | 1908-1916 |
| JAMES H. SHARP | 1949-1958 |
| DAVID A. SHEPARD | 1965-1975 |
| RAYMOND E. SNYDER | 1971-1977 |
| HENRY STEIN | 1930-1934 |
| CHARLES C. TILLINGHAST, JR. | 1962-1983 |
| MAX TISHLER | 1962-1970 |
| P. ROY VAGELOS | 1984- |
| DENNIS WEATHERSTONE | 1988- |
| JOHN S. ZINSSER | 1953-1960 |

*The Merck Board of Directors, Company officers, and guests at Elkton, Virginia, October 22, 1946. Back row (left to right): George W. Perkins, Executive Vice President, Treasurer, and Director; Dr. Henry D. Dakin, Director; Frederic Rosengarten, Chairman of the Board; Edward H. Green, Director; Verne Burnett, Public Relations Counsel; Oscar R. Ewing, Secretary; George W. Merck, President and Director. Second row (left to right): Adolph G. Rosengarten Jr., Director; Carl M. Anderson, Executive Assistant to the President; James J. Kerrigan, Vice President and Director; Edward W. Higgins, Controller; Henry W. Johnstone, Vice President. First row (left to right): Walter E. Sachs, Director; Harry R. Neilson, Director; John H. Gage, Assistant Treasurer; Orville H. Schell, Legal Counsel.*

# CORPORATE OFFICERS, 1908-1991

| POSITION | YEARS IN OFFICE |
|---|---|

## CHAIRMAN

| | |
|---|---|
| P. ROY VAGELOS | 1986- |
| JOHN L. HUCK | 1985-1986 |
| JOHN J. HORAN | 1976-1985 |
| HENRY W. GADSDEN | 1971-1976 |
| CHARLES S. GARLAND | 1962-1971 |
| VANNEVAR BUSH | 1957-1962 |
| GEORGE W. MERCK | 1949-1957 |
| FREDERIC ROSENGARTEN | 1927-1949 |
| GEORGE MERCK | 1925-1926 |

## CHIEF EXECUTIVE OFFICER

| | |
|---|---|
| P. ROY VAGELOS | 1985- |
| JOHN J. HORAN | 1976-1985 |
| HENRY W. GADSDEN | 1965-1976 |
| JOHN T. CONNOR | 1955-1965 |

## PRESIDENT

| | |
|---|---|
| P. ROY VAGELOS | 1985- |
| JOHN L. HUCK | 1978-1985 |
| JOHN J. HORAN | 1975-1978 |
| HENRY W. GADSDEN | 1965-1971, 1974-1975 |
| ANTONIE T. KNOPPERS | 1971-1973 |
| HENRY W. GADSDEN | 1965-1971 |
| JOHN T. CONNOR | 1955-1965 |
| JAMES J. KERRIGAN | 1950-1955 |
| GEORGE W. MERCK | 1925-1950 |
| GEORGE MERCK | 1908-1925 |

## VICE CHAIRMAN

| | |
|---|---|
| JOHN E. LYONS | 1988-1991 |
| ANTONIE T. KNOPPERS | 1973-1975 |
| ADOLPH G. ROSENGARTEN, JR. | 1971-1972 |
| JOHN S. ZINSSER | 1953-1957 |

## EXECUTIVE VICE PRESIDENT

| | |
|---|---|
| JOHN E. LYONS | 1985-1988 |
| P. ROY VAGELOS | 1984-1985 |
| HUSKEL EKAIREB | 1977-1981 |
| JOHN L. HUCK | 1977-1978 |
| RAYMOND E. SNYDER | 1974-1976 |
| JOHN J. HORAN | 1974-1975 |
| HENRY W. GADSDEN | 1955-1965 |
| GEORGE W. PERKINS | 1934-1942, 1945-1948 |

## SENIOR VICE PRESIDENT

| | |
|---|---|
| JERRY T. JACKSON | 1991- |
| RICHARD J. MARKHAM | 1991- |
| EDWARD M. SCOLNICK | 1991- |
| JOHN L. ZABRISKIE | 1991- |
| DOUGLAS J. MacMASTER JR. | 1988-1991 |
| FRANCIS H. SPIEGEL, JR. | 1987- |
| ROBERT L. BANSE | 1986- |
| HOWARD F. POWERS | 1985-1988 |
| ABRAHAM E. COHEN | 1982- |
| ROBERT F. HENDRICKSON | 1981-1985 |
| SPENCER A. STOUFFER | 1980 |
| PHILIP H. ROY | 1976-1985 |
| HUSKEL EKAIREB | 1975-1976 |
| JOHN L. HUCK | 1975-1976 |
| JOHN J. HORAN | 1972-1973 |
| RAYMOND E. SNYDER | 1970-1973 |
| LUTHER S. ROEHM | 1969-1976 |
| HUBERT N. FIACCONE | 1967-1981 |
| ANTONIE T. KNOPPERS | 1967-1971 |
| HENRY W. JOHNSTONE | 1950-1957 |

## ADMINISTRATIVE VICE PRESIDENT

| | |
|---|---|
| FRED BARTENSTEIN, JR. | 1961-1972 |
| HENRY W. GADSDEN | 1955 |
| JOHN T. CONNOR | 1953-1955 |

## SENIOR VICE PRESIDENT - ENGINEERING & TECHNOLOGY

| | |
|---|---|
| STANLEY J. FIDELMAN | 1990- |

## SENIOR VICE PRESIDENT - HUMAN HEALTH MARKETING

| | |
|---|---|
| JERRY T. JACKSON | 1986-1988 |

## SENIOR VICE PRESIDENT - MANUFACTURING & TECHNOLOGY

| | |
|---|---|
| ROBERT F. HENDRICKSON | 1985-1989 |

## SENIOR VICE PRESIDENT - RESEARCH & DEVELOPMENT

| | |
|---|---|
| MAX TISHLER | 1969-1970 |

## SENIOR VICE PRESIDENT - SCIENCE & TECHNOLOGY

| | |
|---|---|
| LEWIS H. SARETT | 1976-1982 |

## GROUP VICE PRESIDENT

| | |
|---|---|
| HOWARD F. POWERS | 1975-1981 |

## GROUP VICE PRESIDENT - INDUSTRIAL & ENVIRONMENTAL

| | |
|---|---|
| JOHN T. RILEY | 1979-1980 |

## VICE PRESIDENT

| | |
|---|---|
| WILLIAM H. McLEAN | 1963-1964 |
| JAMES H. SHARP | 1956-1957 |
| HENRY W. JOHNSTONE | 1936-1949 |
| JOSEPH ROSIN | 1927-1948 |
| JESSE H. AMBLER | 1929-1941 |
| RUDOLF E. GRUBER | 1925-1948 |
| JAMES J. KERRIGAN | 1925-1927, 1936-1949 |
| BENJAMIN L. MURRAY | 1925-1930 |
| L. F. GREGORY | 1919-1920 |
| GEORGE W. MERCK | 1915-1925 |
| ERNEST KAUDER | 1908-1915 |

*In honor of the Merck Centennial, the members of Merck's Management Council pose beside a portrait of company founder George Merck, October 1990. These 25 senior executives coordinate and integrate company activities. The members of the Operating Review Committee, a key advisory group to the Chief Executive Officer, are in the first row (from left): P. Roy Vagelos, M.D., David W. Anstice, Robert L. Banse, A. E. Cohen, Jerry T. Jackson, Judy C. Lewent, John E.*

*Lyons, Douglas J. MacMaster Jr., Richard J. Markham, Edward M. Scolnick, M.D., Francis H. Spiegel, Jr., John L. Zabriskie, Ph.D. Second row (left to right): Clarence A. Abramson, Albert D. Angel, Michael G. Atieh, David A. Conklin, Steven M. Darien, Stanley J. Fidelman, Joseph M. Fox, Joseph W. Keating, G. Theodore Mascott, Eugene F. McCabe, Francis X. McDermott, Edward J. Sot, Walter R. Trosin.*

## VICE PRESIDENT - COMPUTER RESOURCES

| | |
|---|---|
| ALBERT C. CINORRE | 1986-1991 |

## VICE PRESIDENT - CORPORATE LICENSING

| | |
|---|---|
| EDGAR H. PHILBRICK | 1982-1985 |

## VICE PRESIDENT - DOMESTIC SALES

| | |
|---|---|
| JOSEPH L. K. SNYDER | 1948-1950 |

## VICE PRESIDENT - EMPLOYEE RELATIONS

| | |
|---|---|
| STEVEN M. DARIEN | 1985-1989 |

## VICE PRESIDENT - FINANCE

| | |
|---|---|
| JUDY C. LEWENT | 1990- |
| ALFRED P. SMITH | 1987-1989 |
| FRANCIS H. SPIEGEL, JR. | 1985-1987 |
| EDWIN C. SAGURTON | 1976-1985 |
| PHILIP H. ROY | 1972-1976 |
| RAYMOND E. SNYDER | 1953-1970 |
| JAMES H. SHARP | 1951-1953 |

## VICE PRESIDENT - FOREIGN RELATIONS

| | |
|---|---|
| RUDOLF E. GRUBER | 1948-1952 |

## VICE PRESIDENT - HUMAN RESOURCES

| | |
|---|---|
| STEVEN M. DARIEN | 1990- |
| WALTER R. TROSIN | 1977-1990 |

## VICE PRESIDENT - MANAGEMENT INFORMATION SYSTEMS

| | |
|---|---|
| HERBERT H. BLEVINS | 1968-1978 |

## VICE PRESIDENT - MARKETING

| | |
|---|---|
| WILLIAM H. McLEAN | 1951-1953 |

## VICE PRESIDENT - OPERATIONS

| | |
|---|---|
| BLYTHE M. REYNOLDS | 1953 |

## VICE PRESIDENT - PERSONNEL RELATIONS

| | |
|---|---|
| JOHN J. RADIGAN | 1967-1980 |
| EUGENE J. LYONS | 1948-1953 |

## VICE PRESIDENT - PLANNING & DEVELOPMENT

| | |
|---|---|
| EDGAR H. PHILBRICK | 1985-1987 |
| FRANCIS H. SPIEGEL, JR. | 1981-1985 |

## VICE PRESIDENT - PRODUCTION

| | |
|---|---|
| REGINALD P. LUKENS | 1948-1952 |

## VICE PRESIDENT - PUBLIC AFFAIRS

| | |
|---|---|
| ALBERT D. ANGEL | 1985- |
| ROBERT H. MARIK | 1978-1985 |
| JOHN E. FLETCHER | 1972-1978 |

## VICE PRESIDENT - RESEARCH & DEVELOPMENT

| | |
|---|---|
| PER K. FROLICH | 1948-1953 |

## VICE PRESIDENT - SCIENTIFIC

| | |
|---|---|
| RANDOLPH T. MAJOR | 1947-1956 |

## VICE PRESIDENT - WORLDWIDE PERSONNEL

| | |
|---|---|
| STEVEN M. DARIEN | 1989-1990 |

## SECOND VICE PRESIDENT

| | |
|---|---|
| JOHN W. PARRY | 1918-1924 |

## GENERAL COUNSEL

| | |
|---|---|
| MARY M. McDONALD * | 1991- |
| ROBERT L. BANSE * | 1975-1991 |
| JAMES M. FULTON | 1961-1975 |
| FRED BARTENSTEIN, JR. | 1953-1961 |
| JOHN T. CONNOR * | 1951-1953 |

## CONTROLLER

| | |
|---|---|
| EDWARD J. SOT | 1989- |
| THOMAS L. OSTERBRINK | 1983-1989 |
| ALBERT C. CINORRE | 1981-1983 |
| ALFRED P. SMITH | 1979-1980 |
| FRANCIS H. SPIEGEL, JR. | 1976-1979 |
| EDWIN C. SAGURTON | 1972-1976 |
| PHILIP H. ROY | 1968-1971 |
| HERBERT H. BLEVINS | 1958-1967 |
| STUART T. HENSHALL | 1953-1958 |
| RAYMOND E. SNYDER | 1947-1953 |
| EDWARD W. HIGGINS | 1945-1947 |

## TREASURER

| | |
|---|---|
| MICHAEL G. ATIEH | 1990- |
| JUDY C. LEWENT * | 1987-1990 |
| FRANCIS H. SPIEGEL, JR. | 1979-1980 |
| ALFRED P. SMITH * | 1972-1979, 1981-1987 |
| EDWIN C. SAGURTON | 1968-1971 |
| HAROLD A. ROCKWELL | 1958-1968 |
| RAYMOND E. SNYDER * | 1956-1958 |
| JOHN H. GAGE | 1947-1956 |
| GEORGE W. PERKINS | 1927-1942, 1945-1947 |
| HENRY STEIN | 1926-1927 |
| GEORGE W. MERCK | 1918-1926 |
| GEORGE MERCK | 1916-1918 |
| HENRY SCHENCK | 1908-1916 |

## SECRETARY

| | |
|---|---|
| CLARENCE A. ABRAMSON * | 1989- |
| DANIEL W. BYLES | 1986-1989 |
| WILLIAM B. VAN BUREN * | 1976-1986 |
| JAMES M. FULTON | 1970-1976 |
| CARL M. ANDERSON | 1956-1970 |
| JAMES E. McCABE | 1951-1955 |
| JOHN T. CONNOR | 1947-1951 |
| OSCAR R. EWING | 1928-1947 |
| ALFRED JARETZKI, JR. | 1926-1927 |
| EDWARD H. GREEN | 1918-1926 |
| JOHN W. PARRY | 1916-1918 |
| HENRY SCHENCK | 1908-1916 |

*also a Vice President*

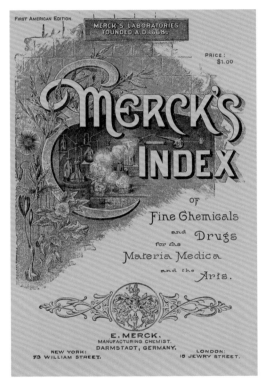

*The first edition of the* Merck Index, *published in 1889, contained an encyclopedic list of over 5,000 chemicals and drugs.*

*The company's founder and first President, George Merck, and Friederike Schenck of Antwerp, Belgium, in Darmstadt, Germany, in July 1892, shortly after the couple had announced their engagement.*

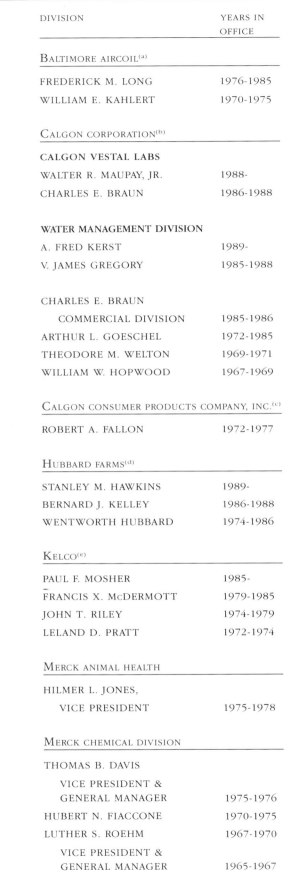

| DIVISION | YEARS IN OFFICE |
|---|---|
| **BALTIMORE AIRCOIL**[a] | |
| FREDERICK M. LONG | 1976-1985 |
| WILLIAM E. KAHLERT | 1970-1975 |
| | |
| **CALGON CORPORATION**[b] | |
| **CALGON VESTAL LABS** | |
| WALTER R. MAUPAY, JR. | 1988- |
| CHARLES E. BRAUN | 1986-1988 |
| | |
| **WATER MANAGEMENT DIVISION** | |
| A. FRED KERST | 1989- |
| V. JAMES GREGORY | 1985-1988 |
| | |
| CHARLES E. BRAUN COMMERCIAL DIVISION | 1985-1986 |
| ARTHUR L. GOESCHEL | 1972-1985 |
| THEODORE M. WELTON | 1969-1971 |
| WILLIAM W. HOPWOOD | 1967-1969 |
| | |
| **CALGON CONSUMER PRODUCTS COMPANY, INC.**[c] | |
| ROBERT A. FALLON | 1972-1977 |
| | |
| **HUBBARD FARMS**[d] | |
| STANLEY M. HAWKINS | 1989- |
| BERNARD J. KELLEY | 1986-1988 |
| WENTWORTH HUBBARD | 1974-1986 |
| | |
| **KELCO**[e] | |
| PAUL F. MOSHER | 1985- |
| FRANCIS X. McDERMOTT | 1979-1985 |
| JOHN T. RILEY | 1974-1979 |
| LELAND D. PRATT | 1972-1974 |
| | |
| **MERCK ANIMAL HEALTH** | |
| HILMER L. JONES, VICE PRESIDENT | 1975-1978 |
| | |
| **MERCK CHEMICAL DIVISION** | |
| THOMAS B. DAVIS VICE PRESIDENT & GENERAL MANAGER | 1975-1976 |
| HUBERT N. FIACCONE | 1970-1975 |
| LUTHER S. ROEHM | 1967-1970 |
| VICE PRESIDENT & GENERAL MANAGER | 1965-1967 |

| WILLIAM H. McLEAN | 1955-1964 |
| HENRY W. JOHNSTONE | 1953-1955 |

## MERCK CHEMICAL MANUFACTURING DIVISION

| DAVID A. CONKLIN | 1987- |
| VICE PRESIDENT & GENERAL MANAGER | 1981-1987 |
| SPENCER A. STOUFFER | |
| VICE PRESIDENT & GENERAL MANAGER | 1975-1980 |
| VICE PRESIDENT, OPERATIONS | 1968-1969 |
| DIRECTOR OF OPERATIONS | 1967- |
| HUBERT N. FIACCONE | |
| VICE PRESIDENT & GENERAL MANAGER | 1965-1967 |

## MERCK CONSUMER HEALTHCARE

| G. THEODORE MASCOTT | 1989-1991 |
| RONALD A. AHRENS | 1991- |

## MERCK FROSST CANADA INC. (f)

| MICHAEL M. TARNOW | 1990- |
| ROBERT A. INGRAM | 1988-1990 |
| JOHN L. ZABRISKIE | 1983-1987 |
| WILLIAM E. BEMBRIDGE | 1980-1982 |

## MERCK HUMAN HEALTH DIVISION

| RICHARD J. MARKHAM | 1991- |

## MERCK PHARMACEUTICAL MANUFACTURING DIVISION

| JOSEPH W. KEATING | 1988- |

## MERCK SHARP & DOHME

| DAVID W. ANSTICE | 1991- |
| JOHN L. ZABRISKIE | 1988-1991 |
| DOUGLAS J. MacMASTER JR. | 1985-1988 |
| JOHN E. LYONS | 1975-1985 |
| JOHN LLOYD HUCK | 1973-1975 |
| JOHN J. HORAN | 1968-1972 |
| STUART T. HENSHALL | 1963-1968 |
| VICE PRESIDENT & GENERAL MANAGER | 1959-1962 |
| JOHN G. BILL | 1955-1959 |
| WILLIAM L. DEMPSEY | 1953-1954 |

## MSD AGVET

| EUGENE F. McCABE | 1987- |
| JAMES GILLIN | 1979-1987 |

## MERCK SHARP & DOHME INTERNATIONAL

| JERRY T. JACKSON | 1988-1991 |
| ABRAHAM E. COHEN | 1977-1987 |
| HUSKEL EKAIREB | 1970-1976 |
| LEO FERNANDEZ | 1968-1970 |
| ANTONIE T. KNOPPERS | 1957-1967 |
| JAMES H. SHARP | 1953-1956 |

## MERCK SHARP & DOHME RESEARCH LABORATORIES

| EDWARD M. SCOLNICK | 1985- |
| P. ROY VAGELOS | 1976-1985 |
| LEWIS H. SARETT | 1969-1976 |
| MAX TISHLER | 1957-1969 |

## MERCK VACCINE DIVISION

| R. GORDON DOUGLAS, JR. | 1991- |

## QUINTON COMPANY

| HARRY J. ROBINSON | 1964-1967 |
| JOHN L. HAMMER, JR. | |
| GENERAL MANAGER | 1962-1964 |

## SPECIALTY CHEMICALS GROUP (g)

| FRANCIS X. McDERMOTT | 1985- |
| HOWARD F. POWERS | 1981-1984 |

\* *Presidents, unless otherwise noted*

NOTES

(a) Acquired 1970, sold to Amstead Industries, Inc. in 1985.
(b) Acquired in 1968.
(c) Sold to Beecham Inc. in 1977.
(d) Acquired in 1974.
(e) Acquired in 1972.
(f) Acquired in 1965.
(g) Specialty Chemical and Environmental Products before 1985.

*The E. Merck exhibit at the World's Columbian Exposition in Chicago, 1893.*

*This 1939 advertisement in
the* Oil Paint & Drug
Reporter *focused on Merck's
commitment to innovation.*

| NAME | YEAR |
|------|------|
| KARL A. FOLKERS | 1951 |
| LEWIS H. SARETT | |
| MAX TISHLER | |
| KARL H. BEYER, JR. | 1959 |
| JAMES M. SPRAGUE | |
| KARL PFISTER | 1964 |
| ASHTON C. CUCKLER | 1969 |
| ROBERT G. DENKEWALTER | |
| MAURICE R. HILLEMAN | |
| TSUNG-YING SHEN | 1976 |
| CHARLES A. WINTER | |
| JOHN M. CHEMERDA | 1978 |
| MAURICE R. HILLEMAN | 1984 |
| RALPH F. HIRSCHMANN | |
| JAMES LAGO | |
| CLEMENT A. STONE | |
| MOHAMMED A. AZIZ | 1987 |
| JEROME BIRNBAUM | |
| WILLIAM C. CAMPBELL | |
| BURTON G. CHRISTENSEN | |
| FREDERICK M. KAHAN | |
| ARTHUR A. PATCHETT | |
| SEEMON H. PINES | |
| CARLOS B. ROSAS | |
| IAN H. SUTHERLAND | |
| CHARLES S. SWEET | |
| GEORG ALBERS-SCHÖNBERG | 1989 |
| ALFRED W. ALBERTS | |
| RICHARD L. MONAGHAN | |
| ARTHUR A. PATCHETT | |
| JONATHAN TOBERT | |

*Microbiologists developing new techniques for the production and purification of antibiotics in the Merck research laboratories, 1942.*

Merck & Co. was established in New York City on January 1, 1891, and incorporated in the State of New York on September 5, 1908. On June 28, 1927, Merck & Co., Inc. adopted the new name of The Merck Corporation. The Merck Corporation and Powers-Weightman-Rosengarten merged on June 30, 1927, to form a new Merck & Co., which was incorporated in New Jersey. On December 29, 1934, the merged companies were consolidated into the present Merck & Co., Inc.

## MAJOR MERGERS
(AND INCREASE IN SHARES OUTSTANDING)

1953: Merck & Co., Inc. merged with Sharp & Dohme (87.5 million shares)

1968: Merck & Co., Inc. merged with Calgon (37.2 million shares)

1972: Merck & Co., Inc. merged with Kelco (6.2 million shares)

1974: Merck & Co., Inc. merged with Hubbard Farms (5.4 million shares)

## STOCK SPLITS

All per share numbers have been adjusted for the following stock splits:

| Date | |
|---|---|
| March 28, 1941 | 3 for 1 |
| April 19, 1949 | 2 for 1 |
| September 10, 1951 | 3 for 1 |
| May 5, 1964 | 3 for 1 |
| May 5, 1972 | 2 for 1 |
| May 1, 1986 | 2 for 1 |
| May 8, 1988 | 3 for 1 |

## MERCK & CO., INC. STOCK DATA, 1935 - 1990

| YEAR | YEARLY LOW ($/SHARE) | YEARLY HIGH ($/SHARE) | YEARLY AVERAGE ($/SHARE) | YEARLY DIVIDEND ($/SHARE) | AVERAGE SHARES OUTSTANDING (THOUSANDS) |
|---|---|---|---|---|---|
| 1935 | 0.04 | 0.06 | 0.05 | 0.00 | 194,400 |
| 1936 | 0.04 | 0.06 | 0.05 | 0.00 | 194,400 |
| 1937 | 0.02 | 0.04 | 0.03 | 0.01 | 194,400 |
| 1938 | 0.03 | 0.05 | 0.04 | 0.00 | 194,400 |
| 1939 | 0.04 | 0.07 | 0.05 | 0.01 | 194,400 |
| 1940 | 0.06 | 0.08 | 0.07 | 0.01 | 194,400 |
| 1941 | 0.04 | 0.06 | 0.05 | 0.00 | 216,000 |
| 1942 | 0.11 | 0.15 | 0.13 | 0.00 | 216,000 |
| 1943 | 0.15 | 0.20 | 0.18 | 0.00 | 216,000 |
| 1944 | 0.16 | 0.20 | 0.18 | 0.00 | 216,000 |
| 1945 | 0.14 | 0.22 | 0.18 | 0.00 | 216,000 |
| 1946 | 0.25 | 0.36 | 0.30 | 0.01 | 237,600 |
| 1947 | 0.20 | 0.30 | 0.25 | 0.01 | 237,600 |
| 1948 | 0.20 | 0.30 | 0.25 | 0.01 | 237,600 |
| 1949 | 0.25 | 0.41 | 0.33 | 0.01 | 241,380 |
| 1950 | 0.36 | 0.62 | 0.49 | 0.02 | 260,280 |
| 1951 | 0.79 | 1.10 | 0.95 | 0.02 | 264,060 |
| 1952 | 0.61 | 0.99 | 0.80 | 0.02 | 264,060 |
| 1953 | 0.47 | 0.72 | 0.60 | 0.02 | 351,540 |
| 1954 | 0.49 | 0.66 | 0.58 | 0.02 | 351,540 |
| 1955 | 0.56 | 0.86 | 0.71 | 0.02 | 351,576 |
| 1956 | 0.68 | 0.97 | 0.83 | 0.03 | 352,080 |
| 1957 | 0.81 | 1.24 | 1.02 | 0.03 | 353,232 |
| 1958 | 1.02 | 2.32 | 1.67 | 0.04 | 364,680 |
| 1959 | 1.86 | 2.55 | 2.20 | 0.05 | 381,672 |
| 1960 | 2.03 | 2.68 | 2.35 | 0.04 | 383,256 |
| 1961 | 2.06 | 2.65 | 2.35 | 0.04 | 384,732 |
| 1962 | 1.68 | 2.64 | 2.16 | 0.05 | 384,660 |
| 1963 | 2.15 | 3.06 | 2.60 | 0.06 | 384,156 |
| 1964 | 2.88 | 4.28 | 3.58 | 0.09 | 385,260 |
| 1965 | 4.04 | 6.25 | 5.15 | 0.10 | 386,784 |
| 1966 | 5.39 | 6.82 | 6.10 | 0.12 | 388,476 |
| 1967 | 6.16 | 7.83 | 6.99 | 0.13 | 426,552 |
| 1968 | 6.15 | 8.06 | 7.10 | 0.15 | 428,304 |
| 1969 | 6.88 | 9.60 | 8.24 | 0.17 | 430,308 |
| 1970 | 6.13 | 9.40 | 7.76 | 0.17 | 437,004 |
| 1971 | 7.86 | 10.94 | 9.40 | 0.18 | 437,544 |
| 1972 | 10.31 | 15.02 | 12.67 | 0.19 | 444,654 |
| 1973 | 12.71 | 16.92 | 14.81 | 0.21 | 445,746 |
| 1974 | 7.77 | 14.33 | 11.05 | 0.23 | 451,800 |
| 1975 | 9.58 | 14.29 | 11.94 | 0.23 | 452,520 |
| 1976 | 10.44 | 13.58 | 12.01 | 0.24 | 452,958 |
| 1977 | 8.33 | 11.38 | 9.85 | 0.26 | 453,276 |
| 1978 | 7.90 | 11.54 | 9.72 | 0.29 | 453,438 |
| 1979 | 10.42 | 12.38 | 11.40 | 0.32 | 452,551 |
| 1980 | 9.71 | 14.33 | 12.02 | 0.38 | 449,742 |
| 1981 | 12.71 | 17.17 | 14.94 | 0.43 | 445,857 |
| 1982 | 10.67 | 14.71 | 12.69 | 0.47 | 443,899 |
| 1983 | 13.63 | 17.44 | 15.53 | 0.47 | 443,661 |
| 1984 | 13.04 | 16.25 | 14.65 | 0.50 | 440,670 |
| 1985 | 15.04 | 22.96 | 19.00 | 0.53 | 427,561 |
| 1986 | 22.38 | 43.17 | 32.77 | 0.63 | 417,978 |
| 1987 | 40.67 | 74.33 | 57.50 | 0.82 | 407,055 |
| 1988 | 48.00 | 59.63 | 53.82 | 1.28 | 395,640 |
| 1989 | 56.25 | 80.75 | 68.50 | 1.64 | 396,099 |
| 1990 | 67.00 | 91.13 | 79.07 | 1.91 | 390,686 |

## Annual Sales, 1891-1990

| Year | Millions of Dollars |
|---|---|
| 1891 | .479 |
| 1892 | .587 |
| 1893 | .523 |
| 1894 | .644 |
| 1895 | .687 |
| 1896 | .809 |
| 1897 | 1.02 |
| 1898 | 1.20 |
| 1899 | 1.33 |
| 1900 | 1.44 |
| 1901 | 1.60 |
| 1902 | 1.58 |
| 1903 | 1.71 |
| 1904 | 1.94 |
| 1905 | 2.04 |
| 1906 | 2.32 |
| 1907 | 2.33 |
| 1908 | 2.55 |
| 1909 | 2.87 |
| 1910 | 3.04 |
| 1911 | 3.14 |
| 1912 | 3.54 |
| 1913 | 3.90 |
| 1914 | 4.23 |
| 1915 | 6.84 |
| 1916 | 6.63 |
| 1917 | 8.15 |
| 1918 | 8.00 |
| 1919 | 7.25 |
| 1920 | 6.52 |
| 1921 | 4.36 |
| 1922 | 5.56 |
| 1923 | 5.60 |
| 1924 | 5.73 |
| 1925 | 6.10 |
| 1926 | 6.40 |
| 1927 | 9.83 |
| 1928 | 13.1 |
| 1929 | 12.6 |
| 1930 | 11.3 |
| 1931 | 10.6 |
| 1932 | 9.21 |
| 1933 | 10.3 |
| 1934 | 11.1 |
| 1935* | 12.5 |
| 1939 | 20.1 |
| 1940 | 23.8 |
| 1941 | 39.6 |
| 1942 | 43.5 |
| 1943 | 57.9 |
| 1944 | 52.8 |
| 1945 | 55.6 |
| 1946 | 57.5 |
| 1947 | 63.3 |
| 1948 | 68.5 |
| 1949 | 110.5 |
| 1950 | 139.2 |
| 1951 | 171.3 |
| 1952 | 160.6 |
| 1953 | 160.0 |
| 1954 | 145.5 |
| 1955 | 157.9 |
| 1956 | 172.4 |
| 1957 | 188.2 |
| 1958 | 242.7 |
| 1959 | 258.7 |
| 1960 | 266.5 |
| 1961 | 284.6 |
| 1962 | 304.8 |
| 1963 | 340.4 |
| 1964 | 376.9 |
| 1965 | 457.4 |
| 1966 | 542.9 |
| 1967 | 590.5 |
| 1968 | 611.2 |
| 1969 | 691.5 |
| 1970 | 761.1 |
| 1971 | 832.4 |
| 1972 | 942.6 |
| 1973 | 1,104.0 |
| 1974 | 1,260.4 |
| 1975 | 1,402.0 |
| 1976 | 1,561.1 |
| 1977 | 1,724.4 |
| 1978 | 1,981.4 |
| 1979 | 2,384.6 |
| 1980 | 2,734.0 |
| 1981 | 2,929.5 |
| 1982 | 3,063.0 |
| 1983 | 3,246.1 |
| 1984 | 3,559.7 |
| 1985 | 3,547.5 |
| 1986 | 4,128.9 |
| 1987 | 5,061.3 |
| 1988 | 5,939.5 |
| 1989 | 6,550.5 |
| 1990 | 7,671.5 |

## Research & Development Expenditures, 1929-1990

| Year | Dollars (Millions) |
|---|---|
| 1929 | .036 |
| 1930 | .062 |
| 1931 | .146 |
| 1932 | .140 |
| 1933 | .213 |
| 1934 | .256 |
| 1935 | .303 |
| 1936** | .357 |
| 1940 | .94 |
| 1941 | 1.5 |
| 1942 | 2.2 |
| 1943 | 2.0 |
| 1944 | 2.5 |
| 1945 | 3.4 |
| 1946 | 3.2 |
| 1947 | 3.4 |
| 1948 | 4.3 |
| 1949 | 3.8 |
| 1950 | 4.1 |
| 1951 | 4.7 |
| 1952 | 5.6 |
| 1953 | 7.0 |
| 1954 | 7.3 |
| 1955 | 10.3 |
| 1956 | 11.5 |
| 1957 | 14.9 |
| 1958 | 17.1 |
| 1959 | 18.6 |
| 1960 | 21.0 |
| 1961 | 21.3 |
| 1962 | 26.1 |
| 1963 | 27.8 |
| 1964 | 30.1 |
| 1965 | 34.9 |
| 1966 | 42.2 |
| 1967 | 48.3 |
| 1968 | 56.0 |
| 1969 | 60.8 |
| 1970 | 69.0 |
| 1971 | 71.6 |
| 1972 | 79.7 |
| 1973 | 89.2 |
| 1974 | 101.0 |
| 1975 | 121.9 |
| 1976 | 133.8 |
| 1977 | 144.9 |
| 1978 | 161.4 |
| 1979 | 188.1 |
| 1980 | 233.9 |
| 1981 | 274.2 |
| 1982 | 320.2 |
| 1983 | 356.0 |
| 1984 | 393.1 |
| 1985 | 426.3 |
| 1986 | 479.8 |
| 1987 | 565.7 |
| 1988 | 668.8 |
| 1989 | 751.0 |
| 1990 | 855.0 |

## Number of Employees, 1939-1990

| Year | Employees (Thousands) |
|---|---|
| 1939 | 1.892 |
| 1940 | 2.203 |
| 1941 | 3.154 |
| 1942 | 3.742 |
| 1943 | 4.049 |
| 1944 | 3.843 |
| 1945 | 4.2 |
| 1946 | 5.2 |
| 1947 | 5.2 |
| 1948 | 5.8 |
| 1949 | 5.5 |
| 1950 | 6.0 |
| 1951 | 7.3 |
| 1952 | 6.4 |
| 1953 | 10.1 |
| 1954 | 10.2 |
| 1955 | 10.0 |
| 1956 | 10.3 |
| 1957 | 10.8 |
| 1958 | 11.5 |
| 1959 | 11.6 |
| 1960 | 11.3 |
| 1961 | 11.7 |
| 1962 | 14.2 |
| 1963 | 14.1 |
| 1964 | 14.6 |
| 1965 | 16.9 |
| 1966 | 18.6 |
| 1967 | 19.5 |
| 1968 | 19.8 |
| 1969 | 22.2 |
| 1970 | 23.0 |
| 1971 | 23.2 |
| 1972 | 24.1 |
| 1973 | 25.1 |
| 1974 | 26.5 |
| 1975 | 26.3 |
| 1976 | 26.8 |
| 1977 | 28.1 |
| 1978 | 28.7 |
| 1979 | 30.8 |
| 1980 | 31.6 |
| 1981 | 32.4 |
| 1982 | 32.0 |
| 1983 | 32.6 |
| 1984 | 34.8 |
| 1985 | 30.9 |
| 1986 | 30.7 |
| 1987 | 31.1 |
| 1988 | 32.0 |
| 1989 | 34.4 |
| 1990 | 36.9 |

* Data for 1936, 1937, 1938 unavailable.

** Data for 1937, 1938, 1939 unavailable.

# ACKNOWLEDGMENTS

In the best Merck tradition, the creation of *Values & Visions: A Merck Century* has been a collaborative enterprise. The book has been two years in the making, involving the efforts of dozens of people from Tokyo to Terlings Park.

The Merck Historical Advisory Committee provided strong support throughout the project. Committee members helped to document the history of their divisions and staff areas and reviewed the manuscript of the book. Current and former members of this group, chaired by Albert D. Angel, include James J. Behen, Simon X. Benito, Burton G. Christensen, C. Boyd Clarke, Stanley J. Fidelman, Robert F. Hendrickson, James P. Hoffman, Charles R. Hogen, Jr., Alfred H. Link, Mary M. McDonald, Robert G. Ruark, Jeffrey L. Sturchio, Michael M. Tarnow, Walter R. Trosin, and Anthony Viscusi. Robert L. Banse gave his enthusiastic support--reading outlines and drafts and offering many helpful insights.

The Merck Archives Working Group also helped in important ways: they included Evelyn W. Armstrong, Jeanne C. Brelle, Vincent J. Cirillo, Alan M. Gardiner, Kenneth J. Gibilisco, Jeffrey M. Goldstein, William H. Helfand, Catherine J. Knight, Mary Lou Oliva, Nancy C. Paulikens, Arlene C. Peterson, and James W. Wallace. We also thank William H. Helfand, John L. Huck, Dr. Koichi Iwadare, Albert W. Merck, Benjamin Rosin, and Mrs. Diana Vagelos for generously providing illustrations; and Doris Ferraro for help in identifying individuals in some of those photographs. Virginia Bergey, Fred Lewandowski, and Jeff Supp supplied samples of current Merck products for use in the still life pictures in the book. Additional photographs and background material on Calgon, Calgon Vestal, Hubbard Farms, Kelco, Merck Frosst, and the history of the Stonewall plant were provided by Bill Hill, Anna M. Ptacek, Gaye Frankenfeld, R. H. Garland, Ann Jenkins, Al McDonald, and Dan Nardi.

Within Public Affairs, Al Angel, Dick Bostwick, Robin Hogen, and Clyde Roche provided thoughtful guidance, astute criticism, and unflagging support. Noel Howard, Joan Jones, and Russ Taylor also made valuable contributions. Louise Wisniewski's assistance has been indispensable to all aspects of the Centennial history project from the beginning; she also took on primary responsibility for compiling the Appendix, with help from J. F. Hinrichs, Dolores Rosinski, Debra Bollwage, Janet Salmons, and Susanne Oberschewen. Members of the Merck Archives and Public Affairs Information Center staff deserve thanks for their efforts: interns Erin Marshall and Lynda Osborne for conducting a survey and preliminary selection of photographs for the book; and Debra Blumstein, Rosemarie Caroselli, Eileen Carter, Janet Jackson, Brendan McNamara, and Barbara Stass for ferreting out information in response to our myriad queries. Janet Jackson also compiled the Index. Eleanor Semanchik kept our computers working, and Frank Drust's expertise enabled us to transmit the book electronically to Rahway for typesetting.

The Business History Group has been central to all of the research and writing associated with the Merck Centennial. Louis Galambos and Robert G. Lewis helped us early on to shape the structure of *Values & Visions*, conducted several of the oral histories, and were always available for advice and counsel. Lou Galambos wrote the "Values" section of the narrative, with research support from David J. S. King and Patricia A. Watson, who also coauthored the chapter on "Merck People." Robert O'Connell conducted several interviews for that chapter, and Elizabeth Roach expertly transcribed dozens of interviews for use in our work. Leon Gortler of Brooklyn College did several valuable oral histories with retired Merck executives and scientists. Ms. Kazuko Kamiya of MSD Japan interviewed Dr. Kiyofumi Ishikawa for the chapter on "Merck People," and greatly facilitated my visit to Tokyo in May 1990 to conduct an oral history with Dr. Koichi Iwadare.

*Values & Visions* was designed by Carol Bouyoucos of Waters Design Associates. John Waters, Carol, and their colleagues brought rare creativity, equanimity, and a sense of humor to the project, with remarkable results. The visual appeal of the book also owes a great deal to the professionalism of Merck's photographers and audiovisual services, particularly William Vander Decker and Frank Kinney of Corporate Creative Services, John Reminger and Reid Zeigler of MSDRL Visual Communications, and Jim Wallace and his staff at MSD Audiovisual Services, including John Kelly and Peggy Grady. Other illustrations and special photography were provided by Jim Barber, Black Star, Bill Farrell, Rafal Olbinski, Kevin Sprouls and Shonna Valeska.

William J. Anderson, the production manager for the project, worked with L. P. Thebault Company to print *Values & Visions* to exacting standards. He kept a complicated assignment on track, with able support from Phyllis A. DeMichele, Bernice A. Golla, and Bridget M. Sclafani, and procurement assistance from Teresa Casal. Distribution has been handled by Gary Zelko, Pam Barnes, and Jeanne Nilsen in Merck Professional Handbooks. The typesetting was done with efficiency and skill by the staff of Corporate Creative Services, including Gail Cash, Dolores Osborne, and Candace Ritter.

In addition to those whose contributions are acknowledged explicitly above, we would like to express our thanks to the many others who answered our inquiries, tracked down elusive information about Merck's past, unearthed old photographs, guided us to retirees and others who could help, reviewed drafts of chapters, and offered insights and advice based on their own Merck experiences. Without exception, people throughout Merck were willing to take time from busy schedules to help bring this book to fruition. We can all be proud of the result.

Jeffrey L. Sturchio
Editor and Project Manager

# INDEX

Entries with an asterisk before the page number refer to illustrations.

AB Astra, 32, 169

Abamectin, 170

Abramson, Clarence A., *178

Absecon, New Jersey, 85

Acyl carrier protein, 95

Affirmative action: Office of Minority Affairs, 41; Phase III, 51

Albany, Georgia, 115, *117. *See also* Flint River plant

Alberts, Alfred W., 92, 94-96

*Aldomet* (methyldopa), 57, 86, 88, 111, 117, *119, 125, 144, 152

Alginate Industries Limited, 31, 140

Alien Property Custodian, 107

*Altepose* (propadrine hydrochloride), 24

*Amber Forest*, 62

Ambler, J. H., *54

American Aniline, 107

American Society for Pharmacology and Experimental Therapeutics, 23

Amino acid sequence, 161

*Amprol* (amprolium), 88, 111, *143, 151

Anderson, Carl M., *124, *177

Angel, Albert D., *36, 40, 42, *178

Animal health, 28, 31-32, 73, 89, 111, 123, 151-156, 170

Anstice, David W., *178

Anthony, Madeline, *112

Antibiotics, 73-77, 91, 112, *183

*Antigen*, *140

"Antiseptic Club," 1914, *174

*Aramine* (metaraminol bitartrate), 59

Arth, Glen E., *9, *85

Ascorbic acid, 112-113

Atabrine, 111

Atieh, Michael G., *178

Atwater, H. Brewster, Jr., *176

Australia, 56-57, 123, 130, 139, 153-154

Aziz, Mohammed A., 155

Bad Aibling, Germany, *61

Ballydine, Ireland, 46-47, 118

Baltimore Aircoil Co., 28, *30, 31

Banse, Robert L., 54, *178

Banyu Pharmaceutical Co., Ltd., 50, 96, 98, 148-150, 169

Barcaldine, Scotland, 140

Barceloneta, Puerto Rico, 118

Barclay, Louis P., *58

Barnum, A. L., *138

Bartenstein, Fred, 54, 145

Bayer, Gustave, *54

Beecham Inc., 124

Bellani, Piero, *125

*Benemid* (probenecid), 117

Beriberi, 68

Beyer, Karl H., Jr., 30, 81-83, 99

*B.F.I.* (bismuth formic iodide powder), 24

Bill, John G., *138

Biochemistry, 70

Biomedical research, 164-165, 169

Birnbaum, Jerome, 89

Bismuths, 15, 67, 103, 109

Black Employees at Merck (BEAM), 51

*Black Enterprise* magazine, 51

Blevins, Herbert H., 48

B.L.H. Trading Co., 130

*Blocadren* (timolol maleate), 98

Board of Directors, 19, 23, 29; members, 1908-1991, 176-177

Boutet, Jean-Marie, *153

Bowen, William G., *176

Branch, B. Lawrence, 51

Branchburg Farm, 123

BritCair Ltd., *31, 140

British United Turkeys, Ltd., 88, 140, 151

Brown, Michael S., 92; on "The New Biology: New Targets for the New Medicine," 159-165

Burnett, Verne, *177

Bush, Barbara, *42

Bush, George, *42

Bush, Vannevar, 19, *29, 85, 87, *145

Buynak, Eugene B., *90

Byles, Daniel W., *124

Calgon Carbon, 124

Calgon Corporation, 28, 31, 124, 184

Calgon Vestal Laboratories, 124

Campbell, William C., 89

Cancer, 96

Carbidopa-levodopa: *See* Sinemet

Carbonic anhydrase inhibitors, 49

Cardiovascular disease therapies, 83, 86-88, 96, 98-99

Carlisle, J. M., *67

Carroll, Edward J., *138

Cary, Frank T., *176

Casey, H. M., *138

Catalysis, 159

Cavazza, Claudio, *53

Cefoxitin: *See* Mefoxin

Central nervous system diseases, 83, 98

Centro de Investigación Básica de España (CEPA), 91

Chamberlin, Earl, *72

Chase, Edward F., *32

Chemerda, John, *72

Chemical engineering, 88, 115-116, 118, 126, 152

Chen, Julie S., 95

Cherokee plant, 112, 114-*116, 126

Chibret, Ambroise, 98

Chibret, Henri, 98

Chibret, Paul, *98

Chibret Laboratoires, 28, 96, 98, 146-147

Chiesa, Joseph R., *32

Children's Inn opening, *42

Childs, Charles, E., Jr., *124

Chiral molecules, 161

Chittenden, R. H., 23

Chloral hydrate, 67

Chlorothiazide: *See* Diuril

Cholesterol, 35, 92, 94, 160, 162

Christensen, Burton G., 93, 126

Ciba-Geigy, 83

Cicchetti, Rudy, *88

Cilastatin, 126

Cinchona, 20, *142

Cinorre, Albert, 48

Clark, Granville, *45

Clark, Larry, 59

Clermont-Ferrand, France, 98, *146

Cline, J. K., 68, 71

Cocaine, 15, 103

Coccidiosis, 73, 123, 170

Codeine, 103

Coffey, H. L., *110

Cohen, A. E., *32, *149, 150, *178; and growth of MSDI in Europe, 143-144, 146-147

Cohen, Frank L., *115

Colin, Philip, *111, 115, 152

Companion animals, 170

Competition, 166

Competitive advantage, 171

Computer Resources, 48

Computer-controlled manufacturing, 111, 113, 117-119

Computers, 43, 111, 118-119; in sales, *138

Conklin, David A., 114, 119, 127, *178

Connor, Camille, 51

Connor, John T., 19, *22, *28, 41, 48, 54, 65, 85, 116, *152, 156; and development of professional management at Merck, 19, 145; and expansion of international operations, 19, 22, 141-143

Conrey, H. S., *54

Cook, Ian, 57

Copeland, Chris, 48, 56

Corn steep liquor, 113

Cortisone, 27, 42, *80, 148-149

*Cortone* (cortisone), 53, 78, 114, *116, 148; promotional literature for, *137

Cosgrove, Liam, 47

Costner, Franklin W., *35

Cramlington, England, 140, 146

*Creolin-Pearson* (coal-tar oil disinfectant), *13

Crop protection, 170

Currie, George S., *29

Dakin, Henry D., *177

Danville, Pennsylvania, 112, 114. See also Cherokee plant

Darien, Steven M., 41, *178

Darius, Charles A., 54

Darmstadt, Germany, 11, 13, 61, 103, 107

Davis, Carolyne K., *176

Davis, Sharon, 111

*Decadron* (dexamethasone), *85, 115

Defense Supply Agency Craftsmanship Award, *122

Dempsey, William L., *29, *87

Denkewalter, Robert G., *83, 85-86, 88

Deoxyribonucleic acid (DNA), 159, 162-163

Detail men, 135, 137-138

Dickey, Charles D., *29

Diphtheria antitoxin, 24, *30

Directors' Scientific Award recipients, 182

Diuretics, 83

*Diuril* (chlorothiazide), *82, 83, 117, 125, 141, 144

Diversification, 28, 30-31, 124

Dohme, Charles E., 24

Dohme, Louis R., 24

*Dolobid* (diflunisal), 40

Driscoll, Alfred E., Governor of New Jersey, 1953, *70

Drug: design, 160, 166-167; development, 167-168; discovery, 166

Drumm, Charlie, 102-103

Dryer, E. R., first secretary of Merck & Co., *41

Dufy, Raoul, *78

Du Pont, 32, 169

*DuoStrep* (dihydrostreptomycin-streptomycin sulfate), *73

Ekaireb, Huskel, 129-131, 135, 143; and expansion of Merck business in Japan, 146, 148-150

Elam, Lloyd C., *176

*Elavil* (amitriptyline hydrochloride), 83, 144

Elkton, Virginia, 76, 110, 113, 126, *127. See also Stonewall plant

Elliott, Boyce, *58

"Emerald City," 29-30

Enalapril: See Vasotec

Endocytosis, receptor-mediated, 163

Engels, William H., 67, *68, *71, 109

Environmental protection, 127, 168

Enzyme inhibition, 92, 161-162

Enzymes, 92-93, 160, 166-167

*Eqvalan* (ivermectin), 57, *154

Erythropoietin, 164

European Community, 47, 53, 142-143, 167-168

Evans, W. C., *138

Everhart, James K., *124

Ewing, Oscar R., *177

Exley, Charles E., Jr., *176

External growth strategy, 169

"Fair balance," 34, 137, 145

Family Day, 16

Far East, 146, 148-150

Farmitalia, 53

Farr, John, 20

Fee, J., *138

Feenance, J. P., *138

Ferlux, France, 98

Fermentation, 74, 109, 113, 115

Fernandez, Leo, 141-143

Fiaccone, H. N., *111, 116-118, *124

Fidelman, Stanley J., 88, *178

Finance Department, 44, 171

Finasteride, 99. See also Proscar

Finkelstein, J., *68

Fleming, Sir Alexander, *76

Fleming, Guy, 121

Fletcher, John E., 42

*Flexeril* (cyclobenzaprine hydrochloride), 98

Flint River plant, 115, 117, 119

Flower, Ricki, 40

Folkers, Karl, 30, *68, 71-72, 94, 99

Food processing, 170

Foreign markets, 15-18, 28, 52-53, 134-135, 139-144, 146-150

Fox, Joseph, 115-116, *179

France, 146-147

Frolich, Per K., *67, 113, 115

Frosst, Charles E. & Co., 28, 96, 98

Fulton, James M., 54, *124

Funk, Robert N., *48

Gadsden, Henry W., 28, 41, 47, 61, 65, 116, 118-120, *152, 156; and diversification, 30-31, 124

Gage, John H., *177

Garland, Charles S., *29

Gene expression, 163-164

General Bakelite Company, 107

Genes, 160, 162-163

Genest, Jacques, *176

Genetic code, 159, 162-164

Germany, 60-61. See also Darmstadt

Gibson, Augustus, *48

Gibson, Russell, *119

Gillin, James, 113, 115, 152-154

Glaucoma, 34, 98-99

Goldman, Irwin, 142

Goldman Sachs & Co., 107

Goldstein, Joseph L., on "The New Biology: New Targets for the New Medicine," 159-165

Green, Edward H., *29, *177

Growth hormone, 164

Gruber, Rudolf E., 109

Gutte, Bernd, *88

Hatfield, F. E., *138

Heart disease, 160

*Heartgard-30* (ivermectin), 30, 89, 154

Hegarty, Allen G., 114

Heiskell, Marian S., *176

Helfand, William H., 146-147

Hench, Philip S., 81

Hendrickson, Robert F., *35, 120

Henshall, Stuart T., 30, *124, *138

Hepatitis B, 35, 98

*Heptavax-B* (hepatitis B vaccine), 90

*HepZide* (nithiazide), *73

Hercules Company, 124

Herf & Frerichs, 15, *16

Hexylresorcinol: See S.T. 37, Sucrets

Higgins, Edward W., *177

High blood pressure, 96, 98, 167

Hill, H. H., *138

Hilleman, Maurice R., 35, 90

Hirschmann, Ralph E., 88

Histamine receptors, 162

Hoddesdon, England, 125, 140

Hoerter, Klaus, 60

Hoffmann-La Roche, 136

Holcomb, J. H., Jr., *75

Hopwood, William W., *124

Horan, John J., *19, 34, 41-42, 51, 54, 124-125, 145, 150, 156, *176; and affirmative action, 51; and Banyu, 150; and creation of MSD AGVET, 153; and establishment of strategic planning process, 145; and expansion of Merck research, 94, 145; and principle of fair balance, 137, 145

Hormones, 159, 161

Hubbard Farms, 88, 151, 184

Huck, John Lloyd, 34, *122, 136; and transformation of marketing at MSD, 137-138

Hudson, I. P., *138

Hulse, Stephen J., *139

Human Genome Initiative, 160, 167

Human Resources, 41, 171-172

Hunter, William G., *58

Hydrochlorothiazide, 125

*Hydrocortone* (hydrocortisone), *80, 148-149

Hydroquinone, 105

Hypercholesterolemia, 160

Imipenem, 126. See also Primaxin

"Indirect gene therapy," 162

*Indocin* (indomethacin), 47, 57, 85-86, 144

Infectious disease, 96

Innovation, 63, 65-99, 109, 116, 146-147, 156

Institut Chibret, *146

Insulin, 164

Inter-Union Council, 121

International Chemical Workers Union (ICWU), 121

*Iodabs* (iodine applicators), *105

Iodides, 15, 103, 106

Iodine, 109

Ishikawa, Kiyofumi, *50

Istituto di Richerche di Biologia Molecolare (IRBM), 53

Italy, 52-53

Ivermectin, 89, 91, 113, 154-156, 170. See also Eqvalan, Heartgard-30, Ivomec, Mectizan

Iversen, Leslie L., 98

*Ivomec* (ivermectin), 56, *153-*154

Iwadare, Koichi, 148-149

Iwadare, Toru, 148

Jackson, Jerry T., *178

Japan, 32, 50, 96. *See also* Banyu,
    Menuma, Nippon Merck-Banyu, Okazaki

Jennings, Tom, 42

Johnson, Lyndon B., 19

Johnson, Woody, *127

Johnson & Johnson, 32, 169

Johnstone, Henry W., *16, *29, *177

Joint ventures, 32, 172

Jones, Marvin, 121

Kahan, Frederick M., *91

Kahan, Jean, *91

*Kaltostat* (alginate fiber wound
    dressing), 31

Kauder, Ernest, 103, 105

Keating, Joseph W., *125, 127, *179

Keenan, Thomas, *118

Kefauver-Harris amendments, 19, 42

Kefauver hearings, 145

Kelco Biospecialties Ltd., 140

Kelco Co., 28, *31, 62, 140, 184

Kelp, 62, 140

Kendall, Edward C., *19, *78, 81

Keppler, William E., *122

Keresztesy, J. C., *68

Kerrigan, James J., 16, 18, *27, *29,
    64-65, *70, *117, *177

Kessinger, G. E., *138

Kippenberg, Henry, 103

Kitasato Institute, 91

Klodt, Gordon R., *138

Klophaus, Richard, *88

Knoppers, Antonie, 22, 130, 139-142;
    and European strategy for MSDI,
    142-143

Knowsley, England, 140

Krone-Speck, Leslie, 43

Kuryloski, Eugene L., 137, *138

Labor unions, 121

*Lacrisert* (hydroxypropyl cellulose), 45

Lago, James, 119

Lambert, Warren J., *139

Larsen, Ralph S., *32

Latin America, 141-142

La Vallée, France, 46, 98, 147

Legal Department, 54-55, 172

Lehman Brothers, 107

Lehritter, George P., *58

Leone, Mario, *52

Lewent, Judy C., 51, *178

Licensing, 172

Lilly, Eli, & Co., 135

Link, Alfred H., 120, 122

Linn, Melinda, 114

Lipp, Peter, 121

Lisinopril: *See* Prinivil

Livingston, Samuel G., *58

Llewellyn, Charles B., *16

Lovastatin: *See* Mevacor

Lymphocyte, 163

Lyons, John E., 34, *35, 41, *176, *179;
    and evolution of MSD's approach to
    professional communications, 137-138

MacDonald, J. H., *115

MacMaster, Douglas J., Jr., 57, 127, *179;
    as president of MSD, 139

*Macrocystis pyrifera*, 62

Macromolecules, 163

Mahler, Halfdan, *36

Major, Randolph T., 23, *27, 67-68, 71,
    *76, 85, 109

Malaria, 111, 142

Malcolmson, Robert, 119

Management Information Systems (MIS), 48

Mangdon de Camp, William P., *58

Mantz, William M., *122

Manufacturing: 101-127; at Cherokee
    plant, 114; computers in, 111, 113,
    117-119; concurrent production,
    115-116; early consolidation, 103,
    106; expansion to St. Louis, 15, 17;
    expansion to Stonewall, 110-111;
    German influences, 17, 103, 121;
    productivity in, 116-122; quality
    control measures in, 109

Marketing, 29, 34, 101, 129-156, 168-169

Markham, Richard J., *179

Marshall, Sir John, *141

Mascott, G. Theodore, *32, *179

McCabe, Eugene F., *35, 154, *179

McCabe, James E., *83

McCondichie, D. H., 117

McDermott, Francis X., *179

McDonald, Mary M., 55

MCMD: *See* Merck Chemical
    Manufacturing Division

McPeak, Ron, 62

Measles-mumps-rubella vaccine, 90

*Mectizan* (ivermectin), 35, 36, 89, 155

Medical-legal review, 137-138

*Mefoxin* (cefoxitin sodium), 43, 91, 111,
    113, 117, 119, 150

*Melozets* (methylcellulose wafers), 24

Mendelian traits, 160

Menuma, Japan, 150

Merck, Albert W., 51, *176

Merck, Friederike Schenck, 11, *180

Merck, George, *11, 15, 17, 65, 102-103,
    107, 156, *178, *180; and early mar-
    keting strategy, 131-134; in London, 140

Merck, George W., *11-12, 16-17, 19, 25,
    *29, 34, *54, 65, 74, *78, 87, 103, 106,
    109-110, 134, 156, *177; on cover of
    *Time*, *156; and establishment of
    Merck research laboratories, 27; and
    expansion into foreign markets,
    134-135; statement that "medicine is
    for the people...," 34; World War II
    postcard to Merck employees, *18

Merck, Tony, *33

Merck, Wilhelm, 11, 14

Merck, E., Darmstadt, 11, 13-15, 17, *61,
    103, 107, 121; agreement over use of
    Merck name, 143, 145; exhibit at
    World's Columbian Exposition, 1893,
    181; London office, 140

Merck & Co., Inc.: Board of Directors,
    1908-1991, 176-177; centralization of
    manufacturing, 125-126; chemicals
    for cold remedies, 1938, *109;
    corporate mission, 156, 166;
    corporate officers, 1908-1991,
    178-179; diversification, 28, 30-31;
    division heads, 1953-1991, 180-181;
    early years, 13-18, 102-106; early
    products and sales tools, *14, *104,
    *128; employees, number of,
    1939-1990, 185; expansion to St.
    Louis, 15, 17, 102-103; financial
    restructuring in 1980s, 44;
    incorporation history, 184;
    independence from E. Merck, 17,
    107; Management Council,
    *178-*179; manufacturing, 101-127;
    marketing and sales, 129-156; merger
    with Calgon, 124; merger with
    Powers-Weightman-Rosengarten,
    106; merger with Sharp & Dohme,
    12, 18, 29, 33, 70, 135, 140; New

York City headquarters (1896), *6;
    pharmacy interior, *10; prescription
    department, 1898, *132; products
    before 1920, *14; Rahway in 1903,
    *15, in 1933, *69; research and
    development at, 25-32, 65-99;
    research and development
    expenditures, 1929-1990, 185; sales,
    1891-1990, 185; sales staff in 1902,
    *58; stock data, 1935-1990, 184;
    stock splits, 184; trademark
    agreement with E. Merck, 143, 145;
    and tradition of global enterprise,
    13-24, 156; and tradition of
    innovation, 25-32, 156; and tradition
    of serving the health needs of
    society, 33-36, 156; in the 21st
    century, 166-173

Merck Chemical Manufacturing Division,
    43, 53, 114, 117, 119, 125-127, 147

Merck Company Foundation, The, 19

Merck Frosst, 96

Merck Frosst Centre for Therapeutic
    Research, 98

*Merck Index*, 33, 131-132, *180

Merck Institute for Therapeutic
    Research, 23, 27, 68, 70, 74, 81, 141

*Merck Manual of Diagnosis and
    Therapy*, 133

*Merck Manual of Geriatrics*, 33, 133

*Merck Manual of Materia Medica*, 132

Merck North America, 18, 134, 139

Merck Pan America, 18, 134, 139

Merck Pharmaceutical Manufacturing
    Division, 45, 53, 125, 127, 147

*Merck Report*, *134

*Merck Review*, *9, *33

Merck Sharp & Dohme, 34, 45, 59, 115,
    119, 122, 135-139; district sales
    managers meeting, 1959, *138;
    products in 1940s and 1950s, *84

Merck Sharp & Dohme Australia, 57, 153

Merck Sharp & Dohme International, 22,
    28, 123, 125, 129-131, 139-144,
    146-150; and animal health business,
    151-153; and flow of innovations
    from abroad, 146; international
    medical advisory council, 144

Merck Sharp & Dohme Research
    Laboratories, 7, 30, 34, 49, 97;

creative tension between Rahway and West Point, in 1950s, 81-85

Merck Sharp & Dohme Thailand, *130

*Merck Veterinary Manual*, 133

*Merck's Market Report to the Drug Trade*, *13, 131-132

"Merck's Second Century," 166-173

Merrifield, R. Bruce, *88

Messenger RNA, 163

Metalsalts Corp., 28

Methyldopa: *See* Aldomet

Mettler, Ruben F., *176

*Mevacor* (lovastatin), 35-36, 61, 95-97, 113, 167

Mevalonic acid, 94

Mezey, Kalman, 144

Mezrich, Reuben S., *99

Microbiology, 76-77, 89

Milk sugar, *134

Millar, J. N., *115

Minority Affairs, Office of, 41, 51

Mirabel, France, 98

Modular manufacturing, 47, 117-118

*Moduretic* (amiloride hydrochloride-hydrochlorothiazide), 125

Molecular genetics, 159-160

Molecular modeling, 48

Molitor, Hans M., 23, *27, *67, 70, 141

Monosodium glutamate (MSG), *114

Monsanto Chemical Company, 107

Morphine, 15, 103

Morson, Thomas, & Son, Ltd., 140-141, 144

MPMD: *See* Merck Pharmaceutical Manufacturing Division

MSD: *See* Merck Sharp & Dohme

MSD AGVET, 31, 56, 151-156

MSD Italy, 52-53

MSD Sharp & Dohme GmbH, 60-61

MSDA: *See* Merck Sharp & Dohme Australia

MSDI: *See* Merck Sharp & Dohme International

MSDRL: *See* Merck Sharp & Dohme Research Laboratories

Mulford, H. K., Company, 24, *26, 27, 29, *90, 140

Multifactorial diseases, 160

Narcotics production, 15, 19, 103-106, 109

National Cancer Institute, 97

National Institute(s) of Health, 72-73, 82, 92, 94-95, 160, 164, 165

National Organization for Women (NOW), 51

National Pharmacy Week poster (1941), *18

National Science Foundation, 12, 87, 165

Neff, Beverly Jean, *90

Neill, Richard W., *131

Neilson, Harry R., *177

Neuroscience Research Centre, 96, 98, 140

"New Biology: New Targets for the New Medicine," 159-165

New Products Committee, 118

New Zealand, 123, *141, 153

Newberry, W. C., *138

Niacin, 118

Nicarbazin, *123

Nickerson, P. A., *138

*Nicrazin* (nicarbazin), 151

Nippon Merck-Banyu, 32, 148-150

Nirenberg, Marshall, 97

Nolan, E. J., *75

Northern Regional Research Laboratory (USDA), 113

Nuclear magnetic resonance (NMR), 160

Oblendorf, A. V., *138

O'Brien, James, *88

Oden, L. J., *138

Odoul, Pierre, *153

Office of Scientific Research and Development (OSRD), 87

Oil, Chemical & Atomic Workers International Union (OCAW), 121

Oil exploration, 170

Okazaki, Japan, 148-*149

Okmulgee, Oklahoma, 31

Oligonucleotides, 163-164

Olsen, B., *111

Onchocerciasis: *See* River blindness

Ophthalmological research, 98

Orphan drugs, 35

Pacific Pumping Co., 22

Palmer, A. Mitchell, 107

Pangsrivongse, Khasem, *130

Pantothenic acid, 111

Parker, H. W., *138

Parkinson's disease, 34

Patchett, Arthur A., 50, 95, 96

Patents, 172-173

Pater, William, 48

*PedvaxHIB* (haemophilus b conjugate vaccine, meningococcal protein conjugate), 90

*Penalev* (potassium penicillin G), 24

Penicillin, 27, 76-77, *73, *80, 111, 113-114; packaging, in Rahway, *18. *See also* Penalev, Remanden

Perkins, George W., *13, 23, 25, *27, *177

Perth Amboy Chemical Works, 107

Pfister, Karl, III, *83, 86

Pharmacology, 23, 70

Pickett, Cecil, *51, *98

Pike, Charles W., 119-120, *122

Pines, Seemon H., 126

Planning, 44

Plasma membrane, 163-164

*Pneumovax* (pneumococcal vaccine polyvalent), 35, 90

Pomezia, Italy, 53

Ponders End, England, 125, 146

Powers, Thomas, H., *20

Powers & Weightman, Schuylkill Falls laboratory, *21; Philadelphia plant in nineteenth century, *109

Powers-Weightman-Rosengarten (PWR), 12, 20, 25, *26, 27, 54, 184; merger with Merck, 106; Philadelphia headquarters, 1915, *20

Pricing, 171-172

Pride in Quality (PQ) program, 33, 120, 122

*Primaxin* (imipenem-cilastatin sodium), 91, 93, 111, 126, *127, 150, 167

*Prinivil* (lisinopril), 167

Productivity Through Employee Participation (PTEP) program, 119

Professional representatives, 137-139

*Proscar* (finasteride), 9, 97, 167

Proteins: structure, 159-161; as targets for disease treatments, 160-161

*Pseudomonas*, 163

Public Affairs, 42, 172-173

Quality, 109, 113, 116, 119-120, 122, 127, 168. *See also* Pride in Quality, Productivity Through Employee Participation, Zero Defects

Quinine, 106, 111, *142

Radigan, John J., 41

Rahway, 11, 30, 46, 50, 85, 102-103, 105-106, 126; early manufacturing plant, *15, *102; chemical operators at, *17, *100, *108; Factory 31, 118; Grounds Department, 1948, *121; scenes from, circa 1935, *102, *105-*106

Rasmusson, Gary, 7-9, 65

Rational drug design, 93, 166-167

Rayner, T. W., *140

Receptors, 98, 159, 161-163

Recombinant DNA technology, 161, 164

*Recombivax HB* (recombinant hepatitis B vaccine), 35, 90, 96

Reductionist revolution in biology, 159

Regulation, 172-173

Regulatory molecules, 161-162, 164

Reichstein, Tadeus, *71

*Remanden* (potassium penicillin G-probenecid), 24

Renin-angiotensin system, 96

*Renitec*: *See* Vasotec

Res, Marco, *125

Research: 25-32, 65-99, 101; animal health, 73, 88-89; antibiotics, 74-76, 112; expenditures, 1929-1990, 185; penicillin, 77, 111, 113-114; in Rahway, 1916-1930s, 67-68; ribonuclease synthesis, 88; sulfa compounds, 73; in universities, 164-165; untargeted, 164-165; vitamin, 68, 71-72, 112. *See also* Merck Institute for Therapeutic Research, Merck Sharp & Dohme Research Laboratories

Restaino, Carmen, *51

Retinoblastoma, 160

Reynolds, Edward, *29

Riboflavin, 71-72

Ribonuclease synthesis, 88

Richards, Alfred Newton, 23, *27, *29, 70, 77

Rice, Owen, *124

Ricin, 163

Riley, Daniel E., *122

Riom, France, 147

River blindness, 35-36, 155, 170

RNA polymerase, 162

Roberts, I. D., *138

Robbins, Bill, 121

Rogers, Paul G., *176

Rohm and Haas Company, 107

Rosengarten, Adolph G., Jr., 20, *29, *177

Rosengarten, Frederic, 20, *29, *177

Rosengarten, Henry D., *20

Rosengarten & Sons, 20

Rosin, Joseph, 67, 106

Ross, Richard, *176

Roy, Philip, 44

Ruyle, William, *72
Ruzicka, Leopold, *71
Ryan, Ken, *46, 47
Sachs, Walter E., *29, *177
Safety, 168
St. Louis, Missouri, 11, 15, 17, *102, 123
Sales, 129-156, 168-169, 185; transition from detail men to professional representatives, 135-139, 145
Sarett, Lewis H., *9, 78, *83, *85, 93, 99
Scandinavia, 146
Schatz, Albert, 74
Schell, Orville, *177
Schenck, Friederike, 11, *180
Schnaidt, E. C., *138
Schwab, E. F., *138
Scolnick, Edward M., 7, *9, 96-97, *179
Scott, Gwendolyn, *51
Shannon, James, 82-83
Shapiro, Bennett M., 92
Sharif, Ibrabim, *51
Sharp, Alpheus P., 24
Sharp, James H., 22, *29; as first president of MSDI, 139
Sharp & Dohme, 19, 22, 24, *26, 28-30, 57, 81-83, 109-110, 135; early sales tools, *128; export business, 139; merger with Merck & Co., Inc., in 1953, 12, 18, 29, 33, 70, 81, 140, 184; 1886 price list, *135
Shen, T. Y., 85
Shenandoah Valley, 110-111
Shimada, Kaoru, *150
Sigma Tau, 53, 96, 98
Silber, Robert H., *85
Silcox, Herbert, *87, 116, 120
Simvastatin: See Zocor
Sinemet (carbidopa-levodopa), 34-36, 96, 111
Sinotte, Paul, 120, 122
Sita, Gino, *72
Skrek, F., *111
Smallpox vaccine, 24
Smith, George B., *58
Smith, J. L., *138
Snyder, Raymond E., 44, *124
Solar Laboratories, 28
Sot, Edward J., *179
Spafas, Inc., 88, 151
Spain, 91

Specialty Chemicals, *31, 124, 170. See also Calgon, Calgon Vestal, Kelco
Spiegel, Francis H., Jr., 32, 44, *179
Sprague, James M., 30, 82-83
Springdale, Arkansas, *153
S.Q. (sulfaquinoxaline), 73, 111, 123, 151, 170
Squibb, 135
S.T. 37 (hexylresorcinol), 24, *84
Stadtman, Earl, 92
Stallard, Dewey, 57, 120, 140
Stapley, Edward O., 89
Stauffen, Ernst, 24
Stebbins, W. N., *138
Sterile Packaging, *51
Steroids, 8-9, 78, 111, 148-149
Stewart, Aaron W., *58
Stiller, E. T., *68
Stoner, Elizabeth, *99
Stonewall plant, 43, 110-112
Strategic alliances, 32, 169
Streptomycin, 27, 74-76, *80, 111-113; in Japan after World War II, 148-149. See also DuoStrep, VetStrep
Strikes, 121
Sucrets (hexylresorcinol tablets), 24, *84
Sulfa drugs, 24, 29, 73, 82-83
Sulfamerazine, 82
Sulfanilamide, 73
Sulfaquinoxaline: See S. Q.
Sulfathiazole, 82
Sullivan, Louis, *42
Sutton, Charles E., *58
Suzuki, Yoshie, 32
Tanaka, Nobuo, *149
TBZ (thiabendazole), 56-57, *88, 118, 123, 151-153
Teamwork, 63
Terlings Park, England, 98
Thailand, 130-131
Thiabendazole: See TBZ
Thiamine, 68
Thibenzole: See TBZ
Thyroid hormone, 162
Timolol maleate: See Blocadren, Timoptic, Timpilo
Timoptic (timolol maleate), 34-36, 96
Timpilo (timolol maleate-pilocarpine), *127
Tishler, Max, 19, 30, 65-67, 71-72, *83, 85-86, 99, 109, 123; and vitamin research, 112; becomes president of MSDRL, 85

Tissue plasminogen activator, 164
Tonocard (tocainide hydrochloride), 117
Tope, Jess J., *124
Toyama, Noriyuki, *149
Transcription factors, 161-162
Trembley, Harry, Jr., *107
Triavil (perphenazine-amitriptyline hydrochloride), 83
Trosin, Walter R., 41, *179
Tsukuba, Japan, 98
Unions, 121
United Gas, Coke and Chemical Workers of America (UGCCWA), 121
United Kingdom, 125, 140, 146
U. S. Department of Agriculture, 113
Upjohn, 135
Upper Merion High School Band, *120
Vaccines, 24-29, 90. See also Heptavax-B, Pneumovax, Recombivax HB
Vagelos, P. Roy, iv, 9, *32, *36, *42, 51-52, *53, 55, 92-96, 99, 125, 145, 156, *176, *178; on animal health, 170; on challenges of biomedical research, 166-167; on the changing healthcare environment, 169-170; on contributions of Merck people, 4, 171-173; on crop protection, 170; on drug design, 167; on environmental protection, 168; and fellow interns at Massachusetts General Hospital, *93; on finance, 171; on global marketing and sales, 168-169; on Japan, 150, 169; on legal and regulatory issues, 172; on manufacturing, 168; on Merck in 2091, 173; on "Merck's Second Century," 166-173; on public affairs and public policy, 172-173; and research group at Washington University (St. Louis), *94; as summer intern at Merck, 1951, *93; on safety, 168; on service to customers, 170; on strategic alliances, 169; on worldwide drug development, 167-168
Van Buren, William, *124
Van de Kamp, Jacob, *78
Vasotec (enalapril maleate), 57, 96, 147, 150, 167
VetStrep (streptomycin sulfate), *73
Viral diseases, 98

Viscusi, Anthony, 153-154
Vitamin B$_1$, 27, 67-68, 110-112
Vitamin B$_2$, 71-72, 111-113
Vitamin B$_{12}$, 27, 72, *73, *80, 81, 113-114, 152
Vitamin C, 112-113
"Vitamin valley," 111
Vitamins, 27, 67-68, 71-72, 81, *84, 110-114
Wagner, H. H., *110
Waksman, Selman, *70, 74-76, 81, 91; cooperative venture with Merck, 74-76
Wald, George, 97
Walker, Ann M. Weightman, 20
Walton, Frank, *138
Wasson, Burton W., 98
Water treatment, 170
Weatherstone, Dennis, *176
Webb, T. J., *71
Weicker, Theodore, 11
Weightman, William, *20
Wells, Barry, *138
Wells, J. A., *138
West Point, Pennsylvania, 29-30, 49, 85
"West Point gang," 30
Whitman, William J., *58
Williams, Peter, 49
Williams, Robert R., 68
Williams, Theresa, 49
Wilson, Evelyn, *72
Winter, Charles A., 85-86
Women of Merck (WOM) organization, 51
Woodruff, H. Boyd, 77, 112-113, 115
Woodruff, John C., 112
Woods, L. C., *138
Working Mother magazine, 51
X-ray crystallography, 160-161
Xanthan gum, 31
Yoneyama, Jun, *150
Young, Robert, *98
"Young Turks" in MSDI, 139-140
Zabriskie, John L., *179
Zero Defects, *122
Zeitler & Rosengarten, 20
Zinc stearate powder, *15
Zinsser, John S., 29-30, 135
Zocor (simvastatin), 117, 167

Copyright © 1991 by Merck & Co., Inc., Rahway, N. J.
All rights reserved.
ISBN 0911910-91-3
First edition — July 1991
Printed in the United States of America

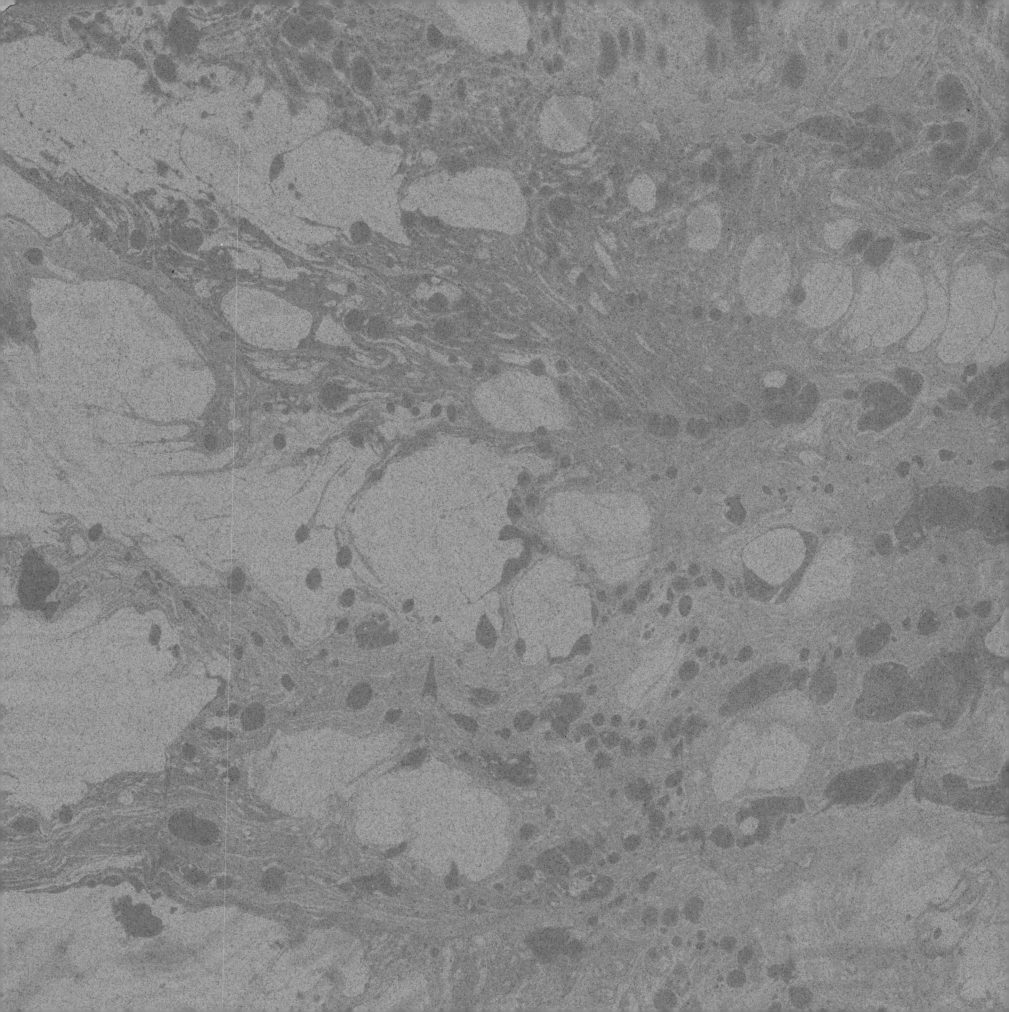